THE WISDOM
of
MODERN RABBIS

THE WISDOM

of

MODERN RABBIS

A Treasury of Guidance and Inspiration

Rabbi Sidney Greenberg

CITADEL PRESS
KENSINGTON BOOKS
www.kensingtonbooks.com

CITADEL PRESS BOOKS are published by

Kensington Publishing Corp.
850 Third Avenue
New York, NY 10022

All Kensington titles, imprints, and distributed lines are
available at special quantity discounts for bulk purchases for
sales promotions, premiums, fund-raising, educational,
or institutional use. Special book excerpts or customized printings
can also be created to fit specific needs. For details, write or
phone the office of the Kensington special sales manager:
Kensington Publishing Corp., 850 Third Avenue, New York, NY
10022, attn: Special Sales Department, phone 1-800-221-2647.

Citadel Press and the Citadel Logo are trademarks of Kensington
Publishing Corp.

First Citadel Printing: October 2001

10   9   8   7   6   5   4   3   2   1

Printed in the United States of America

Library of Congress Control Number: 2001091875

ISBN 0-8065-2241-0

Dedicated with warm affection to my dear, longtime friends,
Marilyn and Heshy Stock.
With special thanks to their family,
Jane, Allan, Zoe, and Noah Stock;
Caryn, Norman, and Sofia Klar; and Lois Cramer.

Contents

CHAPTER 1

ON BEING ALONE

No One Is Alone

NO ONE PERSON is alone when he can cling to a chain of tradition in which he is the latest link.

Joseph H. Lookstein

Shabbat Reminds Us We Need Never Stand Alone

SHABBAT IS MORE than a private time for introspection. *Shabbat* is more than a pleasant day away from the office.

Shabbat is an intrinsically Jewish experience, which means that the rest and refreshment of *Shabbat* take on added dimension because they are structured in a Jewish fashion. *Shabbat* allows us to deal with the turmoil of contemporary life in the context of Judaism.

In our society, where the pace of life is hectic and where the moral ground shifts so rapidly, *Shabbat* is important because it can anchor us weekly in ceremonies and values sanctified by centuries of Jewish life.

Shabbat reminds us that Jews need never stand alone. We can always draw [strength from] our roots in the Jewish experience, our connections to other Jews, our relationship to Torah and the covenant with God.

Mark Dov Shapiro

Man Alone Is Not Enough

DURING ALL THESE years there came a time when I thought that man was enough and that humanism was the answer. Traditionally emphasis upon man and humanistic values is one of the fundamental Jewish concepts; yet I have come to see that humanism is not enough to explain man. Neither his mind nor his creative powers can be truly understood except as the offspring of some universal Parent. I have come to feel that the whole human story, with all its tragedy and its triumph, is like a page torn from the middle of a book without beginning or end—an undecipherable page when cut out of its context. The context of man is the power greater than man. The human adventure is part of a universal sonnet—one line in a deathless poem. Without faith that our human intelligence and haunting human conscience are a reflection of a greater intelligence and a vaster creative power, the key to the cipher is lost and the episode of mankind on earth becomes a hidden code—a meaningless jumble of vowels and consonants.

Joshua Loth Liebman

We Are Not Alone in the Storm

WE DO NOT all have our setbacks at the same time, but it is a fact that we all have our sorrows. It seems difficult for us to believe this at times. We see so many with smiling faces and cheerful countenances. Like Jonah, we think that the storm has engulfed only us while the sun is shining on everyone else. It simply isn't true. We know it could not have been true that there should be a storm which endangered only Jonah's ship. Storms are not selective nor discriminatory in that way. So it is with the storms which come into our lives. We are not alone. The wave merely strikes one ship before it reaches another. If we could only understand this, the sense of being alone would not be so strong within us.

Many of you are familiar with the old folk-legend about the little village in which one person after another came to the rabbi with his troubles. Each one felt it was only his ship which was in the storm. You recall how, when each of the complaining persons was given an opportunity to exchange his bundle of troubles with those of others in the community, he sheepishly decided to keep his own. How much wisdom there is in that little story!

So it is with all of us, my friends. From time to time we find ourselves in the midst of a storm which threatens to engulf us. In our unhappiness it seems to us that only our ship is beset by the storm and that others have clear skies and smooth sailing. But as we look more carefully we realize it isn't so. It is merely a mirage, an optical illusion. We need not feel all alone.

Eli A. Bohnen

We Are Never Alone in This World

PRAYER PROCLAIMS THAT *man is not alone in this world.* There is a great Power which rules over us, a power Who, in His infinity, incorporates every striving and every aspiration of finite humanity. Man, however, must learn to pray properly. If we do not pray in the right way, then we have missed the entire meaning of prayer and shall have failed to communicate with our God. Here, again, the genius of Judaism expresses itself. The word *prayer* comes from the Latin *precare,* which means to *beg, to ask.* Many of us, unfortunately, look upon prayer only as an occasion for asking things of God, for making promises to Him in return for gifts which we expect from the Almighty. The Hebrew word for prayer is *t'filah,* and it expresses a higher motivation. It is derived from the word *his-palel,* which means to *judge oneself.* This is the true purpose of prayer. Rather than an occasion for us to seek favors from God, prayer is the opportunity for us to judge and examine ourselves before Him, to see whether we, by our conduct, have measured up to the standards set up by God and by His law. Once we attain this higher concept of prayer, we can come to realize that faith is reciprocal, that while we rely upon God and His goodness, we must endeavor to prove to Him that He can rely upon us and upon our loyalty to Him. This, then, is the second dimension of humanity, that through prayer—the right kind of prayer—we measure our own spiritual stature and come to understand that we are never alone in this world.

Benzion C. Kaganoff

When the Jew Is Never Alone

COMMUNAL WORSHIP MADE it possible to note the major occasions of a person's life. An individual's grief was shared by the congregation. So were his joys. The communal service was even tailored in parts to reflect the special occasion of one's personal life. Jews may have known much suffering, known too the empty feeling of being a people isolated in the world, but a Jew who regularly worshiped with a congregation was never alone.

Hayim Halevy Donin

We Are Released from a Sense of Isolation

JEWS HAVE LONG considered that God speaks to man through the events of history. The Decalogue begins with an assertion that is no commandment at all: "I am the Lord thy God, who brought thee out of the land of Egypt, out of the house of bondage" [Exodus 20:2].

The reminder of the Exodus from Egypt permeates every Jewish holiday and religious service. This was, for us, a dramatic period of God-discovery, and it has helped to sustain us for thousands of years, in spite of suffering and wandering. The Exodus has eternally etched on the Jewish soul the conviction that "There is One who helps to save. There is a Power that makes for freedom." The burning memory of our historically recorded relationship with God has helped to keep us alive. This memory is not a detached one. It is a recall of personal experience. It happened to us! We experienced the power of God!

Our Bible states that every Jew, including those yet to be born, stood at Sinai. All Jews are bidden to make the revelation at Sinai a personal experience. Our prayer service today is deliberately conceived to prepare the worshiper to enter into and to make personal to himself the experience of his fathers. This is why so much of our prayer seems to he a historic lesson, a method of teaching, rather than of petition. This is a unique feature of Hebraic prayer. It joins the individual to the community of past, present, and future, and insists that this is one ongoing community.

So much of our Synagogue prayer is in this spirit. Those who participate in our services in an understanding way are released from their sense of isolation and loneliness, and they are linked to the continuing history of an ancient people whose ultimate goals are uplifting to the spirit. In Jewish prayer, the limited strength of the individual is bound to the strength of an enduring Israel and to the eternal God to whom Israel has always related.

Herbert A. Baumgard

CHAPTER 2

THE BOOK OF BOOKS

Praising the Bible and Following It

MORE PEOPLE PRAISE the Bible than read it, more read it than understand it, and more understand it than follow it.

Samuel Sandmel

The True Prophet

THE TRUE PROPHET can be described no more accurately than by using Chesterton's statement on Swift: "He hated his perverse generation enough to want to change it, and yet he loved it enough to think it worth changing."

Mordecai M. Kaplan

When a People Enters Universal History

A PEOPLE'S ENTRY into universal history is marked by the moment at which it makes the Bible its own in a translation.

Franz Rosenzweig

The Bible—Our Claim to Mankind's Gratitude

OUR GREAT CLAIM to the gratitude of mankind is that we gave to the world the word of God, the Bible. We stormed heaven to snatch down this heavenly gift; we threw ourselves into the breach and covered it with our bodies against every attack; we allowed ourselves to be slain by hundreds and thousands rather than become unfaithful to it; and bore witness to its truth and watched over its purity in the face of a hostile world.

Solomon Schechter

The Biblical Basis for Democracy

THE FIRST AND noblest expression of the democratic faith is the Biblical narrative of creation. "And God created man in his own image . . . the Lord formed man of the dust of the ground, and breathed into his nostrils the breath of life, and man became a living soul." This is the text and inspiration of all true democracy. As a child of God, man is endowed with dignity; he is born free, equal in his rights before man and God. To focus the lesson of racial equality more sharply, an early Hebrew legend adds this embellishment. The precious bit of earth from which God formed man was gathered from the north and the south, the east and the west, so that no country might at some future time say: "Of us alone did God create the human race."

Abraham A. Neuman

The People and the Book

THE JEW HAS left behind no monuments of stone, no temples or triumphal arches. Even the stone tablets that Moses carried were important only because of the words written upon them. *We are the people of the Book, and without the Book we are no people.*

Robert Gordis

What Is Torah?

TORAH IS THE attempt of a people covenanted with God to fulfill its obligation. It is the quest of the mind for understanding and of the spirit for fulfillment. Torah is the ladder by which the Jew seeks to ascend to God. It is the bridge he builds between himself and humanity. Torah is the worship of God by means of study. It is the prayer of the mind. It is the science which seeks to discover the laws of the moral universe, and thus it deals with the realities that lie above and beyond the world of visible nature. It is man's pilgrimage through life in search of himself. Torah is the shrine which the Jew builds of thought and feeling and aspiration. It is the tree of life and in its shade alone can the Jew find completeness, peace and serenity.

Morris Adler

CHAPTER 3

COMPASSION

When We Are Near the Divine

MAN IS NEVER nearer the Divine than in his compassionate moments.

Joseph H. Hertz

Reaching Out to a Needy Stranger

THERE IS NOTHING so glorious, nothing so rewarding, and nothing so needed as reaching out to a needy stranger. In caring for an anonymous creature in the image of God, we uncover a new reflection of God's precious love, and we illuminate our own lives by the light of that beauty. And we also make someone else's life a little more pleasant too.

Brad Artson

Duties to Animals

IN JUDAISM MAN owes certain duties not only to God and his fellow-men, but also to his fellow-animals. Kindness to animals is with the Jews no mere sentimentality. Like charity it is part and parcel of justice, of righteousness, of piety. They advocate it as a religious injunction to be obeyed not for the sake of economic or material benefit. They feel that sympathy with the weak and dependent of any species reflects back, and promotes, as is pointed out in a Talmudic parable, peace and happiness among human species. Above all they believe that the best service one could render Him is in being kind to His handiwork, that . . .

> He prayeth best who loveth best
> All things, both great and small;
> For the dear God who loveth us
> He made and loveth all.
>
> *Jacob S. Raisin*

Judaism—A Religion of Compassion

JUDAISM DOES NOT neglect a single opportunity to stress the importance of developing a compassionate heart. It is one of the magnificent obsessions of our religion. Judaism is a religion of *rachamanut*. The Almighty is often referred to as the *Ha-Rachaman*—the All-Merciful or the All-Compassionate. In our liturgy, God is described as occupying the "seat of Mercy." The mystical strains of the Shofar are intended to remind the Judge of the Universe to transfer His heavenly seat from the "Chair of Justice" to the "Chair of Mercy."

Baruch Silverstein

The Unfilled Cup

ONE MUST EXTEND the quality of mercy even to one's enemies. It may be necessary to punish those who wronged us, but one must not rejoice at their suffering. When the Egyptians were drowning in the sea, the angels wanted to sing songs of exaltation, but the Holy One, blessed be He, disapproved, saying: "The work of my hands are drowning in the sea, and you are singing!"

The same thought is expressed in a quaint custom of the Passover

Eve Seder ritual. When the Jew recites the story of the plagues suffered by the Egyptians, he pours out from his cup of wine a drop for each plague. For the Jew does not consider his "cup of Salvation" complete when it comes through the suffering of any of God's children. Hence, the more plagues the Egyptians suffered, the less full is the Jewish cup and the less complete his happiness.

David Aronson

What Is Compassion?

COMPASSION IS THE pain a father feels when his son hurts his hand playing ball; the pang a mother knows when her daughter is not invited to a party she had her heart set on; the concern a lover has for the least concern of his beloved; the anguish which touches a man when his friend bares his troubles to him; the tears a child sheds for the limp foot of his dog or the broken arm of her doll; the sigh a judge heaves when he must pronounce a strong sentence; the care a doctor exerts toward a patient in pain; the dull tug at the heart of a soldier when he sees the destruction he has wrought; the help a businessman extends toward a failing competitor; the forgiveness a man grants toward one who has hurt him; the pleading of Moses when the people were to be destroyed because of their golden idol; the weeping of Rachel for the exiles who trudged by her grave on the bloody way to Babylon. It is the eternal mercy of the Lord toward the folly and misery of man.

Samuel H. Dresner

God to Jonah

Do not be impatient, Jonah.
Burning cities will not bring a better day,
Only death.
Those are people!

I love them. I made them.
I do not ask them to be perfect,
Just to try a little harder.

Jonah, Jonah, little man,
Stupid man,
I did not make the world
As a place for perfect cities.
I made it for men—just like you.
I want their love, not their death.

Jonah, are you good and angry?
I am sorry to disappoint you.
But those are people!

Michael Hecht

The Message of Jonah

WHAT IS THE book saying? It is saying that non-Jews should be shown loving-kindness and pity, even as Jews should. Jonah was a most reluctant prophet. He declared the redemption of Nineveh most unwillingly.

So the book proclaims a universalism that is every man's portion. That universalism is emphasized in Jonah's deliverance from the whale. He was delivered so that the universalistic word would not perish. Again, in His anger over the destruction of the gourd, God is clearly rebuking His half-hearted prophet, sharply making clear the sanctity of every life, Jew or non-Jew, in every city, every Nineveh on earth.

Salvation shall be the portion of every repentant soul; and every prophet shall keep the flame of the divine word burning on the altar of all mankind.

Jacob Philip Rudin

Fasting as a Means of Awakening Compassion

BY KNOWING WHAT it means to go hungry, albeit for a day, our hearts are moved for those who suffer. By fasting we are moved to think of the needs of others and to alleviate their suffering. In the *Yom Kippur* morning *Haphtarah,* this idea is given its classic expression. The prophet Isaiah castigates his people for their neglect of the poor. Their fasting and their pretense of piety is not acceptable to God if it serves merely as a cloak for inhumanity.

Louis Jacobs

The Gift of Compassion

THERE IS A Zen parable about a woman who loses a child and goes to the master demanding that life be fair. "Go" the master says, "bring me a mustard seed from a house that has never seen sorrow, and I will promise you a life of fairness." So she journeys from town to town and knocks on doors, searching for a family with no tale of woe. In this house she meets a starving child, in that one, a sick husband, in the next one, two brothers who have not spoken to each other in years, and in the next one, a bride and groom separated by war. She comes back to the master. "Have you found the mustard seed from the house that has never seen suffering?" he asks. "No," she says, "but I have found the gift of compassion."

Elyse Goldstein

The Rabbi and the Shoemaker

THERE IS A classical Hasidic story. A rabbi, a great scholar and sage, filled his whole life with acts of piety. He knew that he would be justly rewarded in the world to come. So he prayed to God to let him see who would sit next to him in the next world, who would be his study partner? And God granted him his wish.

God took him to a little shop where a poor shoemaker slaved away. All day and far into the night the man made shoes, and yet he seemed to have little to show for it. The shop was poor. The man never took time to study; he badly needed to bathe and change clothes. The rabbi was outraged. "O God, after all my acts of piety, this man is to be my neighbor and study partner! What kind of justice is this?" God answered, "Go talk to the shoemaker."

The rabbi introduced himself. The shoemaker answered, "I have heard of your great piety. I wish I had time to learn with you. But who has the time. All day I work hard to make shoes for the rich; they pay my living. And then, when there is leather left over, all night I work hard to make shoes for the poor. Nobody should be without shoes because they cannot afford it." The rabbi turned to God, "*Ribono shel olam.*" (Master of the World, I am not worthy to sit with him.)

Michael Gold

CHAPTER 4

THE REDEEMING DEED

Chain Reactions

CHAIN REACTION IS popularly associated with the atomic bomb, but it is not less gigantic a force in your daily life. Every word you speak, every action you perform sets up a chain of reaction that can end in a damaging explosion or in a shower of blessings.

Harold S. Kahn

How Abraham Brought People to God

ABRAHAM, IN THE Jewish tradition, is the man of compassion, sitting at the door of his tent ready to welcome the hungry and needy. On the verse: 'Abraham planted a tamarisk tree (*eshel*) in Beersheba and called there on the name of God,' the Rabbis remark that the initial letters of the word *eshel* represent the Hebrew words for 'eating,' 'drinking' and 'accompanying on the way.' Abraham, say the Rabbis, loved to provide all men with their basic needs irrespective of their way of life. Those he benefited were generally so impressed that they cast aside their idols to become worshippers of the true God. Religion has all too often suffered severe setbacks because of the repellent quality of some of its representatives. The Abrahamic ideal is that of the religious man of goodwill who brings men to God by his simple goodness.

Louis Jacobs

One Deed

BETTER ONE DEED than a thousand sighs.

Shalom Dov Ber of Lubavitch

Not Theology but One's Life

THE DIVINE TEST of a man's worth is not his theology but his life.

Morris Joseph

Why Mount Moriah?

TWO OF THE most important mountains in Biblical history are Mount Sinai, the site of the revelation, and Mount Moriah, on which Abraham bound his son in fulfillment of the Divine mandate. Many commentators have noted that when the time came for the Temple to be built, the site chosen was not Sinai but Moriah, despite the impressive case that could be made for the primacy of the mountain on which the Israelites accepted the Torah and Commandments.

The choice of Mount Moriah was apparently designed to remind us that the Temple was to be linked not primarily with instruction but with deeds of grandeur and self-surrender. Important as it is to absorb human instruction, it is more important to perform deeds of valor. Perhaps in some way this lesson can be linked with the rabbinic aphorism, "*Lo hamidrash ha-ee-kar ela hamaaseh.*" Not learning but action is of supreme significance.

Sidney Greenberg

Twin Paths

RELIGION HAS ALWAYS insisted that the highway of God is open to every man. He is free to walk the twin paths of worship and of action. Action expresses itself through ritual and through the ethical life; worship, pre-eminently through prayer.

Robert Gordis

Religion Is Not Creed but Conduct

THE REAL BUSINESS of religion is not God but man. Does that sound blasphemous? Then, let us summon Scripture to our support. When Moses pleaded with God, "Show me Thy glory," what response did he receive? Did he get a candid snapshot of God? Did he receive an oil painting of the Divine? Was he made to listen to a theological discourse or a philosophic analysis?

Nothing of the kind! "Thou canst not see My face," he was told. Instead, he was given two tablets upon which were inscribed the duties of man. He was given the law by which human conduct should be regulated. He was handed a pattern of life according to which men should live.

That is religion. Not speculation but behavior. Not creed, but conduct. Not a reaching upward to bring God closer to man, but a delving inward to pull man nearer to God. Oh, how wisely a Talmudic sage put it: "Would that they forsake me," saith the Lord, "but that they keep my law." In reality, he was merely repeating the prophet's religious ideal: "What doth the Lord require of thee, but to do justice and to love kindness, and to walk humbly with thy God."

Joseph H. Lookstein

Social Action Is Religiousness

IN JUDAISM SOCIAL action is religiousness, and religiousness implies social action.

Leo Baeck

We Are Saved Not by Creed but by Deed

IT IS IN accordance with the conception of Judaism that man is not saved by creed, but by deed. Therefore, the ethics of Judaism is an ethics for all men, though all men need not observe the Jewish ceremonial law or accept the historic obligation imposed upon Israel to witness as a distinct religious community to God. The righteousness amongst the Gentiles is their sin-offering. That is to say, it is as valuable in the eyes of God as any particular ceremonial service of the Jew. It is not only as valuable, but it is quite sufficient. The law, we are told, is given not to priest, not to Levite, not to Israelite, but to man.

Samuel Schulman

Amen

THERE IS AN extraordinary root in Hebrew, *Aleph-Mem-Nun*: Amen. Its original meaning, as in other Semitic languages, is "strong, persevering, steady." The second meaning of *Aleph-Mem-Nun*: Amen, in the Bible, is "truth." When the congregation asserts that all that has been said is true, we say "Amen."

I think it is instructive that the same root can move between the concept of strength and steadiness, justice and honesty, faith and practice. I think we have in these three letters—amen—the secret of Jewish spiritual practice. The word for faith (*emunah*) is inextricably bound up with practice and behavior. Spiritual practice entails peeling off layers of falsehood, illusion, and deception. It requires a steadfastness and regularity, a community of comrades and colleagues who support us when our own commitment flickers. It is grounded in the wisdom that knows that each small step requires a choice and takes courage. It understands that one primary goal of spiritual practice is not to make us believers (*maaminim*) in some dogma or doctrine but to make us men and women who are *aminim*—trustworthy and reliable individuals.

Sheila Peltz Weinberg

Abraham Did More Than Profess His Belief

ABRAHAM DIDN'T ONLY profess his belief in God, or his love for God. He immediately took the ram and made it an offering. He molded his life and that of his children in the ways of God. He taught his son to "go out into the fields and pray." He went to great trouble to find a suitable wife for Isaac and left nothing to chance, or fate. I can seldom tell the difference between Jews when I see them in the synagogue. But when I see how they observe the Sabbath under the greatest difficulties, keep the dietary laws in all places and at all times and observe the laws of the *Shulchan Aruch* despite all temptation, then I know who enjoys only the holy days and who enjoys a holy life.

Solomon J. Sharfman

The True Test of Righteousness

JUDAISM SPEAKS OF thirty-six righteous people who populate the world. Without these people, the world could not exist. These righteous people, we're told, are hidden even from themselves. They go about their lives in a fairly ordinary fashion. They might be a store owner or a cashier in the local grocery store. Yet their actions have a profound effect on the world. They're not saints. Our tradition does not claim that they're perfect.

But it does suggest that their lives are permeated by a passion for righteousness. Who knows, one of the thirty-six may be sitting next to you in the synagogue right now, you'll never know.

Righteousness, then, is down-to-earth, accessible, and worldly. The quintessential Jewish hero is not the saint, but the *mench*. Righteousness is something for which we can all strive. It doesn't demand perfection; it does challenge us to do good in humble and unassuming ways. Whether we walk with God or before God, righteousness is a reminder to us that we recognize our role as servants who can fulfill God's will.

Whether you strive to be a righteous person in the manner of Noah or in the manner of Abraham, I say, go for it! The Bible says, "*Tzaddik be'emunato yicheh*—a righteous person lives by his faith." In the end, that's all we have—our faith in God and our faith in ourselves. Maybe we ought to ask ourselves, "When we look in the mirror each morning, do we like the person looking back?"

That's the true test of righteousness!

Mark B. Greenspan

CHAPTER 5

The Destiny of the Jew

The Perpetual Role of the Jew

HAS THIS NOT been the role of the Jew through the centuries? Has he not been the perpetual dissenter against every political and religious totalitarianism that secular and religious rulers have sought to impose upon men? When Hellenism or Rome or the church or the mosque demanded complete conformity and tried to impose a coercive uniformity, was it not the Jew who alone resisted these imperialisms, the Jew who served as the lone heckler in a mass chorus, the Jew who was repeatedly the Mordecai who would not bow down?

Sidney Greenberg

Our Ancestors Stood at Mount Sinai

RECENTLY AT A public banquet I happened to sit next to a lady who tried to impress me by letting me know that one of her ancestors witnessed the signing of the Declaration of Independence. I could not resist replying: "Mine were present at the Giving of the Ten Commandments."

Stephen S. Wise

Show Me a Miracle

THE COURT PHILOSOPHER, we are told, had just completed his lecture on miracles, and after the applause ended the king turned to him with the challenge: "Show me a miracle." The philosopher reflected briefly and answered: "Sire, the Jews."

Ephraim Bennet

Being a Jew—Miracle and Mystery

BEING A JEW is not that simple a matter. It is both miracle and mystery. A Jew is a living witness to God's presence on earth and to His concern with it. And that kind of witnessing is dangerous. And not all the signs of danger are behind us; they lie ahead too. And I may say, in passing, that the English word for witness, derived from the Greek, is *martyr*.

William G. Braude

The Torah—Our Magnificent Obsession

SHAVUOT, "THE TIME of the giving of our Torah," has extraordinary significance for our people. It commemorates the event which burned itself into our soul, molded our character, regulated our behavior and shaped our destiny.

Whatever the impact of Sinai on the course of the subsequent history of mankind in general, one thing is certain. For our people something profoundly revolutionary and irreversible happened there. After Sinai the Jewish people would never be the same.

It was at Sinai that our ancestors heard the heavenly verdict: "On this day you have become a people." A horde of ex-slaves, so recently liberated, was elevated into a consecrated people and given a priceless gift—the Torah. And that made all the difference.

We did not become a people when we threw off the chains of Pharaoh; we became a people when we enlisted in the service of God.

Centuries later the Jewish philosopher Saadiah could write with every justification: "Our people is a people only by virtue of our possession of the Torah."

To possess the Torah meant to be possessed by it. Torah for our people became our magnificent obsession.

Sidney Greenberg

How a People Gains Help and Respect

HELP AND RESPECT can come to a people only through self-help and self-respect.

Stephen S. Wise

If There Were Another Great Flood

SHOULD THE EARTH be submerged under another Great Flood, the Jewish people would learn to live underwater.

Benjamin Kahn

What the World Owes the Jew

IT BECOMES OBVIOUS that we are not discussing a dogma incapable of verification, but the recognition of sober historical fact. The world owes Israel the idea of the One God of righteousness and holiness. Clearly God used Israel for this great purpose.

Louis Jacobs

Why Dictators Are Anti-Semitic

DICTATORS ARE ANTI-SEMITIC because they know or sense that liberty is Semitic in origin and character.

Abba Hillel Silver

The Jew Was the Prophet

THE GREEK GRASPED the present moment, and was the artist; the Jew worshipped the timeless spirit, and was the prophet.

Isaac M. Wise

The Real Miracle of Hanukkah

JEWISH SURVIVAL IN the face of the most monstrous odds and towering threats has indeed been a massive miracle. The real miracle that we celebrate on Hanukkah is not the tiny cruse of oil that lasted so much longer than expected. The fact that we are still celebrating Hanukkah twenty-one and a half centuries later—that is the miracle. But that miracle was not made possible by casual Jews. Casual Jews too easily become Jewish casualties. In every age the miracle was renewed by the dedication, devotion and sacrificial love of men and women who cared enough to give their very best.

Sidney Greenberg

We Ought to Be Better

WE THEREFORE AFFIRM, not that we are better, but that we ought to be better.

Morris Joseph

Chosenness Demands Service

THE ELECTION OF Israel is not a divine favor extended to a people but a task imposed upon it. It does not bestow privilege; it demands service.

Alfred Jospe

What the Rebirth of Israel Has Meant

THE REBIRTH OF Israel has meant the rebirth of our faith in the power of ideals. It has reaffirmed our faith in the reality of spiritual forces in the world. It has rekindled our belief in miracles.

Who would have dared to believe possible what we have seen with our own eyes? Any "realistic" student of history could have advanced a thousand cogent reasons to deny the possibility of such a consummation. For here was a people divorced from its land for almost two thousand years, exposed to the corrosive acids of human brutality, a people whose very existence was called into question by a historian who labeled it a "fossil," a people whose dreams of restoration had been mocked by circumstance and even repudiated by many of its own members. That such a people could achieve the fulfillment of its most cherished and long-deferred hope at the precise moment when the hand of despair lay most heavily upon it—this is an achievement to convert the most skeptical and cynical of men into passionate believers in the invincibility of the human spirit when wedded to an imperishable ideal.

In the face of a miracle of such incredible dimensions, our will to believe receives most powerful stimulation. With the rebirth of Israel there has been reborn the faith of decent men and women everywhere that God is not mocked, that ultimately it is "not by might and not by power but by My spirit," says the Lord of Hosts.

Sidney Greenberg

Why Be Jewish?

WHY BE JEWISH? Why Judaism? Because of the greatness of the past molded by Moses and Isaiah, by Akiba and by Maimonides, by the mystics and the Hassidim, they are our fathers. So you belong to a people that brought a knowledge of God and the ethics of righteousness to civilize a pagan world and redeem it with the blessings of truth and faith. The Jew should be proud of that past and want to identify with it.

Why be Jewish? Why Judaism? Because there is still a long road ahead of us to finish what we began to do. We started to teach but our teaching is not yet fulfilled. So we must go on living to herald the coming of the Messiah by working for peace and justice, for mercy.

Chaim Pearl

The Jew Alone Has Been Committed to a Moral Purpose

HITLER TALKS ABOUT a thousand years. He is merely talking. The Jew, when he speaks of a thousand years, has the warrant of four thousand years of history to which to point. He knows how to wait—a thousand years if need be.

Kol Nidre summons us to remember that there are verities which transcend the changes of time, that there are ageless truths and tasks, that of all the peoples which have trodden the stage of world history, the Jew alone has been from the beginning, a people committed to a moral and ethical purpose, that we, of this age, must continue to hold the banner high and refuse to bow to the seeming necessities of our age even as our forebears refused in their day.

Israel Goldstein

We Need Our Religion

THE INFORMED JEW always looks at the world around him not only as something of a clear-eyed stranger, but as one who has lived through so much before that he can tell the transient from the lasting. To be a Jew means to have lived through Egypt and Palestine, Babylonia and Spain, Poland and Germany. It means to think in terms of centuries and millennia rather than, at the most, of five- or ten-year plans of business expansion. It means the ability to think of our problems in the context of Jewish suffering, and of our goals in the framework of human destiny.

Eugene Borowitz

Two Most Precious Possessions

IN A MOVING book published in Israel called *Nizozei Gevuurah*, "Sparks of Heroism," which contains accounts of Jewish martyrdom in Nazi Europe, the following story is related. In one of the concentration camps in France where French, Belgian and Dutch Jews were rounded up, an order was issued to transport them to the extermination camps in Poland. Among them was the distinguished rabbi of Antwerp. This venerable old figure was marching to the train which would carry him to his death. He walked with steady gait, his head held high. Even the Nazi storm troopers looked at him in astonishment. With his left hand the rabbi was leading a Jewish orphan whom he had picked up in Belgium. In his right arm he was carrying a Torah aloft. He boarded the train with the two most precious possessions of our people, a child and a Torah, the symbols of Jewish survival. When I read this story it was as though I heard the voice of that rabbi saying to us in America: they burned the child and two million more like him. They burned me and the Torah; but they couldn't destroy the Torah because you have it. Hold it dear, cherish it, study and teach it, live by it, so that the spirit of our faith may flower in all its beauty and grandeur in your free and blessed land. Our death as Jews will not then be in vain, for we shall live on through you. Even as the heritage of our fathers survived the centuries and reached us in all its majesty, so will it continue unto the farthest generation as long as you and those who come after you will give heed to the words: *Etz chayim hi la-machazikim boh vesomcheho meushar.* It is a tree of life to them that hold fast to it and everyone that upholds it is happy.

Israel J. Kazis

The Barometer of Civilization

HERE IS A people upon which all the forces of fear, ignorance, and brutality have fastened, decreeing its elimination. If it lives, it proves that these demoniacal forces cannot permanently triumph in human affairs. Not because of his individual virtues, but because of his position, the Jew has been aptly described as the barometer of civilization, or, more aptly still, as the defender of the front-line trenches in the battle for human ideals. If he be destroyed, the furies of hell will be let loose on all groups that dare to think for themselves or cherish their own traditions, that seek to worship God or abstain from worship, in accordance with their own conscience. No religious sect, no national group, no scientific or philosophical seeker after the truth would long be safe in a world where the Jew, the world's most striking minority, has been annihilated. The Jewish people has a duty to live, in order that man's inalienable right to freedom may not die. In the words of an ancient prayer, "If we perish, who will sanctify thy Name?"

Robert Gordis

True Emancipation

OUR EMANCIPATION WILL not be complete until we are free of the fear of being Jews.

Mordecai M. Kaplan

CHAPTER 6

THE MEANING OF FAITH

Faith Is Acquired Slowly

A GENUINE FAITH in God is a distant goal. We do not believe in instant conversions or spontaneous spiritual combustion. Like Jonah's gourd, that which grows in a day perishes in a day. A genuine faith in God, an appreciation of the wealth of our heritage and its noble beauty, have to be acquired slowly, painstakingly, in regular daily doses.

Religion is a quiet dimension of daily living: it is not a spectacular explosion. Its symbol is the soft eternal light, not the dramatic fire-cracker.

Sidney Greenberg

Faith Must Be Acquired Every Moment

FAITH IS NOT something that we acquire once and for all. Faith is an insight that must be acquired at every single moment.

Abraham J. Heschel

What Faith Is

FAITH IS AN act of man who, transcending himself, responds to Him who transcends the world.

Abraham J. Heschel

What Faith Cannot Do

TRUE FAITH DOES not require us to believe the absurd or to shut our eyes to the realities of life, the discoveries of science, or the evidence of reason. Albert Einstein put it accurately: "Science without religion is lame; religion without science is blind." Moreover, those who believe absurdities will practice atrocities. One of God's greatest gifts to us is the power of reason, and when we use it properly we pay highest tribute to Him who, in the words of our prayer book, "mercifully endows the human being with understanding."

In the second place, faith cannot exempt us from Toil. To believe in God does not mean to sit back and wait for Him to do for us what we must do for ourselves. An old adage offers sound advice: "Trust in God but row away from the rocks."

Faith is not meant to be a narcotic but a stimulant: it is a call to action, not a substitute for it. Faith does not mean "God's in His Heaven, all's right with the world." It does mean God who is in Heaven urges us to work with Him in righting what is wrong with the world.

Sidney Greenberg

The Faith We Need

WE NEED FAITH that life is worth living; that the world is not a blind accident with no meaning; faith that there is a Power which is responsible for life and man; faith that this Power, whom we address as our God and the God of our fathers, has given us and mankind the task of perfecting His creation through our work and our love; faith that when we live lovingly and constructively, exercising our minds and our capacities, He is with us because we are with Him. And that is what atonement, or at-one-ment, is all about!

Mervin B. Tomsky

The Lesson of Religion through the Ages

THIS HAS BEEN the lesson of religion through the ages . . . that time . . . may be swallowed up in the splendor of eternity, that experience . . . may be elevated into unconquerable immortality, that little men and women, born of earth, may rise to the heavenly throne of glory by losing themselves in an overbounding love of humanity.

Joseph Baron

The Power of the Will

IN JERUSALEM, ONE day, I learned again the power of faith and will. The man who told his story was a prisoner in Bergen-Belsen. He contracted typhus and became dreadfully ill. The camp doctor predicted he would not live through the night and listed him as dead on the camp roster. The Jew heard the prediction and tossed through the night thinking, "How can this be?" When the war broke out he had been childless. He had traveled to the Belzer Rebbe who gave him a blessing that he would have children. How could he die? The Rebbe's blessing would be unful-filled. Summoning all his remaining strength, he got off the bed and walked a few steps. With an iron will he resolved that he must live. The Rebbe's blessing could not be in vain. In the morning, the camp doctor was amazed that he still lived and was recovering. "It's a miracle!" the doctor said. The man survived the death camp, married, has children now and lives in Jerusalem.

Solomon J. Sharfman

Faith and Action

THROUGH FAITH WE experience the world, through action we give the world meaning.

Leo Baeck

We Must Live Our Faith

A NATIONAL POLL a while ago showed that the overwhelming majority of Americans believe in God. But when they were asked whether it made any difference in their behavior more than half said it did not.

These figures justify the complaint of Dr. Melvin E. Wheatly: "Great hosts of people worship a God of religion who is not at all the God of all life. He is a pious presence in the sacraments but an impudent intruder in the science lab. He is a point of reference of prayers, but an unemployed consultant on business contracts."

Religion, to be alive, must be acted out in the arena of life. Its concern is not only to keep the Sabbath holy, but to keep the weekdays honest.

One of the teachers at the Jewish theological seminary cautioned that the feast of the sermon is always followed by spiritual indigestion unless it is followed by religious exercise. And then he added: "Remember, one kind act will teach more love of God than a thousand sermons."

The matter was summed up best by a prophet whose literary remains are only three chapters in our Bible. But he put us in his everlasting debt in three Hebrew words which are translated: "The righteous shall live by his faith" [Habakkuk 2:4].

Sidney Greenberg

What Is Faith?

WHAT IS FAITH? As the word is generally understood it means acknowledgement of the existence of a supreme being and the reality of a divine order in the world. It means a religious system or a religious group to which one belongs. But faith means more than this. It means also fidelity to our promises. It conveys the idea of the certainty of goodness. To have faith in some person or thing means to be sure of his or its goodness. It means to accept as true that which cannot be demonstrated by rational proof or tangible evidence.

What is faith? It is the ability to say in the hour of sorrow that life is good, and that pain and bereavement are a natural part thereof. It is a rendering of thanks for the blessings we have enjoyed rather than a vain yearning after those we might have had.

What is faith? It is the recognition that the quality of a life is infinitely more important than its number of years. It is the memory of precious moments stored up in the heart, unforgettable experiences which punctuate the ordinary prose of life and give it meaning.

What is faith? It is the determination to make ideals live long after one who professed them is no longer in existence. It is the ability to find solace in the association of the afflicted.

What is faith? It has the ability to feel the touch of a hand made cold by death, to hear across the great barrier the gentle, soothing voice of those we loved. It is the ability to face the trials of life with courage and to confront its problems with undimmed eyes.

This is the meaning of faith.

Harry Halpern

What Faith Is

IN JUDAISM FAITH is the capacity of the soul to perceive the abiding in the transitory, the invisible in the visible.

Leo Baeck

What Is Faith?

FAITH MEANS TO hold small things great, to take light matters seriously, to distinguish the common and the passing from the aspect of the lasting.

Faith is an awareness of divine mutuality and companionship, a form of communion between God and man.

To regard all that happens as workings of Providence is to deny human responsibility. We must not idolize history.

This world is more frequently subject to the power of man than to the love of God.

Its power is revealed when man is able to exercise defiance in the face of adversity.

Our task is to act, not only to enjoy; to change, not only to accept; to augment, not only to discover the glory of God.

What is it that makes us worthy of life, if not our compassion and ability to help?

We do not exist for our own sake. Life would be preposterous if not for the love it confers.

Faith is a dynamic, personal act, flowing between the heart of man and the love of God.

The man of faith will know when to consent and when to defy.

It is faith from which we draw the sweetness of life, the taste of the sacred, the joy of the imperishably dear. It is faith that offers us a share in eternity.

Faith is the insight that life is not a self-maintaining, private affair, not a chaos of whims and instincts, but an aspiration, a way, not a refuge.

Faith is real only when it is not one-sided but reciprocal. Man can rely on God, if God can rely on man.

We may trust in Him because He trusts in us. Our trustworthiness for God is the measure of the integrity of our faith.

Abraham J. Heschel

There Are No Handouts from Heaven

YOU SEE, THERE aren't any handouts from heaven even for parents—and I can't offer sweet and packaged platitudes to youth to be good, to be obedient, to be reverent; I can't separate youth from their parents because Judaism is a family religion—and without the help of the parents our youth will continue to look one upon the other in perplexity and doubt. It is a Jewish family that we go forth in search of God and share the mystery and adventure of the quest for a living faith.

Let no one deceive himself that faith is to be acquired as spiritual manna from above, a gift of God, a handout from heaven. The great spiritual teachers of mankind had to struggle, wrestle, and suffer to achieve their faith. Let no one think that a love of Judaism as a living faith can be acquired without practice, study, thought, and even the agony of doubt. Let no one delude himself into thinking that all we have to do is shout, "God! God!," and because we have rubbed the cover of a prayer book or repeated the magic words, God will appear to inspire us, help us, and solve our problems for us offering faith as a handout from heaven.

William B. Silverman

Even When He Is Silent

ON THE WALL of a cellar in Cologne, where a number of escaped prisoners hid out for the duration, there was found this inscription: "I believe in the sun, even when it is not shining. I believe in love, even when feeling it not. I believe in God, even when He is silent."

Louis Binstock

What Our Faith Should Do for Us

MANY OF US have a faith that shrinks when it is washed in the waters of adversity. We forget that trouble and sorrow have a passkey to every home in the land: no one is exempt from suffering. To believe in God does not mean that we and those who are dear to us will be spared those burdens that are the common lot of all of us.

To believe in Him does mean that we should live by His commandments so that our deeds bring no harvest of pain, remorse, or fear. Out faith should also give us the strength to go on in the face of adversity and the understanding that we may even emerge from our trials wiser and more humane because of what we have endured.

Sidney Greenberg

When Vision Becomes Faith

Vision looks inward and becomes duty.
Vision looks outward and becomes aspiration.
Vision looks upward and becomes faith.

Stephen S. Wise

To Keep Alive That Little Spark

LET US REDISCOVER a place where we can pray together, study together, and work together for the fulfillment of that beautiful dream. Let us try to recapture that sense of *kavanah*, that sense of piety and inner devotion so that whatever we do will become a sacred act. Let us strive to keep alive that little spark that brings us here each year at this time. May the spark become ignited and may the torch of our faith burn more brightly in the days that lie ahead.

The story is not over. A new chapter will be written this year as we are inscribed, individually and collectively, in the Book of Life. With faith in God and confidence in our people, I believe that we shall one day climb the mountain and view at close range, the cloud of glory.

Norman Kahan

The High Use of Skepticism

A PUPIL ONCE asked his rabbi why the Almighty endowed man with skepticism. "After all," he asked, "we have been taught that everything He created has some beneficial purpose, but what possible purpose could skepticism serve? It only leads to doubt and denial of faith."

The rabbi was ready with his answer. "There are times," he answered, "when it is better not to have too much faith in the Almighty. When a poor man comes to you for help because he and his children are hungry, do not send him away with the assurance that the *Ribbono Shel Olam* (Master of the Universe) will perform some miracle for him. That is when you use the skepticism. Act independently. You help the poor man yourself."

Sidney Greenberg

Faith Involves Sacrifice

AND WHAT DID God say to Abraham when the trial was over? *Atto Yadatti*—"Now I know that you are a God-fearing man."

You see, discovering God was but the first step, the first stage in religion. But it was not enough. Only when Abraham showed that he was ready to put aside every personal consideration was the test complete and the relationship established. For belief in God may be, paradoxically enough, a man-centered belief. Akeidas Yitzchok demonstrated that it must be a God-centered commitment.

Our whole culture today must shift its polarity from man to God, from pleasures to ideals, from matter to spirit.

If the religious revival in America is eventually to have meaning, it will do so only when we are cognizant that faith involves sacrifice. Only then will the Almighty say of this revival and of our profession of faith: *atto yadatti*—"Now I know that this is a generation of God-fearing men and women!"

Samuel S. Stollman

CHAPTER 7

THE IMPORTANCE OF THE FAMILY

The Basic Jewish Institution

THE FIRST TWO letters of the Hebrew alphabet spell *Av*, father. In truth, from our fathers, from our home, we learn the alphabet of life. The Jewish home is the basic institution of Jewish life, for it has the first chance and prime responsibility of shaping and molding the Jewish attitudes and enthusiasms of the child. If the home fails, no other agency can make up for this failure.

Saul I. Teplitz

Being the Right Mate

SUCCESS IN MARRIAGE does not come merely through finding the right mate, but through being the right mate.

Barnett Brickner

A Covenant with Posterity

WE NEED TO think of the home as the cradle into which the future is born, and the family as the nursery in which the new social order is being reared. The family is a covenant with posterity.

Sidney Goldstein

A Dying Father's Letter to His Children

I SAW THIS year a letter that a father who knew his death was imminent wrote to his children in which he said, "I bid you a fond farewell and ask you not to mourn my passing, but live together harmoniously respecting the memories of your loving, loyal and devoted parents." Of how many families has this been true, and of how many not true? How many families have been drawn more closely together, and how many have quarreled and fallen apart? In how many situations have we been worthy of their memories, and in how many have we been petty and selfish and unworthy?

Philip S. Bernstein

Isaac's Greater Fear

WHEN WAS ISAAC more afraid? When his father bound him on the altar of sacrifice or when he beheld his son, Esau, untutored in the ways of his people? By far the greater fear of Isaac was that his son would depart from the traditions of his people.

Edward E. Klein

The Family Needs Shabbat

AT A TIME when the integrity of the Jewish family has been seriously undermined, do we not need more than ever before the powerful help of Shabbat to preserve the cohesiveness and promote the togetherness of the family?

At a time when so many worries gnaw at us, so many problems weigh on us, and so many cares feed on us, can we afford to dispense with the joy and the delight the Shabbat can bring us?

The Shabbat, the Torah tells us, is the day that God blessed. It is more. It is the day that blesses those who have the wisdom to observe it.

Sidney Greenberg

Roots and Wings

THE TWO MOST precious gifts we can give our children are Roots and Wings—to be firmly rooted in our rich Judaic heritage, and to be inspired to reach one's fullest potential.

Joseph H. Lookstein

How to Restore the Jewish Family and Home

THE ELEMENTARY MORAL foundation upon which the Jewish home and the Jewish family must be rebuilt is not male imperative nor female imperative but parent imperative, making for physical and emotional and spiritual security for the children in the home.

Ultimate joy and fulfillment of purpose and meaning in life came from the gratification of being good parents to growing, good children. And this natural and universal cornerstone of being is the beginning of wisdom as we ponder what can we do to restore the strength and the beauty, the wholeness and the wholesomeness of the Jewish family.

Ely E. Pilchik

The Impact of Jewish Family Life

IN MARRIED LIFE it is the attitude toward the institution of the family on the part of husband and wife that determines not only their relationship to each other, but their ambitions and achievements in every one of their other relationships.

What family integrity has contributed to the perpetuation of Judaism, and what Judaism in turn has done to perfect the institution of the family as a socializing and spiritualizing agency in the life of the Jew are matters that should have been given scientific study. But we are on terra firma when we say that, as a factor for moral purity, Jewish family life has been without equal. Judaism's influence upon the attitude of the greater part of mankind toward chastity has been more far-reaching, perhaps, than upon the attitude toward any other human or cosmic relationship.

Mordecai M. Kaplan

CHAPTER 8

OVERCOMING FEARS

Proceed and Fear Not

EACH MORNING, A Jew is told to open his eyes upon a new world created especially afresh, renewed each day in grace and in love and to say, "Blessed are Thou, our Lord our God, who createst light and brings on the darkness, Who makes peace and creates everything." And to sense the opportunities for creativity that are present in the world and the opportunity for purposeful enjoyment of it. It is as if some wizened old man were to put his hand upon our shoulder, face leathery from the seasons, to tell us, "calm down there young feller, everything proceeds in its season and things make sense in their time. Sure, life is a challenge and certainly we all need a little *mazal*, but those who drop out are hardly fulfilling their own purpose or that of their people. Proceed," the old man prods us, "and fear not, for in His hand you may place your spirit when you lie down to sleep and to rise in the morning and even if some time between that your soul were to depart, the Lord is with you, you need not fear."

Myron Fenster

What Not to Fear

THOU SHALT NOT be afraid of thy hidden impulses.

Joshua Loth Liebman

The Cardinal Irreverence

THE CARDINAL IRREVERENCE in Judaism is to be afraid of life, for when we fear life we betray a lack of faith in God. Faith in God does not mean to believe that sorrow will never invade our homes, or illness never strike us and our loved ones. Many people who cherish such a naive belief are due for heart-breaking disillusionment. It is these people who will say to you: "When my mother died, I stopped believing in God." They believed the wrong things about God to begin with. To believe in God is to have faith that He will give us, amidst all vicissitudes, the strength to endure, and the power to hold on and see it through, the capacity to translate even our trials and our tribulations into moral and spiritual victories.

Sidney Greenberg

Faith Masters Fear

WE MASTER FEAR through faith—faith in the worthwhileness of life and the trustworthiness of God; faith in the meaning of our pain and our striving, and confidence that God will not cast us aside but will use each one of us as a piece of priceless mosaic in the design of His universe.

Joshua Loth Liebman

CHAPTER 9

FORGIVENESS

To Rule Over Two

WHO AVENGES SUBDUES one, who forgives rules over two.

Isachar Hurwitz

Sweetest Revenge

THE SWEETEST REVENGE is to forgive.

Isaac Friedman

Forgive Those Who Hurt You

EVERY NIGHT BEFORE you sleep, you should forgive those who have sinned against you.

Moshe Teitelbaum

The Great Error of Our Day

UNFORTUNATELY, RELIGION HAS been turned into a handmaiden of the circumstances of life. Whatever we do is correct, and religion is called upon to sanction our deeds. This is the great error of our day. And this is what Yom Kippur cries out against. The Torah says that on this day you will be forgiven. One day has been set aside to forgive us because we are human, frail and mortal; but, at least, this minimum is asked of us: to recognize that we need forgiveness. He who will not admit that he is wrong cannot be forgiven.

Morris Bekritsky

The Courage to Move On

FORGIVENESS IS THE courage to let go and to move on and not be trapped in the past. It is the power to project ourselves sympathetically, empathetically into the position of the offender. The French say "to understand all is to forgive all."

Forgiveness is the courage to see the whole person rather than to focus and fixate on the bad. Forgiveness is about remembering the kindnesses that someone did for us, not the errors they made. Forgiveness is the ability to understand that people change and mature.

To ignore the possibility that people can improve and develop is the essence of atheism. Humanity is made in the image of God, so to demean people and to deny this chance to change is to demean and deny God.

Charles P. Sherman

If We Want to Change Our World

IF WE WANT TO change our world, and who of us is not unhappy about the situation in which we find ourselves, then there must, to begin with, come the declaration of our bankruptcy, our recognition of our failure, and then as persons seeking forgiveness, we must seek the fresh start and an opportunity to do new things with the benefit of our experience behind us.

Emanuel Rackman

God Gave Us Three Gifts

GOD GAVE MAN three gifts: the gift of wisdom, the gift of generosity, and the gift of forgiveness. These were to remain forever the tokens of the divine in man.

These are the gifts that Yom Kippur pleads with us to apply to our lives: the wisdom of self-control against the appetites which would destroy our bodies; the gift of generosity as antidote to our greed and our envy; and the gift of forgiveness to dissolve the anger and the hatred which poison our lives. Take these three gifts this Kol Nidre Eve and let Yom Kippur work their magic into your lives.

Aaron M. Wise

CHAPTER 10

WE ARE FREE TO CHOOSE AND TO CHANGE

We Can Choose Life's Colors

ONE OF THE heavy burdens of being human is the need to make choices—choices that are often as desperately difficult as they are decisive. Edwin Markham, the twentieth-century American poet, wrote of these agonizing dilemmas:

> I will leave man to make the fateful guess
> Will leave him torn between No and Yes
> Leave him in the tragic loneliness to choose
> With all in life to win or lose

The most fateful choices are made in tragic loneliness. In the valley of decision, we stand alone, accompanied only by our haunting fears or our stubborn hopes, by dread despair or gritty faith.

Yet, though we appear to stand solitary, in truth we are accompanied by the tall and brave spirits who have stood where we stand and who, when torn between "No" and "Yes" have said "Yes" to life and its infinite possibilities; by those who have had the wisdom to focus not on what they had lost but on what they had left; by those who understood that fate is what life gives to us and that destiny is what we do with what's given; and by those who, therefore, grasped the liberating truth that while we have no control over our fate, we do have an astonishing amount of control over our destiny.

When a blind man was asked by a sympathetic woman, "Doesn't being blind rather color your life?" he answered, "Yes, but thank God, I can choose the color."

Sidney Greenberg

Yes, I Can Change Myself and Another

AND THE ANSWER seems to emerge from the misty depths of both our faith and our scientific perceptions: yes, I can change, if I know that someone loves me enough, if I realize that someone in this world has confidence in my potentiality for growth and for fulfillment as a human being! And one further illumination blazes forth: not only can I be changed; but even more important, I can do something that only God can do, I can change another human being by being lavish in my love for him, by being extravagant in the affection and the devotion that I pour upon him. I can transform him if I envelop him with the knowledge that someone cares enough about him, hopes for him, prays for him, believes that there is within him immeasurable possibilities for growth.

Morris N. Kertzer

How to Live Meaningful Lives

TO BE SURE, our biological inheritance, our childhood experiences, our environmental conditioning do exercise a vital influence upon us. These factors are real and powerful, but the human will is no less powerful.

We are not only shaped by our environment; we shape it. We are not only the creatures of circumstance; we are also the creators of circumstance.

Our genes may determine whether our eyes are blue or brown, but whether we look upon each other with cold indifference or warm compassion is for us to choose.

Our physical height may be biologically determined but our human stature we fashion ourselves.

Our environment determines the language we speak and the pronunciation we use, but whether our words are cruel or gentle, carping or comforting depends squarely upon us. Our passions, appetites and instincts are part of our animal equipment, but whether they rule us or we rule them is left for each of us to determine.

One of the hallmark verses of the Torah tells us: "I have set before you life and death, the blessing and the curse; choose life . . ."

It is only when we believe that there are indeed moral choices and that we have the power to make moral choices that we can truly live meaningful lives.

Sidney Greenberg

We Are Responsible for Our Thoughts and Acts

ROSH HASHANAH EMPHASIZES the central truth that our destiny is not controlled by blind fate nor by luck or superstitious practices but by man's responsible thoughts and acts. Rosh Hashanah does not stress the comfort of faith but its challenges.

Lothar Lubasch

We Do Not Live by Facts Alone

WE HUMAN BEINGS not only react, we also respond, and the measure of a human being is to be found in the nature of that response. Any clergyman can cite from his personal experience so many illustrations of people whom sorrow made bitter. He can also cite as many or more illustrations of people whom sorrow made better.

There are people who emerge from an encounter with grief richer human beings, taller in stature, more compassionate, more sensitive, more appreciative of the gift of life. They can then say with the poet William Wordsworth: "A deep distress hath humanized my soul."

The same fire that melts the butter hardens the egg. The same wind that extinguishes a match will fan a flame into a strong blaze. Man does not live by facts alone.

An aggressive atheist in a mood to advertise his point of view painted these words on a roadside billboard: "God is nowhere." A seven-year-old girl riding in the family car passed the billboard. She was thrilled and excited, for she read these words: "God is now here."

Sidney Greenberg

Direction

THE HUMAN BEING, if not quite captain of his fate, can yet steer himself in a new direction.

Arnold A. Lasker

Blaming Circumstances

NO PERSON SUCCEEDS in any enterprise until he takes responsibility for his choices, until he knows with unwavering certainty that he has choices, and that upon the outcome of those choices his entire destiny will depend.

"People," wrote George Bernard Shaw, "are always blaming their circumstances for what they are. I can't believe in circumstances. The people who get on in this world are the people who get up and look for the circumstances they want, and if they can't find them, make them."

Sidney Greenberg

We Are Free to Change

MAN IS NOT forever doomed to the errors and the consequences of his past conduct. He is free to repent and through repentance to nullify the evil influences of his past over him. One of the noblest and most inspiring contributions which Judaism made to the spiritual development of mankind was the concept of *Teshuvah*, repentance. Repentance means the opportunity of a new start, the chance to correct what man had left crooked, to fill that which is wanting in one's life. Repentance is the central motif of this entire holy season [Rosh Hashanah]. It is the luminous theme around which these heroic spiritual clays revolve.

Not only is man free and able to renew himself and to make a fresh start, but in this enterprise toward newness and regeneration lies the meaning and significance of his life.

Abba Hillel Silver

We Can Begin Anew

JONAH STANDS BETWEEN the seer and the prophet. Conceiving his function as seer and unfailing predictor of the fall of Nineveh, he cannot accept the higher ideal of "return unto Me and I shall return unto you" [Malachi 13:7]. The author of the book of Jonah, unlike the man he describes, has already accepted the prophetic-rabbinic tradition that contrasts the human judge, who cannot revoke his sentence, and God who can. Thus, in the book of Jonah, a new idea is born "and God repented of the evil, which He said He would do unto them; and He did it not" [Jonah 3:10].

This then is the greatness of our book. Jonah defines the true calling of prophecy. The prophet is not a predictor of inevitable destruction. Evil once committed need not pursue man to his end. Repentance is possible. Destruction is avoidable. God prefers penitence to punishment.

All of this was difficult for Jonah, the seer, to accept. It is still rejected by many fearful and guilt-ridden persons who subconsciously or otherwise long to punish or be punished for wrongs long since repented and better forgotten. What more appropriate message can tradition offer for Yom Kippur than that of the book of Jonah? Man can begin anew. Even the infamous Nineveh was spared when it turned from its evil path. In the words of the prayer we repeat on this day, "But repentance, prayer, and charity annul the severe sentence."

Maurice S. Corson

The Promise of Atonement

WE CAN TRANSFORM error separating us from others into a good which brings us together.

At any point in our lives we have the power to regret a mistake, to learn from it.

Not merely to be sorry but to accept responsibility for our errors and for the hurt we cause someone else.

We can atone.

Moshe Davis and Victor Ratner

A New Beginning Can Always Be Made

THE BUOYANT OPTIMISM of Judaism in teaching that a new beginning can always be made feels strange in our day and age. The fashionable philosophies of our time speak of anxiety and frustration, of failure and despair, of man's "creaturely" helplessness and "existential" tragedy, of the knell of doom in the distance, sounding dark and implacable. But we must remember that the message of Judaism always sounds strange to human ears. Even in the ages of faith, when men walked about with long pious faces, mortifying their flesh in penitence and contorting their minds to fit rigid dogmas, the healthy optimism of our faith sounded strange and unbelievable. For Judaism is healthy minded and open-eyed. It does not close its eyes to evil in nature or to sin in human nature, but it asserts with tireless persistence that God is "King" over nature and that man is capable of triumphing over the evil in his makeup. "It is at the door that sin lurks, lusting for you, but you may rule over it." [Genesis 4:7]

Jacob B. Agus

It Depends on What We Are Doing

IN THE MINHA service, we read *Ashray,* in which one of the consoling verses assures us that "God is near to all who call upon Him." But in the Book of Jonah, God's proximity to the Prophet who sought to elude Him is hardly a reassuring thought. For the Psalmist God's nearness is uplifting. For poor Jonah it is a horrible burden.

God either accompanies us or pursues us; He either helps or harasses us. It all depends on what we are doing.

Sidney Greenberg

Each Day Will Present Opportunities

THE PURPOSE OF our Service is to realize that there are countless opportunities which will be given to us in the future to change and improve the situation in which we find ourselves today. The purpose of our Service is to make us realize that each day of the New Year will present opportunities to make those changes. As we pray that we have the strength to bear our responsibilities for yesterday's behavior, the courage to face and take advantage of tomorrow's opportunities, and for the wisdom to make each day's decisions.

Judah Kahn

Slavery in Freedom

IT IS THE task of every free person to liberate himself from those inner tendencies which, without his even knowing about them, make him a slave "in the midst of freedom," as one Hebrew writer put it. To lead a life which is governed by prejudice, by violent likes and hatreds, is to be a slave. To become the victim of an unbending, unyielding point of view—to refuse to grow up or grow out of childish notions and habits—to put a "no trespassing" sign on one's mind and heart so that it is never open to the ideas and perspectives of others—this is an enslavement which needs genuine liberation.

True freedom means to be able to control and dominate our own feelings, impulses and thoughts, so that they can help us to grow into better human beings.

Solomon S. Bernards

The Great Gift

GOD GAVE US an irrevocable gift—free will. Free will is the crown of our humanity; it is the divine gift which we celebrate during these High Holy Days as we evaluate the past and look prayerfully to the future. Humbly I thank God for that infinite patience that enables Him to see us make mistake after mistake—often mistakes of tragic and horrendous proportions—and yet not revoke that gift which makes us human.

Simeon J. Maslin

We Are Able to Make Choices

IN THE BIBLE, there's a verse describing the creation of humanity that reads, *Vayeitzer ha-adam*—"And God created the human being." But the word *vayeitzer* is written in an unusual way, with two *yods* instead of one. Basing himself on this unusual spelling, Rabbi Yossi tells us that human beings are created with two *yetzers*, two inclinations; one toward the good and one toward the bad. And every one of us, not only Adam, is created this way. We're "hardwired" to be able to make choices, to be able to act in different ways.

And if we make the wrong decisions, if we act improperly, we can always turn back. *Teshuvah*, repentance, is part of the structure of the universe. According to the rabbis, it was created before the physical universe. We can always turn back.

Carl M. Perkins

We Have Enormous Control

WE MAY NOT have control over what happens to us, but we actually have enormous control over how we will respond. We have enormous control over what kind of people we are. Our challenge is to exercise that control.

A story in the Talmud teaches that at the moment of conception, an angel named Laila descends and scoops up the embryo and brings it up to God and asks God, "Will this baby grow up to be intelligent or foolish? Will it be strong or weak? Will it become wealthy or poor?" And presumably the angel gets an answer to these questions.

The text goes on to tell us, though, that there is one question that the angel does not ask: "Will this child grow up to become a *tzaddik* or a *rasha*, a good person, or an evil-doer?"

The angel doesn't ask this question because, even though God knows whether the child will become a boy or a girl and presumably knows the answers to all of those other questions, God doesn't know the answer to that question. God doesn't know whether or not any baby will grow up to become a *tzaddik* or a *rasha*. As Rashi puts it in his commentary on this passage, "This is the question that God puts to us, for everything is in His hands except for this, which is in our hands." [B. Niddah 17b, s.v. "Ki im I'yirah." See also B. Berakhot 33b, B. Megillah 25a]. Whether or not we're going to do good is entirely up to us.

Let us focus our attention on what we can influence, which is how we will behave and how we will respond as we live our lives. May we worry less about what is beyond our control, and devote ourselves more fully to what is.

Carl M. Perkins

When We Live Like a Mensch

WHY THIS NEED to affirm the significance of life in moral terms? Because we know that the most important story of our lives is that we are created with the freedom to do good and evil, and we know that we fulfill the deepest meaning of our lives when we are faithful to the covenant, with the Source of our being, when we live like a *mensch* and embrace Torah.

Samuel Egai Karff

What Is the Essence of Living?

FOR WHAT IS the essence of living? Matthew Arnold spelled it out in a very simple and precise sentence. "Life is not a having and a getting but a being and becoming." Life is not expansion in wealth alone but growth in the personal sense. It is not the accumulation of things or the piling on of possessions but the flowering of the spirit within. It is not to impress others with what we have but to reveal to them what we are. Of what value is it to stand on top of the pyramid of financial success when our souls have shrunk to a pygmy height? Why embrace the horizons and set out to conquer other worlds when we are yet slaves to our own folly and greed? Should we find it necessary to fill the emptiness of our hearts with the clatter of new toys, new acquisitions? Is it really essential to hide our deeper sense of worthlessness behind a façade of material possessions? What is life? A having and a getting? A chasing and a hunting? A hoarding and a keeping? Or a being and becoming? A chance to release His divine kernel within us that hungers so much for the true, the good, and the beautiful? Why do we kill this divine need? Why do we choke off this flower of our yearning for the better things in life with the weeds of avarice, envy, and discontent with our lot!

Let us not concentrate so much on making a living. Too often does this involve us in the false, and superficial, the mediocre and second-rate. It is basically a matter of compulsion. We must obtain in some way the means of our existence and often we cannot stop to ask at what price this is done. But while making a living, let us also meditate on the necessity for making a life. For here we build on our strongest assets. Here we confront the true and the genuine in ourselves. Here we have our freedom of choice. We make a life not because we have to, but because we want to, because we want to be a good machine that can be of some use in this world.

Harry Essrig

Rosh Hashanah's Triple Message

THE TRIPLE MESSAGE of Rosh HaShonoh—of creation, of judgment, of redemption—is no abstract dogma, given, as the phrase, goes "for your information." Rosh Hashanah, the birthday of the world, tells us: the Creator God is free, He has conferred on you a measure of freedom: exercise it! Rosh HaShonoh, the Day of Judgment tells us: your conduct is subject to scrutiny in terms of the divine law: therefore do better, strive for nobler and lovelier deeds! Rosh HaShonoh, holding before us the redemptive vision of the Kingdom of God, challenges us: do what you can to make the vision come true. For as we cling to the faith that the universe has a concern for man, that faith must become visible reality through us.

Bernard J. Bamberger

The High Use of Stubbornness

IF WE, THE Jewish People, had not had a capacity for stubbornness, could we have survived to this day? Could we have endured through two *churbonot*, and millennia of oppression and persecution? We are an *am kshei oreff*, a stubborn and stiff-necked people, and thank God that we are!

But there is a world of difference between the stubbornness shown by Jewish leadership and Pharaoh's stubbornness. We were stubborn in clinging tenaciously to the Torah. Pharaoh was stubborn in clinging to tyranny and brutality. The choice was his. All the miracles and plagues could not succeed in weakening Pharaoh's stand. Yes, Pharaoh was stubborn! But he could have used his stubbornness to persuade Egypt that slavery was reprehensible. He chose instead to use his power and influence in another direction. For this the Torah condemns him.

The question "What was Pharaoh's guilt?" is no question at all. He was endowed by God with the finest capacity for leadership, a hard heart and a stiff neck, broad shoulders and unswerving tenacity. He chose to use these traits to reject good and to embrace evil. It was not God who directed his behavior, but Pharaoh himself.

Every man is endowed by God with certain capacities, strengths, weaknesses, fortes and flaws. How he uses them, he alone must choose. And for whatever choice he makes, he alone must remain responsible.

Macy Gordon

I Will Open Myself in the Water

It is between me and the water now
The water is my medium
With it I inscribe my name
Invisible and permanent
The house of Israel becomes my home

Another step of being
A path traced with new eyes

I will open myself in the water
Immerse myself whole
And I will emerge
Complicated and honest as ever
A Jew

Blessed is the Holy One to whom I entrust the transformations of my soul.
Blessed is the Holy One who has chosen me for the people Israel.
Blessed am I, who chooses the people Israel, through the water.

Noa Rachael Kushner

Our Choices

THE SHOFAR IS, as you know, a horn. In the Talmud, our Rabbis note: *keren darko l'hazik*, "The horn of the animal is prone to do damage." Yet, the same horn can become the Shofar which can call man to the heights of Sinai, if he so chooses. It is the instrument of destruction, but it is also the symbol of *akedas yitzchok*, the intended sacrifice of Isaac. Which shall it be?

Let us choose to make Israel the means of enriching the Jewish people, not dividing it. Let us make the family the center of exaltation, not sorrow. Let us seek learning as the avenue for self-development, not as a tool for making money only. If we allow Torah to guide us, we will realize the greater good which can purify us in all these areas as we pray: "Purify our hearts to the greater ideal of serving Thee in truth, for Thou God [not our self] art Truth and Thy word [not our personal interest] is Truth and remains eternally [not a fleeting shadow as the self]."

In this eternity there is a unity. Man and God, man and his fellow-men share as one in hope and promise.

Simon A. Dolgin

The Two Sides of Human Nature

WHEN THE ANCIENTS studied man, they were impressed with the two sides of human nature. They found man capable of doing good, of being warm, tender and friendly; they also observed that he was capable of destructiveness, cruelty and evil. They visualized the spirit of goodness and the spirit of evil as being locked in a bitter struggle for the soul of man.

It is a rather unequal struggle, to be sure. For it is far easier to entice man to jealousy and to inflamed passions than it is to convince him to be humble, to be cooperative, to use reason and common sense.

The evil inclination, the "*yetzer rah*" of the Rabbinic tradition, is a powerful energy source. It must be: else how could it result in such torrents of sadism, fury and hate, as we have seen pour forth from the human heart? And yet, interestingly enough, if this energy source is controlled and disciplined in the right directions, it leads to constructive achievement! It is the aggressive energy drives, properly tamed, which have stirred ambition, which have made men resourceful and courageous, which have led people on the high road of adventure and discovery.

The "*yetzer tov*," the good inclination, is powerful too. It is undeveloped stages, it may lead to such undesirable traits as the over-possessive love of some mothers for their children—"smother love" they call it. Another primitive manifestation is the self-love which preoccupies some people—they are so concerned with their own care, their own beauty, that no one else can truly communicate feeling to them.

But when the impulse to goodness is trained and disciplined, it opens up the genuinely creative facets of life for us. Not only do we begin to like people, but we harness our energies to the tasks of building stronger bonds of understanding and cooperation with others.

We then discover the true meaning of the verse in Deuteronomy: "I have placed before Thee life and death—the blessing and the curse—therefore choose life.

Solomon S. Bernards

CHAPTER 11

FREEDOM AND DEMOCRACY

To Get Out of Egypt

RABBI NAHMAN OF Bratzlav comments on "and they made no provisions for the way": "When you are about to leave Egypt—any Egypt—do not stop to think 'But how will I earn a living out there? . . .' One who stops to 'make provisions for the way' will never get out of Egypt."

Charles I. Kraus

Truth Needs Freedom

THE TRUTH, TO be sure, makes us free. But we have to be free to get at the truth.

Mordecai M. Kaplan

Our Actions Can Make a Difference

WHAT IS CRUCIAL to understand is that the actions we choose to take in the face of adversity can make a difference in our lives. They can avert the severity of the decree, not the decree itself. Our actions can allow us to do the best we can with whatever we have to work with. We may not be able to change the objective reality, but we do have the ability—like

Avraham—to transform meaninglessness into meaning, and the profane into the sacred.

Shoshana Gelfand

American Fair Play

AMERICAN FAIR PLAY would guarantee to every man the right to worship God according to his own convictions and not according to the persuasions or prejudices of his neighbor.

Stephen S. Wise

Who's Driving?

WE DON'T MIND being slaves as long as we are our own slave drivers.

Mordecai M. Kaplan

Freedom Speaks with a Jewish Accent

OUR BIBLE TELLS of a God who wants man to be free. He is a God who hears the groaning of the slaves and sends a messenger to remind them in their agony that their cries have been heard.

He is a God who threatens destruction upon every tyrant who hardens his heart to the call of compassion and the demands of justice. He is a God who reveals Himself to the humiliated, the despised, the oppressed.

When He proclaims his commandments, He introduces Himself by saying: "I am the Lord your God who brought you out of the land of Egypt, out of the house of bondage." This is His signature. He is a God of freedom.

God spoke to our people first about freedom. Ever since, freedom has spoken with a Jewish accent. Passover renews our faith in the coming of a day when all will be free, and Passover rekindles our determination to work for that day.

Sidney Greenberg

Food Before Freedom

THE PASSOVER HAGGADAH has the right idea of freedom. Before it has anything to say about freedom, it wants to make sure that "all who are hungry" are provided for.

Mordecai M. Kaplan

We Are Co-Authors of Our Story

WE ARE FREE, we matter and in the most significant sense our life is in our own hands. This is the message of the season. Though none of us is without sin, yet none of us need surrender to hopelessness. We are not here acting out a script that has been written for us. We are co-authors of the story of our life and should resolutely bear our responsibility for it. It is a responsibility which gives us the precious opportunity to revise, edit, renew, and construct the drama in which we have the principal part.

Let us be worthy of such an opportunity.

Morris Adler

The Chains We Forge

THE SAD TRUTH about many of us is that, though we live in the freest country in the world, we are held in bondage by inner pharaohs. Some of us are the serfs of the pharaoh of tyrannical habits. Some of us are the serfs of the pharaoh of prejudice and greed. Some of us pay excessive tribute to the pharaoh of success or pleasure.

The invisible chains these despots fashion are as real as any imposed by a human dictator. Our task is to discipline ourselves, to take control over our lives, and to remove the shackles we ourselves have forged.

Sidney Greenberg

Freedom Needs Opportunity

FREEDOM WITHOUT OPPORTUNITY is like appetite without food. Opportunity without freedom is like food without appetite.

Mordecai M. Kaplan

I Chose Life

WHEN MY DEAR wife, Gillian, died of cancer, our little son, Zach was just thirteen months old. My world was black. I wanted to join her in the grave. I had no desire to live. Then I held my son in my arms and knew that I had a job to do, and that Gillian would expect me to do it. I chose life.

One Shabbat, when Zach was three, I blessed him, as I do each week, with the ancient words used by Aaron and his sons. When I finished, he looked up to me, smiled, and said, "Now let me bless you, Abba!" And so I received life's blessings, sacred and sweet. And I know that I am blessed.

Kenneth Cohen

When Our Freedom Is Complete

OUR EMANCIPATION WILL not be complete until we are free of the fear of being Jews.

Mordecai M. Kaplan

Please Untie Our Knots

Dear God,
We are bound with very tight knots.
They choke off air and stop the blood from pulsating freely. The knots make us like computers with carefully controlled circuitry. The

knots in our brains tie our creativity—our link with You. We follow the knot around in its intricacy—but it remains a knot.

The knots in our hearts keep us from crying and dancing when we long to—

They tie us to the posts of the fences that separate us from each other.

The knots in our muscles keep our teeth clenched, our jaws locked, our legs crossed, our shoulders stooped, our backs bent, our chests from inhaling and exhaling the full sweetness of life's breath.

O, God, untie all our knots!

Sheila Peltz Weinberg

Because God Freed Us from Egypt

RASHI, AT THE very beginning of the Book of Genesis, writes that God should not have begun the Torah with the story of the creation, but with the commandment of the *paschal* sacrifice, for that was the first "*mitzvah*" He gave Israel. Because our peoplehood began on the very eve of the liberation from Egypt, whenever God commands us to fulfill His law, He constantly refers to the fact that He brought us out of Egypt, rather than that He was the creator of the world. The laws of the Torah apply to us, not because they came from the creator of the world, for then, they would be applicable to all mankind, but because God freed us from Egypt.

Meyer Kramer

True Freedom for All

WHEN THE FAMILY gathers around the Seder table, the simple ceremonies, beginning with the pronouncement, "Lo this is the bread of affliction which our forefathers ate in the land of Egypt," then continuing with the drops of wine removed with the finger as symbols of sorrow for the loss of Egyptian life in the Exodus, and ending with the profound hope that next year may all humanity be free from the chains of slavery, convey a message that deeply touches the heart of the human being. For it speaks of the freedom that will not only gain for the individual release from the oppression of his neighbor, but release from his own handicaps of blindness and ignorance and prejudice which produce the injustices and the wars and the slaveries that plague the human race.

Charles E. Shulman

Without Law There Is No Freedom

THE EXODUS IS only the first chapter of the saga of liberty. It reached its climax when a horde of erstwhile slaves proclaimed in unison at the foot of Sinai, "We shall do and we shall listen." No wonder that Jewish tradition ties up the Festival of Passover, which commemorates the emancipation from Egypt, with the holiday of Pentecost, which commemorates the giving of the Law. Without law there is no freedom. As the irons of bondage are broken, the hands must be free to grasp the tablets on which are inscribed the divine commandments. Else liberty degenerates into license and freedom into servitude to a new tyranny. No man is free, say the Jewish sages in the Talmud, save one who lives by the Law.

Let us view the matter thus: Freedom is like a mighty torrent. Permitted to flow uncontrolled, it can flood the countryside and bring destruction and havoc and ruin. Properly harnessed, it can fertilize the plain, water the field, and yield power and energy by which life may be enriched. The poet must have had that image in mind when he sang: "Only in fetters is liberty. Without its banks, could a river be?"

Joseph H. Lookstein

Are You a Slave or Free?

THERE'S A SIMPLE test you can give yourself to check your status; slave or free. Just answer the following questions. First, "For whom do I work?" Certainly we all have responsibilities, but if we're not working for our own satisfaction, then we're not free. Work should be a mission, not a burden.

The second question is, "For what do I work?" If we see our work merely as a means of amassing wealth, then we are not free. Our work must have meaning or it will become oppressive.

And, finally, we must ask ourselves, "Do I know when to stop?" After all, even God knew when to stop, He created the world in six days and rested on the seventh. For a slave, there are no limits, no boundaries, and no time to stop.

Too many of us are suffering beneath a burden of "*kotzer ruach and avodah kasha.*" It's time for us to rebel against the modern slave mentality of the work ethic. It's time to stop and smell the roses!

Mark B. Greenspan

CHAPTER 12

THE GIFTS OF FRIENDSHIP

What We Get from Friendship

FRIENDSHIP IS LIKE a treasury: you cannot take from it more than you put into it.

Benjamin Mandelstamm

What Friendship Is

FRIENDSHIP—ONE HEART in two bodies.

Joseph Zabara

Our Real Friends

DO YOU HAVE at least one friend (it could be your spouse) who speaks honestly to you, and who can criticize you? If you don't, then you don't have any real friends.

Joseph Telushkin

Old Friends Are Best

Cherish friendship in your breast—
New is good, but old is best;
Make new friends, but keep the old;
Those are silver, these are gold.

Joseph Parry

CHAPTER 13

GOD AND WE

How We Serve God

SERVICE OF GOD consists in what we do to our neighbor.

Leo Baeck

To Love God

TO LOVE GOD is to refuse to let oneself be depressed by the world.

Mordecai M. Kaplan

Bringing Order out of Chaos

BRINGING ORDER OUT of chaos is the work of God. And we give some evidence that we are made in His image when we go and do likewise.

Albert S. Goldstein

The World Has a Creator

RABBI AKIBA USED to say that just as a door testifies that it had a carpenter and a coat testifies that it had a weaver, so does the existence of the world testify that it had a Creator.

Joseph Klein

God Is the Attributes We Assign to Him

WHEN WE SPEAK of God's attributes, we should mean not that God has those attributes but that He *is* those attributes.

Mordecai M. Kaplan

What God Wants of Us

GOD DOES NOT want us to do extraordinary things; he wants us to do ordinary things extraordinarily well.

Bernard S. Raskas

Putting God in the Center of Life

IT IS WORTH noting that the Hebrew word for life is a four-letter word. It is *hayyim*. But unlike its English counterpart, which has *if* in the middle of it, the Hebrew word for life has two *yuds* in the middle. And two *yuds*, as we know, spell the name of God.

If we put God in the vital center of our lives, we can meet any contingency without being defeated or overwhelmed. And we can then live with the certainty that life has meaning, purpose and unlimited possibilities of fulfillment.

Sidney Greenberg

My God

WE DO BELIEVE that the God of the Universe, the one and only God, is also *our* God. He is the God of you and me. Great as he is, he is not too great to be *my* God, too great for me to pray to him, too great for him to help and care for me. On the contrary: just because he is so great, just because he is so perfect and unique, do we *also* believe that he can be, and is, *also* the God of each individual man.

C. G. Montefiore

Our Divine Quest

WE ARE COMMITTED to a divine quest. We are summoned to go forth in search of divinity. A divinity we will never completely find. But the quest itself will sanctify our aspirations, our future, beyond the edge of mystery, in the direction of God.

William B. Silverman

God of Truth

From the cowardice that shrinks from new truth,
From the laziness that is content with half-truths,
From the arrogance that thinks it knows all truth,
O, God of truth, deliver us.

Mordecai M. Kaplan

Where Is God in Tragedy?

Where is God in a terrible tragedy?
God is in the compassion we feel for the bereaved.
God is in the sympathy and in the support that kind friends extend to the survivors.
God is in our resolve to apprehend the murderer and to prevent further shedding of innocent blood.
God is in the strength that the victim's loved ones will somehow find as they make their way through the valley of the shadow.
God is in the healing that will come to them ever so slowly but ever so surely.
God is in the power of the human spirit to rise above sorrow and to transmute suffering into song, adversity into artistry, and pain into poetry.
We come from God and we return to Him and with the Source of life no soul is ever lost. God is also in the great gift of remembrance. As the poet said, "God gave us memory so that we might have roses in December."

Sidney Greenberg

Something to Hold On To

THE WOMAN IN the subway who suddenly fell forward when the car came to a stop explained in embarrassment, "I had nothing to hold on to." In our journey through life we are frequently jostled as we take a curve, or halt suddenly. What do we "hold on to?" Holding on to someone can be precarious since a person can fall, or move away. Some people hold on to their money to attain stability as life sways precariously. They think that by having a "bank balance" they will attain a spiritual balance.

In fact, the surest anchorage in life is our confidence and trust in God, who is our rock and redeemer. Our religious faith provides us with the greatest equilibrium. If you want something to hold on to, grasp the Bible, embrace the *mitzvot*.

We live in anxious and tense times, and we are in for a rocky ride. Hold on.

Stanley M. Wagner

God Hears Even the Unuttered Cry

NO APPEAL TO God, no cry of distress goes unanswered. "God hears a cry of sorrow even when it is unuttered," said Rabbi Mendel. Commenting on the verse, "And God heard the voice of the lad," he explained it in this way: "Nothing in the preceding verses indicates that Ismael cried out. No, it was a soundless cry, but God heard it."

Sidney Greenberg

In Defeat, Triumph

OTHER NATIONS OF antiquity, when they were defeated, acknowledged that their gods had been defeated. The Jews always saw in their defeat the triumph of their God.

Abba Hillel Silver

What the "Loving Father" Wants of Us

THE MATURE PERSON who refers to God as his "loving Father" does not expect a cosmic lollipop; he is simply expressing his awareness of the moral, mental, physical and aesthetic possibilities which the Lord put within him, and which God ardently wishes him to fulfill.

Harold L. Krantzler

What I Share with God

THROUGH HIS IMAGE implanted within me, I share with God a brief terrestrial excursion here on earth.

Alexander Alan Steinbach

Meeting God

BEAUTY AND HOLINESS are the mirror of God's countenance; music is the echo of His voice.

Alexander Alan Steinbach

To Help Live Is Divine

THE WILL TO live is animal; the will to let live is human; the will to help live is divine.

Mordecai M. Kaplan

God Is Personal but Not a Person

TO SAY THAT God is personal does not necessarily mean that God is a person. Many things that are not persons are personal: love, honor, friendship, loyalty. None of these ideals is impersonal; they have meaning only as they are manifest in personality. In the same sense, God is personal. God is indeed the very source and sponsor of human personality.

Eugene Kohn

Young Enough and Old Enough

WE CAN BE young enough to seek companionship, but old enough to appreciate solitude.

We can be young enough to crave happiness, but old enough to know that the harvest of happiness is usually reaped by the hands of helpfulness.

We can be young enough to want to be loved, but old enough to strive to be lovable.

We can be young enough to pray as if everything depended on God, but old enough to act as if everything depended on us.

Sidney Greenberg

How We Prove God's Existence

THE BEST ARGUMENT for the existence of God is a godlike human life.

Mordecai M. Kaplan

Where God Stands

GOD SAID, "I will stand there before you on the rock" [Exodus 17:6]. This implies: In every place where a man leaves his footprint, there *I* too will stand.

The Midrash

What Revelation Is

REVELATION IS THE silent, imperceptible manifestations of God in history. It is the still, small voice.

Herbert M. Loewe

Man's Innate Dignity

THE RECOGNITION OF man's innate dignity as God's coworker is basic to a proper understanding of his nature, as manifested in his creative ability, his moral responsibility, and his untapped potentialities.

Robert Gordis

Always There Is God

A RELIGIOUS PERSON structures his life around the experiences of God. He knows that God is in commandments, in actions of righteousness, as well as in the beauty of the world. When I fulfill myself, there is God. When I bring right and justice to others, when I create joy and happiness, there is God. The sensitive person lives his life in the presence of God at all times.

Alan Hammer

God's Co-Partner

THE MOST PROFOUND teaching of the Jewish tradition is that man is neither a helpless being or a worthless creature. He is, in the words of the Talmud, "the co-partner of G-d in the work of creation." He is created in the image of G-d. And this means that man possesses part of the nature of G-d—the gift of reason and thought, the power to choose between good and evil, the unconquerable yearning for righteousness, and above all, the capacity to bridge the gulf between "what is" and "what can be." The evil that man has made, he can unmake, so he is fashioned in the image of G-d.

Morton L. Gordon

What the Meaning of God Can Be

REVERENCE FOR HUMAN personality—that can be our religion. That can be, for us, the meaning of God.

Abraham Cronbach

God Makes Nature Creative

GOD IS THE force in life that makes nature creative and not merely mechanical.

Robert Blinder

Where God Exists

"WHERE DOES GOD exist?" The Kotzker rebbe asked several of his followers.

"Everywhere," the surprised disciples responded.

"No," the rebbe answered. "God exists only where man lets Him in."

Joseph Telushkin

The High Use of Atheism

"WHY ARE THERE atheists in the world?" The disciples asked Rabbi Mosheh Leib, "Why did God create atheism or permit it to exist?"

"God has need for atheism," Rabbi Mosheh answered, "for the sake of man. If someone seeks your aid, you must act as if there were no God to help. Act as if you alone can help. In that way, even atheism can be exalted. Even atheism can be sanctified."

Stanley Yedwab

God Suffers with the Sufferers

GOD WAS THERE in the concentration camps, suffering with the sufferers, hanging on the gallows with the victims, suffocating in the gas chambers, and stealing bread for the sick. It was because God was there that some were able to survive. It was because God was there that some were able to hug and kiss their wives and husbands and children as the gas seeped in around them. It was because God was there—a palpable presence to many—that some were able to face their final moments with nobility, knowing that they had defeated death. It was because the young Elie Wiesel felt God hanging on the gallows next to that little boy that he is able today, after seeing his entire civilization annihilated, to believe in God, to question God, and to cry with God.

Simeon J. Maslin

Recognition of God Influences Everything

TO THE AUTHENTIC Jew the recognition of God is not an abstract or mystic idea. It influences everything he does. It expresses itself not only in prayer, in Shabbos and kashruth, in shofar and fasting, but in the study of Torah and reverence for parents, in honorable business practices and in proper language. It is attained not by renouncing the world and isolating oneself from humanity, but by being an integral part of a family, a community, a society, and emulating Moses, the godly man.

Israel Miller

We Need God

WE ARE NOT enough by ourselves. We don't see enough. We don't know enough or understand enough. We don't have vision enough or wisdom enough.

We need God. We need the hope which is from Him; the great distances from our eyes, His wisdom for our hearts, His eternal truths for our spirits.

We need God: for the sense of timelessness beyond our time, for the sense of eternity to cradle our brief hours.

We need His arms to uphold us.

We need His presence to know that the world eternally has a place for memory and for life whose years are ended.

Jacob Philip Rudin

God Urges Us to Become Fully Human

GOD IS THE goal that impels man to become fully human.

Mordecai M. Kaplan

Caesar's and God's

WE CANNOT RENDER anything to Caesar which is not also God's.

Arnold Wolf

Worshipping God and Obeying Him

IT IS INCOMPARABLY easier to venerate the truth than to speak it, to admire righteousness than to practice it, to worship God than to obey Him.

Mordecai M. Kaplan

One Life in a Deathless Poem

MAN IS NOT alone and neither his mind nor his conscience nor his creative powers can be truly understood if they are regarded as orphans without some universal Parent. I have come to feel that the whole human story, with all its tragedy and triumph, is like a page torn from the middle of a book, without beginning or end—an undecipherable page, when cut out of its context.

The context of man is the Power greater than man. The human adventure is part of a universal sonnet—one line is a deathless poem.

Joshua Loth Liebman

The Captain Is My Father

A COLLEAGUE OF mine tells the story of a youngster, standing on the banks of the Mississippi holding a long pole with a red flag at its end, waving down a steamboat. A stranger, passing by, said to him, "You foolish youngster, do you really expect to stop that boat?" "It'll stop, mister," the boy replied, "I ain't worried." To his surprise, the stranger noticed the boat swerve toward the bank, the gangplank was dropped and the boy walked up, "You see, mister," the boy said, turning to the stranger, "the captain of the boat is my father."

We have a Heavenly Father, ever ready to receive us, if only we earnestly wave in his direction. This makes the passing of another week, the ushering of a new year, meaningful.

As we direct ourselves toward the divine course, we will hear the father-captain repond, *solachti kidvorecho*, "I have forgiven as you have spoken, that the New Year be good and blessed—*shana tova umvurechet*."

Simon A. Dolgin

Things God Cannot Do Without Us

WE MUST NOT permit our faith in God to grow so mighty that we forget the things that God cannot do without us.

God cannot make a peaceful world unless we, His children, help Him by rooting out the hatred from our hearts, the prejudice from our minds, the injustice from our society.

God cannot promote the security of the State of Israel unless we permit our abundance to work with Him in this enterprise of redemption.

God cannot build a happy home unless husband and wife work with Him by bringing to it a spirit of sharing, mutual respect, a binding loyalty, constancy and compassion.

God cannot give us a peaceful night's sleep unless we cooperate with Him by doing an honest day's work.

God cannot forgive our sins unless we help Him by genuine contrition for what has been and firm resolve for what we mean to accomplish. "How do we know our sins have been forgiven?" a pupil asked his Rabbi. "When we don't repeat them," he answered.

God heals the sick but not without the doctor's medicine, the surgeon's hands, the nurse's vigilance, the encouragement of loved ones and friends.

God brings forth bread from the earth but not without the farmer who prepares the soil, plants the seed, harvests the crop.

God helps the poor with the charity we give, cheers the lonely with the visits we make, comforts the bereaved with the words we speak, guides our children with the examples we set, ennobles our lives with the Mitzvot we perform.

And here ultimately is the reason why you and I are here on this earth. God needs us, each of us. We are joined with Him in a great partnership.

May neither an excess of humility nor a surplus of faith keep us from performing nobly our assignments in this partnership.

Sidney Greenberg

How We Reveal God

SPIRITUAL SEEKING IS the human drive to make meaning out of the fact of existence. We name what we seek "God." By creating holiness/wholeness in life, we reveal the face of God.

Meryl M. Crean

The Yeast of the Universe

Yeast, mixed with the dough itself, is an inner force, causing the loaf to rise. I mean no irreverent heresy in suggesting that God is the yeast of the universe.

Roland B. Gittelsohn

God Wrote Half

I composed a song about life.
But God wrote half,
He gave me wings,
I soared on high
And saw the world.
I acclaimed love
And derided hate,
But He guided my heart
To choose.
He gave me a joy and a pain,
My spirit brooded on them,

And they released a light.
Time turned what I knew into words,
The words came together
And gave birth
To the song.

Ben Zion Bokser

We Must Fix the Cracks

JUDAISM DESCRIBES A complex process of collective redemption; Jewish Messianism has numerous strands and is not easily described. But its basic structure goes something like this: first, the world was created whole; then it was broken; and in the future, it will be restored once more to wholeness. We can actually hear this process replicated in the notes of the *shofar: tekiah, shevarim, tekiah*—whole, broken, and whole. We live in the middle, in the fractured reality of human history, in the broken state of human imperfection. Our role as human beings is, with God's help, to fix the cracks within ourselves and within God's world.

Marc Margolis

God Goads Us

GOD IS THE goad that impels man to become fully human.

Mordecai M. Kaplan

Reckoning with the Will of God

WE OWE IT to ourselves to consider what our relationship to God shall be. If it is not more than a relationship between a three-year-old child who wants things, then contemporary man will have to concede that his religious experience and motivation are infantile. If, however, God will help us to act at least as eight- or ten-year-old children who are aware of the fact that there should be a reciprocal relationship between parents and children, and that it is important for children to reckon with the will of their parents, then contemporary man will begin to think of reckoning with the Will of God and do the things every day of his life which have no purpose other than to indicate that he is submitting himself to the Will of God.

Emanuel Rackman

God Is of Supreme Importance

GOD IS OF no importance unless He is of supreme importance.

Abraham J. Heschel

Three Whom God Loves

GOD LOVES THESE three: the person who does not get angry; the one who does not get drunk; and the one who does not insist upon his privileges.

The Talmud

Serve the Creator with Joy

PURIFY ALL YOUR ideas and thoughts, and do not think many thoughts, but one alone: to serve your Creator with joy. And let all the thoughts that come to you be included in that one thought.

Shneur Zalman of Ladi

Divine Accessibility and Human Behavior

LEVITICUS BELIEVES THAT divine accessibility is coordinated with human behavior. We have the power through the morality of our behavior to make God imminent or transcendent. Divine intimacy with humanity depends upon the quality of human action. If, by polluting the sanctuary, we can make it unfit, as it were, for divine living, just think what we could do by sanctifying it.

Sylvan Kamens

The Bragging Farmer

A FARMER WAS showing the boy his acreage and bragged extravagantly about his accomplishments. He concluded his monologue of self-congratulation with the proud boast: "I grew it all by myself, Sonny. And I started out with nothing!"

"With nothing?" the young fellow asked in amazement. "Golly, sir without even a seed?"

Sidney Greenberg

We See God in What He Does

WE CANNOT SEE God. We can see only what God does.

Sidney H. Brooks

What God Dreams

GOD'S DREAM IS . . . to have mankind as a partner in the drama of continuous creation.

Abraham J. Heschel

We Can Serve God Through Everything

THE WORLD IS teeming with God. Since God is in everything, we can serve God through everything.

Daniel C. Matt

What God and Man Need

MAN CANNOT GET along without God who cares, and God cannot get along without a man who cares.

Ely. E. Pilchik

When You Are Alone with God

OUR PROPHETS TEACH us on the contrary. "*He* declared unto you, o man, what is good and what the Lord seeks from you: Only to practice justice, and the love of mercy, and to walk humbly with your God" [Micah 6:8]. It is God who defines "what is good," not man.

The crux of our understanding of the knowledge of God lies in the last phrase, usually rendered "to walk humbly with God." Literally the phrase has an entirely different meaning. The Hebrew word *hatznea* has the same root as *tzniuth* which denotes something hidden or secret. *Hatznea lechet im elokecho* really means, therefore: "To walk with your God even when you are in secret, quite alone with Him."

Immanuel Jakobovitz

God Elicits Our Best

GOD IS THAT aspect of reality which elicits from us the best that is in us and enables us to bear the worst that can befall us.

Mordecai M. Kaplan

Religion Calls a Sin a Sin

IT IS TRUE that the word "sin" is old-fashioned. But it can never become out-of-date, because it expresses a basic reality. Truth driven out through the door re-enters through the window. Modern psychology dismissed the idea of sin as meaningless, but then it found that it needed the concept. Wishing to avoid "contamination" with religion, psychologists avoid the term "sin" and prefer "guilt," because it is a basic element in human experience. What is guilt, as used in the jargon of our day? It may be defined, not unfairly, as an overpowering feeling that something is wrong, without any clear understanding of what is right! Religion calls a spade a spade, and a sin a sin.

What is sin? It is an act of rebellion against God and the laws of His world. Sin is man's failure to render obedience to God's law of righteousness in the universe. In Solomon Schechter's words, "Sin taints the divine in man, breaking all communion with heaven."

Robert Gordis

The Lenient Rabbi

MANY WOMEN CAME to a hasidic rabbi on the eve of Yom Kippur with questions relating to *kashrut*. He replied to each one, without exception, that the food was kosher and could be eaten. When approached by a rabbi colleague who suggested that it might be more proper to be stricter in rendering decisions on the eve of the Day of Atonement, the hasidic rabbi responded: "On the contrary. If I should declare a chicken of doubtful *kashrut* unfit for eating, I may be guilty of sinning against my brethren who may not have anything else to eat before the fast, and a sin against man will not be expiated on Yom Kippur. However, if I declare the chicken to be kosher even though there may be some doubt, I am sinning only against God, and as you know, the Day of Atonement brings pardon for sins against Him."

Philip Goodman

Each Jew Must Plead His Own Cause Before the Divine Judge

THE JEW MUST stand upright on his own two feet before the Judge of all. He has no patron saints to plead his cause, no Father Confessor to grant indulgences, absolutions, or dispensations. He is, in the fullest sense, the "master of his fate, the captain of his soul." He neither has, nor asks for, any intermediary to bear his brief before the Judge of Heaven. Each man is his own barrister. He must plead his own cause, with a sincere heart that is truly repentant, to God alone.

Abraham Carmel

Leave a Little to God

"ON THIS DAY of Rosh Hashanah the world came into being." The majestic *Musaf* Service in its threefold structure proclaims the life-giving truth of man's relationship to God as co-partner in creation. The *Malkhuyot* proclaim the sovereignty of God—God rules the world as our Father and our King. Nor do we have to go it alone. For the *Zikhronot* recall that God is mindful of man's struggles and agonies, his weaknesses and frustrations, his capacity for goodness and greatness. Out of the sovereignty of God and the significance of man comes the third section of the Service, the *Shofarot*, paying a tribute to the shofar, which was sounded on Sinai at the giving of the Law and will be heard again proclaiming the Messianic age.

The shofar is symbolic of the cosmic partnership of God and man. On Mount Sinai it was said: *Mosheh yedabber veha'elohim ya'anenu bekol*, "Moses spoke and God answered him with a loud voice." Let us speak and act for the right and then leave a little to God, knowing that He will not fail us. Together we can go forward to build a world worthy of God's greatness and man's hopes.

Robert Gordis

Moral Law—Principal Self-Revelation of God

THE UNIQUE ELEMENT in the Jewish religion consisted in the conscious recognition that the chief function of the belief in God was to affirm and fortify the moral law . . . that the moral law is the principal manifestation of God in the world. The identification of God as the author of righteousness was thus translated into the identification of God as the author of *Torah Min Hashamayim*, of the Torah as divinely revealed, the original prophetic discovery of the moral law as the principal self-revelation of God.

Mordecai M. Kaplan

God—The Healing Fact

GOD'S ESSENCE, BUT His attributes of activity—namely, the universal laws of social, mental, and moral health—these we can possess. God, as [William Ernest] Hocking insists, is not the Healing Fiction but the Healing Fact, and we come upon Him at work in the majesty of nature and the fruitfulness of mind, in the laws of atoms and the goals of men.

Joshua Loth Liebman

God Needs to Help to Make Cosmos out of Chaos

IT IS REALLY amazing how easily we succumb to the tragedy of focusing our gaze on insignificant goals when there are such great causes to champion, so many relationships to establish, so many great books waiting to illumine our darkness. How can we continue to grovel in the mire of small ends, arrogant selfishness and sordid motives when life ebbs so swiftly away and God is summoning us to become coworkers with Him in fashioning a cosmos out of chaos?

Leon D. Stitskin

God Is Our Ally

HOW DO WE know that a man's sins have been forgiven?" asked a Hassidic rabbi. And he answered: "When he no longer commits the sin." We are free to break with what we have been; to be what the better angels of our nature assure us we can become.

And in this struggle we are not alone. God is our ally. God who gave us the power to repent helps us in this endeavor. Our sages picture God as saying to us: "If you open the door of repentance only as wide as a needle's eye, I will open it wide enough to permit carriages and wagons to pass through." God helps those who want to remake themselves, to refine their character, to redirect their lives.

In brief then this is the two-fold meaning of this day: responsibility for yesterday, opportunity for tomorrow. But the choice must be made today.

"Behold I set before you the choice today." God grant us the will to choose, and the wisdom to choose wisely.

Sidney Greenberg

When We Are Near to God

JUDAISM TEACHES THAT man is never nearer to God than when he serves the best interests of his fellows. The whole thrust of the Akedah story is to emphasize that service to God by harming one's fellows is revolting to God.

Philip Lipis

Hold with Open Arms

ALL OF LIFE is the more treasurable because a great and Holy Spirit is in it.

And yet, it is easier for me to let go.

For these things are not and never have been mine. They belong to the Universe and the God who stands behind it. True, I have been privileged to enjoy them for an hour but they were always a loan due to be recalled.

And I let go of them the more easily because I know that as parts of the divine economy they will not be lost. The sunset, the bird's song, the baby's smile, the thunder of music, the surge of great poetry, the dreams of the heart, and my own being, dear to me as every man's is to him, all these I can well trust to Him who made them. There is poignancy and regret about giving them up, but no anxiety. When they slip from my hands they will pass to hands better, stronger, and wiser than mine.

This then is the insight which came to me as I stood some months ago in a blaze of sunlight: Life is dear, let us then hold it tight while we yet may; but we must hold it loosely also!

Only with God can we ease the intolerable tension of our existence. For only when He is given, can we hold life at once infinitely precious and yet as a thing lightly to be surrendered. Only because of Him is it made possible for us to clap the world, but with relaxed hands, to embrace it, but with open arms.

Milton Steinberg

When the Torah Is Complete

THERE ARE SIX hundred thousand letters in the Torah, and in the Torah we find that there were six hundred thousand Israelites. Thus each person is a letter of the Torah; without him, the Torah will never be complete. Each person has his own indispensable role to play. If he sins, he has lost that precious moment and has rendered himself unable to be the letter which he is. All Israel suffers as a result, for the Torah is incomplete.

And thus when one man repents, all Israel, and God, are joyous, because in turning from sin to good, he has written his letter again in the Torah and in the now, the moment which has its own sacredness and significance, the Torah is complete, and God and Israel are at peace.

Arthur Hertzberg

Service of God Is Service of Man

THERE IS NO service of God without the service of man. God reveals Himself to us as a mirror high above us wherein we see ourselves reflected. We see Him as a Helper when we are helpers. We see Him as a Redeemer and Protector when we are redeemers and protectors. The love of man, in short, is the substance whereof the love of God is made and the service of man is the stuff whereof the service of God is made.

Abraham Cronbach

Prayer Unifies

PRAYER IS THE energy feedback God gets from us, His creation. Prayer completes the circuit of God's energy to the entire system, for we are integral parts of the universe. Praying for our well-being, and ultimately for our own perfection, is equal to praying for the universe, since it is composed of its parts—of us! Prayer unifies. It unites us with our fellow human beings and all the other beings in God's universe. Taken in our totality—gentile and Jew; woman and man; child and adult; animal and plant; the earth below and the heavens above—we are the likeness of God.

Zalman Schachter Shlomi

The Ultimate Test

ARE OUR SUPPLICATIONS to God heard and answered? This question takes us back to the fundamental question regarding the nature of the universe as a whole. Are they right to say "The Lord does not see it, the God of Jacob does not pay heed" [Psalm 94:7], or is there a self-evident cogency to the argument "Shall He who implants the ear not hear, He who forms the eye not see?" [Psalm 94:9]? But even assuming that He does "hear" and "see," is He *concerned*, and does He respond in accordance with the standards of justice and mercy?

We do not *know*, and we cannot possibly ever know, the answer to these questions. We either believe that "more things are wrought by prayer than this world dreams of"—and that God hears the cry of the stranger, the widow, and the fatherless who are wronged and afflicted, and responds to their cry [Exodus 22:20–23], and that "The Lord is near to all who call upon Him, to all who call Him with sincerity" [Psalm 145:18]—or we do not. No amount of "proof" can validate either position beyond a reasonable doubt, nor even establish a reasonable preponderance of proof in favor of the one position over the other.

But there are some things that we know about prayer with a certainty that is at least as great, if not greater, than the certainty with which we know the phenomena brought to our attention by our five senses. We know that the ability and the privilege of reciting our needs before God is our ultimate defense against being overwhelmed by utter despair. For we would not have uttered the prayer at all if it were not for a glimmer of hope that moves us to do so. And we know from the testimony of others, and many of us from our own experience, that the heartfelt utterance of a prayer can ignite that glimmer into a flame that brightens, at least for a moment, the darkness which surrounds us.

In that moment of illumination, we may see with persuasive clarity that God owes us nothing, that "His thoughts are not our thoughts" [Isaiah 58:8], that what we may be praying for may not be to our advantage, and that He has ways of exercising His love, justice, and mercy which are beyond our knowledge or power to comprehend. In such a moment of illumination, we may see that to love God means, among other things, to subdue our will to His, so that we accept what we deem to be His favorable response to our supplications without self-righteousness, and what to us may appear as His unfavorable response without resentment. For the ultimate test of whether our prayers have or have not been answered is whether we rise from them reinvigorated in our belief that life is good and more firm if committed to living the good life. All else is of secondary importance.

Simon Greenberg

A Potent Instrument of Survival

THE SIDDUR, AS the Jewish prayer book is called in Hebrew, gives voice to the depth of Jewish faith. It is marked by an all-pervading and radiant optimism. It greets each new-born day with the ringing assertion that the soul with which God has endowed man is pure. It maintains an unyielding faith in the basic goodness of the human soul. A somber note is seldom heard.

The exiled Jew has trudged indeflectibly forward through the leaden-footed centuries, ever carrying joyously in his heart prayer for the regeneration of his people and the rebuilding of Zion. He has had an unwavering religious faith in the divine destiny that will override the man-made cataclysms of history. His prayer book has been for him a potent instrument for survival. In recurrent affirmations it promises that he will be comforted for the sorrows he has borne.

The prayers are irradiated by a glorious universalism and an unfailing vision of hope and betterment for all men. The Messianic concept of an ideal Golden Age is set not in the past but in the future. Blessings and prayers are addressed to God not only as our God and God of our fathers, but also to Him as *Avinu shebashamayim*, our Father who are in heaven, *Meleh haolam*, the King of the universe, and *Ribbono shel olam*, universal Lord.

The prayer book is a manual of intense personal devotion and piety; but it is no less the expression of Jewish social idealism. It voices the religious aspirations of the whole people and the aim to achieve an ennobled spiritual society. The prayers, overwhelmingly in the plural, express the striving of all the Jewish people to reach their God. In unifying brotherhood of worship the individual draws inspiration and strength from the communal praying, through which he brings to the congregation his increment of spiritual purpose and devotion.

David De Sola Pool

Prayer Allows Us to Be Alone with God

TO FEEL THE proximity of God we need intervals of withdrawal from other men. If we are not to lose ourselves in that real loneliness which is remoteness from God, we must have periods of loneliness upon earth when our soul is left to itself and we are remote from other men. If we are not to go astray in the world, we must look into ourselves and remember our souls and God. In the innermost recesses of the human heart there dwells a desire for such loneliness, which, incidentally, is one of the strongest roots of asceticism. It is a historical achievement of Israel that through prayer it satisfied this human need and religious necessity. The purpose of prayer is to allow us to be alone with God and apart from other men, to give us seclusion in the midst of the world. We are to seek loneliness also in the house of God even when it is crowded with men, to be alone there also with ourselves and our God. If our life is to be filled with devoutness, we must from time to time abandon the ways of the world so that we may enjoy the peace of God.

Leo Baeck

We Become What We Pray For

THE MAN WHO prays passionately and unremittingly for money may never attain wealth. But he will acquire a monetary soul, a character whose actions are governed consistently by mercenary motives, whose judgement of all things is not their value but their price.

He who prays ardently, ceaselessly for fame, may never achieve renown. But he will become transformed by his prayers into a creature whose very food is flattery, who quails at criticism, who revels in the bubble glory of reputation, who dies in his soul at the slightest neglect to his vanity; a constant prey to every foolish breath of gossip, to all the vacillating whimsicalities of popular opinion.

While he who longs to be an artist or a poet may never hold a brush and palette, or pen a single line of verse or music; but his prayers will create in him the artist's soul alive to all the wonder and loveliness and grace that are in existence.

Albert S. Goldstein

These Words Can Bring Us into the Presence of God

WHEN WE ENTER the synagogue and open our prayer books, we find words printed on paper. They can mean little or nothing, if so we are disposed. But the imaginative mind and the sensitive spirit and the intelligent heart may find tremendous power in these words . . . through them he will link himself to all the generations of his fathers in a golden chain of piety . . . he will join his fellows of the house of Israel everywhere, and time and space will be no hindrance as he pours out his soul together with his fathers and his brothers toward heaven. He will find words soothing and peaceful—and words rousing and challenging to the conscience.

But above all, these words, laden with the tears and joys of centuries, have the power to bring us into the presence of God. Not all at once, not easily, not every time: but somehow, sometime the faithful worshipers who take heart and soul into their hands and offer them up without reservation—somehow, sometime they will know that they have reached the throne of Glory, and that God has taken them by the hand.

Chaim Stern

The Very Essence of Prayer

PRAYER IS BASICALLY an awareness of man finding himself in the presence of and addressing himself to his Maker, and to pray has one connotation only: to stand before God. To be sure, this awareness has been objectified and crystallized in standardized, definitive texts whose recitation is obligatory. The total faith commitment tends always to transcend the frontiers of fleeting, amorphous subjectivity and to venture into the outside world of the well-formed, objective gesture. However, no matter how important this tendency on the part of the faith commitment is—and it is of enormous significance in the Halakhah, which constantly demands from man that he translate his inner life into external facticity—it remains unalterably true that the very essence of prayer is the covenantal experience of being together with and talking to God and that the concrete performance, such as the recitation of texts, represents the technique of implementation of prayer and not prayer itself.

J.B. Soloveitchik

Prayer Assigned a Place of Primacy in the Life of the Jew

THE RABBIS ASSIGNED to prayer a place of primacy in the life of the Jew. The Jew is required not only to participate in the prescribed daily services in synagogue and at home, but also to pronounce blessings on all events and experiences. As the famous scholar M. Steinschneider aptly put it: "The Jew's whole life became a divine service with interruptions." And these rabbinic prayers have withstood the vicissitudes of time and fashion and have survived the onslaughts of both persecution and prosperity. It is only in our times that these prayers have been challenged. If the challenge is to be met successfully, an understanding of these prayers is urgently needed.

Abraham Millgram

Pray for the Ability to Pray

WHAT THEN IS left for us to do except to *pray for the ability to pray*, to bewail our ignorance of living in His presence? And even if such prayer is tainted with vanity, His mercy accepts and redeems our feeble efforts. It is the continuity of trying to pray, the unbroken loyalty to our duty to pray, that lends strength to our fragile worship; and it is the holiness of the community that bestows meaning upon our individual acts of worship. These are the three pillars on which our prayer rises to God: our own loyalty, the holiness of Israel, the mercy of God.

Abraham J. Heschel

Prayer Pushes Out the Walls of Normal Existence

PRAYER IS NOT an easy way of getting God to do what He ought to do, and neither is it a way of getting Him to do what we ought to do. There is no escape from the duty that lies upon us. Prayer will not offer us a refuge from the problems that trouble us. Prayer does, however, offer us the opportunity to raise ourselves and our lives to a higher peak. Prayer, if performed in that spirit, will put us in a better position, far better equipped to deal with the harassments and the dilemmas of our lives.

Prayers take us into a large universe. It pushes out the walls of normal existence. How small is the area in which most of us live! During our vacations we may take trips abroad and see distant lands, but most of the time the majority of us lead lives that are local and parochial. All of us live in restricted areas of our own concerns—of our families, of our own offices and needs, of our own resentments, hates, and prejudices. How important it is that now and then we go out into the great open space of the universe and let the vast breezes that come from distant places blow in upon our confined lives. How important it is to capture for a moment the large perspectives that lets us see ourselves as part of a larger universe.

Morris Adler

The Need for Self-Fulfillment

A GREAT CHASIDIC teacher said that a person should always bear two verses in mind: "It is for my sake that the world was created" and "I am but dust and ashes."

If the individual is of supreme importance, the worshiper may well feel that his efforts to deal with his problems and concerns form part of the movement of the world toward the perfection of the "Kingdom of Heaven." As Hillel put it, "If I am not for myself, who will be for me? But if I am for myself only, what am I?" [Ethics of the Fathers 1:14].

A person should see his own needs in the light of his overriding concern for self-fulfillment, and understand that the fulfillment of his self is attained through his integration within the purpose and design of God.

Jacob B. Agus

Prayer Can Satisfy a Very Real Need of the Soul

THOUGH OUR PRAISE and our thanksgiving can confer naught upon "the Most High God, the Possessor of heaven and earth," to us it can ensure much. It can satisfy a very real need of the soul—the need to express itself to the Source of its joys, to the God of its life. Is it not true also that prayer itself begets devotion? "While we meditate the fire kindles." The payment of our tribute to God, far from removing the sense of indebtedness, leaves us more grateful, more humble than ever. In the clear atmosphere of worship, we see more plainly than before the distant heights of the Divine majesty and goodness. For our own sakes, then, for the sake of the fullness it gives to our spiritual life, we must obey the natural promptings of our heart, and, like the Psalmist, "sing unto the Lord as long as we live."

Morris Joseph

A Word Uttered in Prayer Is a Promise

PRAYER MUST NOT be dissonant with the rest of living. The mercifulness, gentleness, which pervades us in moments of prayer is but a ruse or a bluff if it is inconsistent with the way we live at other moments. The divorce of liturgy and living, of prayer and practice, is more than a scandal; it is a disaster. A word uttered in prayer is a promise, an earnest, a commitment. If the promise is not kept, we are guilty of violating a promise.

Abraham J. Heschel

What Real Prayer Requires

REAL PRAYER REQUIRES anguish, a feeling of inadequacy and nothingness in relation to God, a shaken soul, a bleeding heart. "The Lord is near unto them that are of a broken heart, and such as are broken in spirit He saves" [Psalms 34:19]. Thus the Psalmist speaks of *t'filah l'ani* "The prayer of the poor man" [102:1]. This aspect of prayer is so vital that Jewish law, in a truly poignant regulation, requires of the *Chazan*, of the reader who leads the congregation in prayer, "that he shall be married and have children, so that he shall know how to pour out his heart and offer supplications from the depth of his heart."

Perhaps our lives today are too easy to appreciate the essence of prayer. Thank God, we do not know what it means to suffer hunger, to worry whence to take tomorrow's bread for our children, to run to the synagogue of *Shabbat M'vorchim* preceding the new month and cry out for a *chayim shel parnasah*, a life of sustenance.

We must learn again how to *davven*, how to pray properly.

Immanuel Jakobovitz

The God of Mothers and Children

I WILL NEVER forget the first time I was able to *daven* [pray] after my daughter's birth. When I was able to hold the *siddur* in my hands once again, on the second Shabbat of my daughter's life, I found myself reaching out to a different God than ever before.

I found myself talking not to an image of God as the God of law and command and blame . . . I called out to God as the giver of life, the God of mothers and children, of love and care and nourishment, a God who would understand that there was sanctity in nursing and diaper changing and rocking and comforting as surely as there was sanctity in my encounter with the *siddur*.

That night, for the first time in my life, I encountered a feminine image of God who rejoiced in the birth of my daughter and my own rebirth as a mother. This is a gift that will be with me forever.

Amy Eilberg

It Is Preferable to Pray with the Congregation

JEWS CAN PRAY in the privacy of their homes, but it is preferable to do so in the company of co-religionists, whenever possible. Maybe that is why our Sages emphasized the point that God is more inclined to listen to the prayers uttered in a congregation than in private. And if declaration of faith must be recited—such as the *Kaddish* or the *Kedusha*—only in a *Tzibur*, in a congregation, may it be recited, for only there can we sanctify the name of the Lord, not in isolation.

Hayim Halevy Donin

Prayer—A Natural Urge

PRAYER IS THE manifestation of the natural urge in every human being to give expression to his innermost feelings. Primitive man stood in amazement as he scanned the wonderful and mysterious world around him. When he watched the sun burst forth in golden rays he felt an inner urge to express his emotions of awe and wonder. The waters cascading down the mountainside, a mighty river flowing without cease, the peals of thunder reverberating, the flashes of lightning piercing the sky, the multicolored flowers carpeting the landscape, the variety of foods and the diverse vegetation sustaining mankind—all these phenomena brought forth wonder, amazement, fear, reverence and thankfulness. To whom? Very early in history it must have been to the Creator, to God as man conceived of God. The impelling force in man was to express in words his mental and emotional experiences to the Creator, to God. These expressions we call prayer.

Joshua Cohen

God's Invitation to Live in His Presence

JUDAISM IS GOD'S invitation to live in the presence of the Almighty. Man may live in His presence because God desires him so to live. Man may seek God's closeness in prayer because God has made Himself known as the One who is close. Man may call on Him, because He desires to be called by man. "God is desirous of the prayers of Israel"; this is the foundation of the possibility of Jewish prayer. The Jew can pray because God has "opened his lips." Yehuda Halevi said of Judaism that it was begun by God, meaning that it was not a human discovery but a religion of revelation; it commenced with God's self-revelation. So is prayer in Judaism not the original creation of man, but made possible by God, who lets us come near by being near us. There is a temptation to compare revelation and prayer and to say that in revelation, God addresses man, whereas in prayer, man addresses God. One must overcome the temptation; it all begins with revelation. It is true that in revelation, God seeks man, and in prayer, man seeks God. However, man may seek God only because he knows that He may be found; and he knows that God may be found because he was first found by God.

Eliezer Berkovits

Prayer—A Method of Cooperation with God

THE IDEA OF cooperation between man and God explains the significance of prayer. Apart from the dependence on God and the sense of reverence and worship of God's wisdom, power and holiness which it expresses, prayer is a method of cooperation with God in enabling a man to meet a difficult situation. How God does His share man cannot presume to tell; but it is to the extent that we surrender ourselves in prayer, and attune our spirit to the spirit of God, that God responds to our calls upon Him, and meets us in our need.

Isidore Epstein

Pulling the Pendulum Back

CREATING NEW RITUALS that celebrate women's experience is only the beginning of the *tikkun* [healing] that can overcome women's marginality and unlock spirituality. There are other dimensions of women's experience that point to a feminist theology, a different way of speaking about God that emerges from a different experience of God. . . .

Translated into theological terms, women's experience of God may be more an experience of immanence than one of the transcendence, the God we experience within and among us as opposed to the God over and against us. There has always been a dialectic tension in Judaism between transcendence and immanence. In Rabbinic Judaism the pendulum swung well over to the side of transcendence; feminist Judaism is pulling the pendulum back. We need to explore these different images of God in our tradition—the image in the midrash of God as a nursing mother with Torah the milk she gives her child Israel, the image of the Shechinah, the God who is the source of *[r]achamim*, womblike compassion, the God Jacob/Israel saw in the face of his brother.

But we cannot stop there; we must find ways to translate them into our prayer. Our liturgy was created by men; it emphasizes those images of God and community that reflected the values of the men who framed it. A new liturgy must be accessible to women as well as men, drawing on all of our experiences of God and community.

Laura Geller

What Prayer Requires

PRAYER REQUIRES THAT we open our hearts to God; that we welcome Him within the innermost recesses of our hearts.

A story is told of the Kotzker Rebbeh, that he asked his Chassidim "Where can God be found?" His Chassidim immediately answered *M'lo chol ha'aretz k'vodo*. ("His glory fills the whole earth.") But the Rebbeh was not satisfied with this intellectual answer. He told his followers "God is to be found wherever you allow him to enter."

If we feel God in this fashion, then we can pray to Him; then we can pray about what we really want. We can enter into a dialogue with Him; we can express our desires and let Him answer us that what we want is truly a worthy desire.

Arthur H. Neulander

Universal Devotion

THE ONE UNIVERSAL God does not require one universal church in which to be worshipped, but one universal devotion. In the realms of ascertainable facts, uniformity can be looked for. In the realms of art and philosophy, there can be only sincerity of quest and expression—only dedication. Religion is the supreme art of humanity. . . .

Their common purpose in the world will not be advanced by merger or amalgamation. Were all arts, philosophies, and religions cast into one mold, mankind would be the poorer for it.

Abba Hillel Silver

As We Speak to God, He Speaks to Us

HUMILITY IS THE consciousness of our place in the world; but it is a place not merely given to us but created by us. Without knowledge of the moral commandment there can therefore be no true humility or faith. Only the two united result in self-knowledge and permit us to experience life in totality; they constitute the religious feeling toward life which unites what is given to us and what we in turn have to give. As man speaks to his God he always hears God's words; during his prayer he always simultaneously hears the commandments to duty. This simultaneity, also characteristic of monotheism, gives to man his inner unity and religiousness.

That is why the Bible places faith and deed together, as a single religious unit. "Keep love and justice, and wait on the God continually" [Hosea 12:7]. Trust in the Lord, and do good" [Psalm 37:3]. "Wait on the Lord, and keep his way" [Psalm 37:34]. "Offer the sacrifices of right-eousness and love put into practice; but at the same time, humility is a beginning, for it is a humility which never rests but always seeks afresh to apply God's word. Arising from the ethical deed it also gives rise to a new ethical deed.

Leo Baeck

The Special Benefits of Public Prayer

THERE ARE TIMES when the religious individual wants to be alone with himself and with God. Some of our most meaningful prayers come at such times. But there are special benefits also to be derived from public collective prayer. When we worship together with others, we counteract the feeling of futility and helplessness which so often afflicts every sensitive individual. We reinforce our identification with our fellowmen. We strengthen our belongingness within humanity, as a step toward perceiving how we belong, all of us together, to the universe and to life. When all is said and done, a primary purpose of prayer for each of us must be to enlarge his horizons. Both his human and his cosmic horizons. Perhaps this is why the Talmud enjoins: "Pray only in a room with windows."

This is also, I think, something of what Martin Buber means: "To begin with oneself, but not to end with oneself, but not to aim at oneself; to comprehend oneself, but not to be preoccupied with oneself."

Roland B. Gittelsohn

The Multiplicity of the Forms of Prayer

PRAYER APPEARS IN history in an astonishing multiplicity of forms; as the calm collectedness of a devout individual soul, and as the ceremonial liturgy of a great congregation; as an original creation of a religious genius, and as an imitation on the part of a simple, average religious person; as the spontaneous expression of upspringing religious experiences, and as the mechanical recitation of an incomprehensible formula; as bliss and ecstasy of heart, and as painful fulfillment of the law; as the involuntary discharge of an overwhelming emotion, and as the voluntary concentration on a religious object; as loud shouting and crying, and as still, silent absorption; as artistic poetry, and as stammering speech; as the flight of the spirit to the supreme Light, and as a cry out of the deep distress of the heart; as joyous thanksgiving and ecstatic praise, and as humble supplication for forgiveness and compassion; as a childlike entreaty for life, health, and happiness, and as an earnest desire for power in the moral struggle for existence; as a simple petition for daily bread, and as an all-consuming yearning for God Himself; as a selfish wish, and as unselfish solicitude for a brother; as wild cursing and vengeful thirst, and as heroic intercession for personal enemies and persecutors; as a stormy clamor and demand, and as joyful renunciation and holy serenity; as a desire to change God's will and make it chime with our petty wishes, and as a self-forgetting vision of and surrender to the Highest Good; as the timid entreaty of the sinner before a stern judge, and as the trustful talk of a child with a kind father; as swelling phrases of politeness and flattery before an unapproachable King, and as a free outpouring in the presence of a Friend who cares.

Max Heiler

In Prayer Our Ancestors Speak Through Us

THE JEWISH PRAYER book is really the expression of the sense of the community. . . . When the Jew prays he does not pray of himself alone and for himself alone. Before his soul is the vision of all Israel. Israel, not merely today, but Israel yesterday and also the Israel of tomorrow. He who expresses what the Jewish prayer book contains avows himself thereby one of a community, one of a historic group. It is not he who speaks but his people; his ancestors speak through him and his children.

Emil G. Hirsch

The Sanctity We Feel in the Social Bond

PUBLIC WORSHIP DRAWS out the latent life in the spirit of the man. Those who, when alone, do not, or cannot, pray, find an impulse to prayer when they worship with others; and some will pray together who cannot pray alone, as many will sing in chorus who would not sing solos. As two walking together in some dark wood feel stronger and braver each for the other's near presence, so many who are spiritually weak in themselves will find spiritual strength in a common spiritual effort. That is the value of public worship for the individual. It has also a social value.

Public worship expresses the sanctity we feel in the social bond. A congregation at worship is a society declaring its devotion to God, a fellowship of men forged by faith in Him. Here is an experience that can deepen the social spirit and strengthen the bond of sympathy among men. If in public worship we realize that our prayers are also the prayers of the man who is by our side, it will make us more effectively aware of our common humanity and implant a spirit which will be potent for social good. They who worship God together bring Him into their mutual relations. If public worship does not produce the result, then it is but private worship in a public place. If it does bring men closer together under the influence of God, then it is a way to the sanctification of human society.

Israel I. Mattuck

I Prayed for Wisdom, Courage, Patience

PRAYER WAS AN important source of strength for me while battling breast cancer. When undergoing treatment, I must confess that I did not always know what to pray for. Because I believe in a living but limited God who does not cause the difficulties of life, it did not seem appropriate to ask now for special dispensation, to beg or bargain with God that my life might be spared. If God is not the cause, I reasoned, then God cannot be the cure.

And so I prayed instead for wisdom not to lose perspective, to remember in the midst of helplessness the blessings that I continued to possess, to remain as even-tempered as possible despite being afraid or in pain. I prayed for courage to cope with whatever lay ahead and for strength to sustain the hopes of my family and friends. And in those moments when I felt absolutely powerless, something particularly difficult for a person as independent as I am, I prayed for patience and the ability to endure a little more. And when I was too weak to pray, I hoped that God's love would envelop me, that God's embrace would bring me comfort and lift me up from the depths of despair.

And for some reason, I kept remembering an episode of the television series *All in the Family*. Archie, who was more a believer than he would ever care to admit, was in real trouble one day, and he just looked up to heaven and said, "Lord, A. Bunker here." That memory continues to bring a smile to my face, knowing as I do that God is our faithful friend, the One who listens, the One who understands.

Sally J. Priesand

CHAPTER 14

The Good Life

Success and Failure

HE IS A success as a human being whose heart is overflowing with pity and tenderness; he is a failure who remains callous to human suffering.

Baruch Silverstein

Hazards of Success

ONE OF THE built-in hazards of being human is the overpowering temptation to greet success in a mood of self-congratulation. The weeds of pride flourish most conspicuously in the soil of prosperity. The Bible speaks of the pride which goes before a fall. It would be no less in order to call attention to the pride which comes after a rise. When life becomes comfortable and upholstered, when our undertakings prosper and our possessions multiply, we are so prone to proclaim ourselves self-made. What further demonstration do we need of our resourcefulness, our wisdom, our ingenuity, our cleverness?

How well Moses understood the need to caution against the all too prevalent tendency to regard our blessings as proof of our ability or our virtue: "Beware, lest you forget the Lord your God. . . . Lest when you have eaten and are satisfied you say in your heart: 'My power and the might of my hand has gotten me this wealth.'" Apparently, Little Jack Horner was not the only one to become persuaded that he was really a very good boy simply because he had managed to pull a few plums out of life's pie. It never occurred to him to reserve a kind thought or word for the one who had baked the pie or the One who made the plums to grow.

Sidney Greenberg

When Life Has Meaning

ACCORDING TO THE teaching of our faith, life has no meaning unless it is filled with deeds. A man living a short life in terms of years, may in terms of the ultimate, live a longer life than the one who has enjoyed longevity. Indeed, our sages tell us that a *rasha* (evil individual) is considered dead even when alive, while a righteous person is considered alive even after his death.

H. Norman Strickman

Gratitude Involves Sharing Blessings

A TRUE PERSPECTIVE on our possessions serves to remind us that they are given to us in trust, to use not only for our own pleasures and gratification but also in the service of others. Gratitude at its highest goes beyond counting blessings. It involves sharing blessings. It leads not only to a sense of thankful dependence upon God but also to an awareness of our duty to our fellow man. It talks not only of indebtedness to be acknowledged but also of debts to be discharged. It takes us beyond saying thanks to giving thanks.

We are not truly grateful until we make it possible for others to experience gratitude, too.

This, after all, is what we really mean when we say "much obliged." We mean that we are much obliged, we have incurred a debt which we are duty-bound to repay. What is involved is not generosity but common honesty.

Sidney Greenberg

The Test

THE DIVINE TEST of a man's worth is not his theology but his life.

Morris Joseph

Be Good to Yourself ✓

SO MANY PEOPLE go through life filling the storeroom of their minds with odds and ends of a grudge here, a jealousy there, a pettiness, a selfishness—all ignoble. The true task of a man is to create a noble memory, a mind filled with grandeur, forgiveness, restless ideals, and the dynamic ethical ferment preached by all religions at their best.

Leo Baeck

The Path to Heaven—A Way to Walk on Earth

WHAT IS NEEDED today is not the reassurance that "God's in His heaven and all's right with the world." Rather we need to be reminded that there's so much wrong with the world that we must try to right.

"Noble discontent," it has been said, "is the path to heaven." It is also a good way to walk the earth.

Sidney Greenberg

What Is the Good Life?

WHILE IT IS man's right and responsibility to stand on his own feet, he must not forget his responsibilities to society. What, then, is the good life? It is the life of the socialized individual—the person who retains his individuality but develops and extends it to embrace humanity.

David Aronson

Our Three Basic Needs

WHAT ARE THESE basic needs of man of which the tradition speaks and to which our attention is drawn as we enter the world of the synagogue and participate in the pageantry of prayer, ritual and ceremony of the High Holy Days?

If we may couch it in modern terminology, our tradition addresses itself to the three basic needs of all human beings: the need to belong, the need to believe, and the need to become. These are the three dimensions of human experience which no one can ignore, except at the cost of personal fulfillment and happiness.

Max Routtenberg

In Giving We Grow Stronger

IF ANY RABBI, veteran or fledgling, or any teacher or parent, feels at times unequal to the task, let him take comfort in the special wording of God's assurance to Moses: "And I will draw from the spirit that is *on you*." If it was to be *ruach*, spirit, why not from God's own inexhaustible supply? Why draw upon Moses, whose spirit was then at its lowest ebb, with almost nothing left to draw upon?

But God, again, knew what He was doing. He was telling Moses, in effect: "Though you say you have reached the end of your rope, with all your patience and spirit seemingly gone—you are wrong! There is still enough *ruach* in you to give to others. Indeed, you will recapture and retain your spiritual power only if you share it—if you endow it to others!"

This is the sublime and redeeming paradox of spiritual influence: In giving of our own faith and moral vigor, we ourselves grow stronger. All great teachers have become the fulfilled human beings that they are only by sharing their spirit and illumination with their students. So we, in the congregations we are called upon to lead, can truly fulfill our best selves as Jews and as human beings, only by sharing our spiritual hunger, by endowing whatever light we possess to those who have grown accustomed to the darkness.

From the very depths of despondency, Moses was saved by sharing his light with others. It was a miracle of redemption, as the Midrash takes pains to tell us: "What was Moses like at that moment? He was like a light that is placed in a candlestick, from which everyone kindles his lamp. *V'en oro haser klum.* Yet its own radiance is not in the least diminished" [Sifri].

Nor will our light be diminished. Indeed, our light, our passion, our faith, will be augmented only as we share our hungers of the spirit with those who look to our ministry. This will be their redemption—and ours.

Jacob E. Segal

We Need Moral Imagination

I BELIEVE THAT the twenty-first century, certainly in its first decades, likely will be dominated more by micro issues than macro ones. If the twentieth century was largely devoted to answering the question, "How can we survive?," the coming years will be devoted to answering the question, "What makes our survival worthwhile?"

I suggest that what we most need now is to articulate a vision for the future, one that can be lived out one day at a time.

Central to this vision is the need for each of us to develop what I like to call "moral imagination." By this, I mean the ability to fully think through the implications of our actions, particularly as to how they will affect others. Over the past century, society has made extraordinary technological advances because of the active imaginations of our scientist and researchers, but we have been slower to advance morally because of a general unwillingness to practice imagination in the moral sphere.

Joseph Telushkin

The Good Life Is Social Centered

OUR TRADITION TEACHES us that, on this day of judgment, the Jew must pray for the well-being of all mankind. Examine our liturgy. "Lord our God, inspire veneration for Thee in all Thy creatures . . . may they all become one fellowship to do Thy will with perfect heart." Look further. "Who is like unto Thee, merciful Father, who in Thy compassion rememberest Thy creatures for life,"—not Thy people alone, but *all* Thy creates. Look still further. "As a shepherd musters his sheep and causes them to pass beneath his staff, so dost Thou pass and record, count and remember every living soul,"—not every *Israelite*, but *every living soul*. We exclude no one from salvation. "The righteous of all people have a share in the world to come"—is the verdict of our sages. We are bidden "to feed the non-Jew, even as we do the Jew." We are admonished that "whosoever saves a single life, it is as though he saved the entire world." The good life can never be self-centered. It must be social-centered.

Joseph Lookstein

Think a Mile Ahead

INVITED TO THE bridge of an Atlantic liner, a woman passenger gazed out at the vast expanse of sea and said, "Captain, you have so much time up here to think. What do you think about?" "Madam," replied the captain, "I think about a mile ahead." Occupying a command post, we too would indicate good judgment if we were to think a mile ahead to prepare for tomorrow.

Solomon Roodman

Charity—Our Obligation to Give

THE TERM FOR charity in Hebrew is *tzedakah*, from the root *tzedek*, meaning "righteousness" or "justice." The English term "charity" is from the Latin *caritas*—"love." In Rabbinic Hebrew, *tzedakah* carries the connotation of both "justice" and "love."

Charity is something that is *due* to those in need. It is an obligation upon the giver; a right of the receiver. The Bible, while praising the charitable and generous of heart, does not leave the needs of the "have-nots" to the whims of the "haves." Charity is a *mitzvah*, a duty commanded by

Jewish law. The Bible does not say "you ought to give charity" but "Thou shalt." Judaism instructs us that, whether we feel in charitable mood or not, "Thou shalt open thy hand . . . to all the needy in the land." It is simply a matter of justice and righteousness.

Simon L. Eckstein

To Live Fully

THE TRADITIONAL JEWISH prayer book instructs us always to revere God, whether in public or in private, to acknowledge the truth, and to speak truth in one's heart. No person can afford to forget for a moment this call to honesty and clear conscience.

During the *Pesukei D'zimra* (the selections, mostly from the Book of Psalms, that build up the mood for community worship), there are a number of references to the quality of all humans and to the destiny of humankind. At one point, the Psalmist offers advice to the person who wishes to live fully. The Psalmist says: "Keep your tongue from evil and your lips from speaking guile. Depart from evil and do good. Seek peace and pursue it" [Psalms 34:14–15]. Ideal humans avoid misusing their power of speech, and they engage actively in the pursuit of peace and in contributing to the welfare of all humans.

Jack J. Cohen

Serving Something Greater Than Self

ELDAD RAN WAS killed in Israel's War of Independence at the age of twenty. Before he died, he left us a legacy containing wisdom that belies the youthfulness of its author. He wrote: "Lately I've been thinking about what the goal of life should be. At best, man's life is short. . . . The years of life do not satisfy the hunger for life. What then shall we do during this time?

"We can reach either of two conclusions. The first is that since life is so short, we should enjoy it as much as possible. The second is that precisely because life is short . . . we should dedicate life to a sacred and worthy goal . . . I am slowly coming to the conclusion that life by itself is worth little unless it serves something greater than itself."

Sidney Greenberg

We Should Acquire Greater Humility

JUST AS THE Copernician revolution deprived the earth of its centrality, so has the disclosure of the vastness of Creation given us pause as to the meaning and purpose of human existence or of existence itself. We can no longer be sure that we humans are the crowning achievement of the creative process. At most, we have a right to hold out hope that the human adventure may eventuate in something more magnificent than it already is. We can extract new meaning from the prescient cry of the Psalmist:

> "O Lord, our Lord/How glorious is Thy name in all the earth!/ Whose majesty is rehearsed above the heavens/ . . . When I behold Thy heavens, the work of Thy fingers,/The moon and the stars, which Thou hast established; /What is man, that Thou art mindful of him?/And the son of man, that Thou thinkest of him?/ Yet Thou hast made him but little lower than the angels,/And has crowned him with glory and honor./Thou has made him to have dominion over the works of Thy hands;/Thou hast put all things under his feet."

Psalms 8:2, 4–7

The Psalmist is right in his grasp of the sublimity of the universe. He is right about our ability to exercise considerable authority as God's creative assistant. But even as we explore the stars and outer space, we acquire or should acquire greater humility before the ever-expanding reality that flees from our grasp. This new realization is both daunting and inspiring.

Jack J. Cohen

Death—A Night Between Two Days

LIFE IS A day that lies between two nights—the night of "not yet," before birth, and the night of "no more," after death. That day may be overcast with pain and frustration, or bright with warmth and contentment. But, inevitably, the night of death must arrive.

Death is a night that lies between two days—the day of life on earth and the day of eternal life in the world to come. That night may come suddenly, in the blink of an eye, or it may come gradually, with a slowly receding sun.

As the day of life is an interlude, so is the night of death an interlude. As the day inevitably proceeds to dusk, so does the darkness inevitably proceed to dawn. Each portion—the foetal existence, and life, and death, and eternal life—is separated by a veil which human understanding cannot pierce.

Maurice Lamm

CHAPTER 15

GRATITUDE

The Blessings We Take for Granted

THE MORE OFTEN and the more regularly we receive any blessing, the less likely we are to be aware of it. What is constantly granted is easily taken for granted.

"I have often thought," Helen Keller wrote, "that it would be a blessing if each human being were stricken blind and deaf for a few days at some time during his adult life. Darkness would make him more appreciative of sight; silence would teach him the joys of sound."

Too often it takes a serious threat to our blessings to make us aware of them.

Sidney Greenberg

Twice a Day I Give Thanks for My House

WHENEVER I CAME home, morning or evening, and reached my house, I always offered thanks to God, aloud, for this, that out of His great kindness He had given me this house, for me and my family, though I did not deserve it.

Alexander Ziskind

The Golden Thread

THE OBLIGATION TO cultivate a lively sense of appreciation for the manifold blessings a gracious God heaps upon us daily runs like a golden thread throughout the fabric of our religious faith. The Jew who adheres faithfully to his spiritual obligations is enjoined to recite no less than one hundred blessings from the time he wakes in the morning to the time he retires at night.

So highly did our Sages prize the mood of thanksgiving that one of them declared: "In the time to come, all the offerings will be abolished except the offering of thanksgiving." Thus the practice of giving thanks enjoyed special preeminence over all other religious disciplines.

Sidney Greenberg

Thanksgiving for the Privilege

THE ANCIENT RABBIS had a special formula of thanksgiving for the *privilege* of prayer, and the saints availed themselves of this privilege to its full extent. Besides the obligatory prayers, the Jewish saint had his own individual prayers, some of which have come down to us. The burden of these is mostly an appeal to God's mercy for help, that He may find him worthy to do His will. "May it be Thy will," runs one of these prayers, "That we be single-hearted in the fear of Thy name; that Thou remove us from all Thou hatest; that Thou bring us near to all Thou lovest, and that Thou deal with us graciously for Thy name's sake."

Solomon Schechter

How to Eat Strawberries

IN ONE OF his letters, Robert Southey tells of a Spaniard who always put on his spectacles when he was about to eat strawberries so that they might look bigger and more tempting. "In just the same way," adds Southey, "I make the most of my enjoyments."

At Sukkot time, we would do well to ponder these words. If only we could learn to magnify our blessings instead of exaggerating our troubles!

Grandma's eyesight wasn't as good as it used to be, but there was nothing wrong with her perspective. When asked about her health, she answered softly: "I have two teeth left, and thank God they are directly opposite one another." Her spectacles were properly focused.

Sidney Greenberg

A Test of Faith

THANKSGIVING IN THANKLESS times provides a real test of faith.

Stanley Rabinowitz

Blessings Bought by Blood

THE TRUTH IS that every blessing we enjoy has been sacrificially paid for by others. We are indebted far beyond our embarrassed means to make adequate recompense. It is no accident that the word "bless" and the word "bleed" come from the same root. Every important blessing we enjoy—our freedom, our health, our heritage, our security—is dipped in the blood of generations of benefactors. There is nothing we can give which we did not at first receive. Such obligations can never be fully liquidated. But neither are we exempt from making some sustained effort at repayment.

If we are truly thankful for our freedom we must be vitally concerned with the plight of those who still wear chains. If we are grateful for our share of God's abundance, we must share that abundance with the ill-fed, the ill-clad, the ill-housed. If we are genuinely appreciative of our own good health, the plight of the handicapped becomes a legitimate claim upon our financial resources. If we are sincere when we exclaim of our spiritual legacy, "happy are we, how goodly is our inheritance," then it becomes incumbent upon us to strengthen the institutions dedicated to disseminating a knowledge of Judaism.

The art of giving thanks means ultimately no appreciation without reciprocation.

Sidney Greenberg

Appreciation and Action

JEWISH TRADITION ASSIGNS a special blessing to be recited on seeing a beautiful spectacle of nature. It specifies, moreover, that even a blind person should recite the blessing thanking God for "opening the eyes of the blind" because, though he himself cannot see, nevertheless he benefits from the sight of others. Judaism has never failed to perceive the connection between appreciation and action. He who is aware of his own good fortune is more likely to share it with the less fortunate than he who takes everything as his due. He who perceives the extent to which his welfare is dependent upon his fellow men will be more apt to serve them in turn than he who is oblivious to their interdependence. And he who regularly reminds himself of the extent to which his whole being is a manifestation of the Creative Power behind and within all things will more probably feel and fulfill his toughest ethical responsibilities. Gratitude for our blessings, then, is more than just a mood worthy on its own account. It also is, or should be, the precursor to that conduct which is the final objective of prayer.

Roland B. Gittelsohn

Given to Us in Trust

A TRUE PERSPECTIVE on our possessions serves to remind us that they are given to us in trust, to use not only for our own pleasures and gratification but also in the service of others. Gratitude at its highest goes beyond counting blessings. It involves sharing blessings. It leads not only to a sense of thankful dependence upon God but also to an awareness of our duty to our fellow man. It talks not only of indebtedness to be acknowledged but also of debts to be discharged. It takes us beyond saying thanks to giving thanks.

We are not truly grateful until we make it possible for others to experience gratitude, too.

This, after all, is what we really mean when we say "much obliged." We mean that we are much obliged, we have incurred a debt which we are duty bound to repay. What is involved is not generosity but common honesty.

Sidney Greenberg

Gratefulness Makes the Soul Great

TO PRAY IS to take notice of the wonder, to regain a sense of the mystery that animates all beings, the divine margin in all attainments. Prayer is our humble answer to the inconceivable surprise of living. It is all we can offer in return for the mystery by which we live. Who is worthy to be present at the constant unfolding of time? Amidst the meditation of mountains, the humility of flowers—wiser than all alphabets—clouds that die constantly for the sake of His glory, we are hating, hunting, hurting. Suddenly we feel ashamed of our clashes and complaints in the face of the tacit glory in nature. It is so embarrassing to live! How strange we are in the world, and how presumptuous our doings! Only one response can maintain us: gratefulness for witnessing the wonder, for the gift of our unearned right to serve, to adore, and to fulfill. It is gratefulness which makes the soul great.

Abraham J. Heschel

Who Am I to Give Thanks to God?

THE STORY IS told of a Chasid who came to visit a famous Chasidic Rebbe, renowned as a man of prayer. On entering the prayer-room, the man found the teacher deep in thought and smoking his pipe. The man waited, then said his own prayers, and still the Rebbe did not move. Timidly the Chasid approached the master and reminded him that it would soon be past the time for praying the morning Shema. "It's all very well for a man like you," said the Rabbe; "you are satisfied to come to synagogue and say your prayers right away. But I began my prayers as soon as I rose this morning with the words: *"Mode Ani,* 'I give thanks before Thee'; and then immediately began to meditate—'Who am I to give thanks to God?'—And I am still pondering this question."

Bernard M. Casper

Thanking God for Commonplace Things

WE CAN ALL appreciate the joy experienced by a woman bearing her first child, particularly after a long period of wedded life. We would naturally expect such a woman to show some form of gratefulness, of her indebtedness to God for realizing her innermost hopes. Similarly, we anticipate such gratefulness from one who has escaped injury while others suffered; one who has encountered unusual success in business, an unexpected popularity, or any extraordinary good fortune. But, do we ever thank the Almighty for the commonplace things; for our life, for our health, for those very simple God-given gifts which humanity has learned to take for granted?

Leah named her fourth son Judah so that he might serve as a symbol of thanksgiving when everything in life was routine, when she had already begotten other children, when she did not experience the anxiety and aspiration of her sister, Rachel. She learned to thank God in comfort as well as in adversity.

Solomon B. Shapiro

CHAPTER 16

MARKS OF GREATNESS

How We Miss Greatness

MANY A MAN might have become great in later years if he had not in his younger years believed himself to be that already.

Daniel Sanders

What Is Greatness?

GREATNESS IS A matter not of size but of quality, and it is within the reach of every one of us. Greatness lies in the faithful performance of whatever duties life places upon us and in the generous performance of the small acts of kindness that God has made possible for us. There is greatness in patient endurance; in unyielding loyalty to a goal; in resistance to the temptation to betray the best we know; in speaking up for the truth when it is assailed; in steadfast adherence to vows given and promises made.

God does not ask us to do extraordinary things. He asks us to do ordinary things extraordinarily well.

Sidney Greenberg

We Can Each Aspire to Greatness

IN JUDAISM WE are each a reflection of divinity, each a bearer of the Divine Image. "There is no great and no small to the soul that maketh all."

And every one of us can aspire to greatness. Greatness is measured not by fame, wealth, status, or power. Some of the most heroic people we all have known have been unsung and untrumpeted. We have known parents who have cared for a handicapped child day after day, week after week, and year after year, compensating for nature's frail endowment with massive doses of inexhaustible love.

We have known young mothers who have borne bravely the heavy burden of widowhood and managed to be both mother and father to their children.

In recent years I have witnessed in a geriatric center the unflagging uncomplaining heroism of some children who devote themselves for years to the comfort of parents who are no longer even aware of the sacrificial devotion being lavished upon them.

We have all known humble people of whom fame has never even heard who have a boundless capacity for bringing cheer into lonely lives, who are drawn by some special instinct to human need, who are always scrubbing the little corner assigned to them to make it brighter and cleaner.

Sidney Greenberg

The Essence of Israel's Dignity

WHAT I HAVE learned from Jewish life is that if a man is not more than human then he is less than human. Judaism is an attempt to prove that, in order to be a man, you have to be more than a man, that, in order to be a people, we have to be more than a people, Israel was made to be a "holy people." This is the essence of its dignity and the essence of its merit. Judaism is a link to eternity, kinship with ultimate reality.

Abraham J. Heschel

CHAPTER 17

GROWING

We Become What We Think

IN PHYSICAL HYGIENE, it is a well-known law that we become what we feed on. Well, this is even more true in mental hygiene. We become what we think!

Asher Block

How We Could Become Nobler

IF WE DEVOTED as much energy to getting away from sin as we do to getting away with sin, how much nobler we would become.

Sidney Greenberg

Why an Acorn Becomes an Oak

WHY DOES AN acorn become an oak, rather than a hippopotamus? There is an inner drive burgeoning in every created thing—from whirling electrons to the mind of man himself—urging it to become that which it is intended to be, to fulfill the pattern of its unique perfection.

Avraham Soltes

We Ought to Be Better

WE AFFIRM, NOT that we are better, but that we ought to be better.

Morris Joseph

Our True Task

JUDAISM IS THE religion of life which makes no cult out of death, which seeks no private salvation from the grave, which accepts with confidence and trust both the miracle of birth and the mystery of death. Our faith does not close its eyes to tragedy and does not deny that we human beings shall never possess the everlastingness of stone, the silent enduring quality of the mountain peak, but we have other gifts, conscious minds, aspiring hearts, far-visioned souls. Our faith tells us that God has given to each human being the ability to paint a portrait large or small, beautiful or ugly, radiant or blooming, and our faith summons us to become a portrait painter of a soul-landscape that shall be worthy to be hung in any art gallery of the spirit. Judaism proclaims that God has arranged our journey so that in years brief or many we can find love, joy and the fruits of fulfillment, partial and relative though they be, and that when our day is finished, we would accept its final note with the same calm trust that we greet the skylark's song at sunrise. True, "each one of us has his toad to swallow every morning." Yet we can become what Goethe once said is the true task of man—"Life-worthy."

Joshua Loth Liebman

From Dust to Divinity

Man is but "little lower than the angels."
He is a *ben adam*—"a child of the dust."
  That is his origin.
He is a *ben Elohim*—"a child of God."
  That is his destiny.
And his life is the measure between these two. Only God is perfect.

Only man is perfectible. In our brief journey through the world we live in we can ascend from dust to Divinity.

Julius J. Nodel

The Preciousness of Being a Jew

I AS A Jew do not know what despair is. Despair means utter futility, being utterly lost. I will never be lost. I know where I came from, I know where I am going. I am the son of Abraham. Despite all my imperfections, deficiencies, faults and sins, I remain a part of that Covenant that God made with Abraham; we are going toward the Kingship of God and the Messianic Era. This is the preciousness of being a Jew.

Abraham J. Heschel

There is No Shortcut to Character

THE DEVELOPMENT OF character is a distant goal. Goethe, the nineteenth-century German poet, once revealed the truth in this matter when he said, "Life is a quarry out of which we are to mold and chisel and complete a character." Notice all those time-consuming verbs. Character is distilled out of our daily confrontation with temptation, out of our regular response to the call of duty. It is formed as we learn to cherish principle and to submit to self-discipline. Character is the sum total of all the little decisions, the small deeds, the daily reactions to the choices that confront us. Character is not obtained instantly. We have to mold and hammer and forge ourselves into character. It is a distant goal to which there is no shortcut.

Sidney Greenberg

How We Grow

VERY EARLY IN our history we were taught that the hallmark of a Jew is a profound feeling of concern for the welfare of other Jews. One of the most striking illustrations of this lesson is found in the opening chapters of the Book of Exodus.

"And Moses grew up and he went out to his brothers and saw their burdens" [Exodus 2:11].

It would have been so natural, so understandable and oh so very practical had Moses chosen not to notice his brothers' travail, to claim no kinship with these degraded slaves. How tempting it must have been to cling to the security, the delights, the prerogatives of the royal palace in which his life was so snugly upholstered. But had Moses done so, God would not have noticed him and history would not have remembered him.

The whole course of human events was radically altered because in a decisive moment, an obscure foundling of a condemned people threw off the anonymity and the protection of Pharaoh's palace and "went out to his brothers and saw their burdens."

From that day to our very own, a crucial index of Jewish maturity is the ability to go out to our brothers and be sensitive to their burdens.

Sidney Greenberg

Grow into Your Ideals

THE GREAT SECRET of success is to go through life as a man who never gets used up. That is possible for him who never argues and strives with men and facts, but in all experiences retires upon himself, and looks for the ultimate cause of things in himself.

Albert Schweitzer

What Growth Requires

ALL GROWTH IS difficult. Our Sages tell us that no blade of grass grows except for an angel which stands over it and commands: "Grow!"

We are born selfish. To the infant the whole world exists for one supreme purpose—to minister to his needs. Growing up is the slow, painful process of learning that we are here not to be ministered to, but to minister; not to be served, but to serve; not to be fed but to feed; not to be imprisoned within ourselves, but to go out to our brothers.

But we are afraid to venture out. Seeing brothers gives them a claim over us. It is easier not to notice them, to acknowledge no kinship with them.

An eight-year-old unintentionally gave expression to this philosophy of evasion. During a Consecration Service, a rabbi addressed a youngster who bore the name of one of Jacob's sons, and the rabbi expressed the hope that the young fellow "would live a life of dedication to your brothers of the House of Israel." Without batting an eyelash, the youngster replied at the top of his voice: "I ain't got no brothers."

We can only hope that when that young fellow grows up he will discover that he does indeed "got" brothers, that he is intimately related to them by a thousand bonds of kinship, fate and loyalty, and that to the extent that he goes out to them will he fulfill his fundamental duty as a Jew and his fundamental need as a human being.

Sidney Greenberg

The Urge to Give

THERE COMES A time in the development of ourselves, when receiving from others, which is the essence of selfishness, gives way to the irresistible urge to give to others—to grow beyond the limits of one's skin.

Joshua Loth Liebman

Keep the Mind Open

AS WE GROW older it is very tempting to develop a permanent mind-set. But minds, like parachutes, are valuable only when open.

To shut the windows of the mind is to court mental and spiritual suffocation. We must literally never stop going to school, broadening our horizons and expanding our knowledge.

As long as we keep our minds open and alert, as long as we are willing to try a new skill, entertain a new thought, develop a new friend, surrender an old prejudice—so long do we remain vital people, so long do we gain ground and move forward in the search for more abundant life.

Sidney Greenberg

Self-Centered Needs

SELF-CENTEREDNESS IS A form of infantilism.

Julius Gordon

How Far We Must Still Go

BERGEN-BELSEN DID NOT lead me to abandon my faith in God's love for man. It made me understand how far man must still go to deserve it.

Maurice L. Zigmond

The Companion of Ignorance

SELF-COMPLACENCY IS THE companion of ignorance.

Solomon Schechter

Needed—Conquest of Human Nature

MEN'S CONQUEST OF nature has been astonishing. His failure to conquer human nature has been tragic.

Julius Mark

When Our Prayers Are Answered

OUR PRAYERS ARE answered not when we are given what we ask but when we are challenged to be what we can be.

Morris Adler

The Road to Moral Perfection

THAT MAN IS best able to advance on the road to moral perfection who starts with the accumulated spiritual heritage of righteous ancestors.

Felix A. Levy

How Our Life Is Fulfilled

OUR LIFE IS fulfilled by what we become, not by what we were at birth. Endowment and heritage mean much . . . and then again nothing; the essential thing is what we make of them.

Leo Baeck

Preparing Now for Our Later Years

WE CAN PREPARE ourselves now for our later years by cultivating worthy goals which will outlive us and give us a sense of pride. Just going to our work jobs, e.g., going to build the arks in our lives, isn't enough to sustain us in our later years. Then retirement can mean the end of a man's productive life, much as the marriage of a woman's youngest child may write "finis" in her own mind to her usefulness.

The question of how to deal with the elderly is not a question of what to do for our parents and our grandparents. The question is: what should we do with and for ourselves? At about the time we learn to make the most of life, most of it is gone. Prepare for advancing years now by making new beginnings, by developing worthwhile interests and by serving others in the community. Then we will be able to feel that like Abraham, even as we are *growing old* our lives are worthy.

Herbert Yoskowitz

Life—A Developing Romance

IF, THEN MY friend, you have made of your life a developing romance, a legend of budding and blossoms; if you have made your past fruitful and your present a seedbed for future growth; if you are striving sunward even though it be through pain and struggle; if every year an added measure of mind- and soul-ripening comes to you: keener perceptions, finer discriminations, sounder judgments, deeper loyalties; if you feel that you are growing, then you are alive, and the greatness and the glory of life are yours, and you are to be called blessed among the children of men.

Abba Hillel Silver

Rest and Grow

TO THAT PART of us which is secular and animal, Shabbat says, "rest"; to that part of us which is spiritual, moral, and human, Shabbat says, "grow."

Sidney Greenberg

Everything Is Opportunity for Growth and Blessing

ABRAHAM DID THE same thing. Directly after reading about Sarah's death and Abraham's purchase of a burial plot for her, we read, ". . . and the Lord had blessed Abraham in all things" [Genesis 24:1]. God had blessed him with his wife's death? Yes, that too, or at least that was how Abraham was able to see things. Everything for him was an opportunity for blessing. Where is it written that all blessings must feel good? Some opportunities for growth hurt like hell, like the death of a loved one. Yet they are opportunities for blessing nonetheless. Such an event is a chance to reach a greater depth within ourselves, to find out what we are made of, how strong we are, how well we can care for those we love, how accepting we can be of their care for us. Everything, Abraham teaches, is an opportunity for growth and blessing.

David E. Fass

To Pray We Must Believe We Can Grow

THE RABBIS OF Eastern Europe, in the eighteenth century, taught, "the greatest evil is when you forget that you are the son of a king!" This was their way of saying that man will live optimistically and creatively only if he remembers, at all times, that he is wonderfully formed by a God who cares. In our highly urbanized and competitive society, it is easy for the individual to conclude that he is an insignificant speck in a swarming mass. The pages of Genesis would teach us otherwise. The text informs us that man is made in the "image of God." While contemporaries of the early Hebrews taught that the king was divine and that his subjects were a mere shadow of the king's being, the Hebrews taught that each man is made of the divine stuff itself!

Prayer is not possible unless one has a reasonable evaluation of his own importance. Those who belittle or hate themselves despair of ever leading meaningful lives and find it difficult to pray. To pray, you must believe yourself capable of change and growth toward the "image of the Divine." Looked at in this light, prayer is an exalted tool leading to the reawakening of the sense of one's own worthwhileness. It is a channel by which the individual river can link itself to the great ocean of life. It is a way of learning, a way of reaffirming the fact that we live in a kingdom greater than the kingdom of the individual. Prayer is a way to the tapping of a power greater than the individual believes he has. It is the process of becoming increasingly a part of the greater life in which we move and which flows through us at all times.

Herbert M. Baumgard

CHAPTER 18

SEARCH FOR HAPPINESS

Treasures at Home

AMONG THE HASIDIM they tell the tale of poor Rabbi Eizik of Cracow. He had a recurring dream that under the bridge which leads to the king's palace in Prague there was a great treasure. If he would journey there and dig he need never know poverty any more.

Rabbi Eizik made the journey, found the bridge, but be did not dare to try to dig because the bridge was guarded day and night. Finally the guard who had observed him asked what he was doing all this time near the bridge. Rabbi Eizik told him of the dream which had brought him here.

Whereupon the guard burst into laughter. "You have faith in dreams! If I believed in dreams I would have had to go to Cracow, because long ago I dreamed that there was a treasure buried beneath the kitchen stove of some Jew named Rabbi Eizik."

Rabbi Eizik took his shovel, returned home and dug up the treasure beneath his own stove. With the money he built a Shul which they called Rabbi Eizik's Shul.

Sidney Greenberg

Those Who Fail to Dare Are Failures

FAILURES ARE MADE only by those who fail to dare, not by those who dare to fail.

Louis Binstock

Service and Happiness Go Together

A BROOK IS going somewhere. It is water on a mission. About to present itself to other waters at its destination, it never neglects little wayside opportunities. On its way to make its final offering, it gaily gives itself all along the way. Deer drink of its refreshing coolness with a deep content. Boys of seven years and of seventy probe its pools and eddies with their lures and return home at the day's end with the brook's gift of speckled trout. Fish, crustaceans, mollusks, and water insects are given a home in its swirling currents and tranquil pools. From its birth in bubbling springs to its arrival and its final goal the brook is selfless and a happy appearing thing. Service and happiness belong together.

Harold E. Kohn

Happiness Is a By-Product

HAPPINESS IS A by-product of cheerful, honest labor dedicated to a worth-while task.

Sidney Greenberg

The Way to Happiness

THE BEST WAY to attain happiness is not to seek it.

Claude G. Montefiore

How to Find Happiness

THIS WOULD BE a much happier world if we recognized this truth—the truth which a social philosopher of the last generation so aptly formulated: "No one can be perfectly happy till all are happy" [Herbert Spencer].

There would be lots more happier marriages and happier homes if we recognized this truth. Many a "misunderstood" husband would be far less misunderstood if he demonstrated a little more understanding for his partner in marriage. Many an unhappy wife would be far happier if she brooded less over *her* unhappiness and concentrated more on how to make a husband happy. Young people would feel less rejected if they did not make their parents feel rejected. Parents would have less cause for disappointment if they, in turn, did not repeatedly let their children down. Happiness is not a one-way experience; it is a reciprocal experience. Invariably, it is the result of an effort to make someone else happy.

Joseph H. Lookstein

When Wealth Brings Joy

WEALTH CAN BE joy. I am not thinking of hilarity, gaiety, levity—states of mind that can be bought with gold. I am thinking of the inner joy that comes to him who dedicates his wealth to the good of his fellow man.

Joseph H. Lookstein

The Flute That Was Covered with Gold

IN THE TEMPLE at Jerusalem there was a flute fashioned out of reeds, an old flute, having come down from the days of Moses. The sound of the flute was sweet and beautiful, ravishing the soul of the worshippers. But one day the priests of the sanctuary decided to decorate the flute and they covered it with gold. The flute was never the same again. Its sweet, clear, cool tones were now harsh, metallic and jarring. Gold had coarsened its melody.

Abba Hillel Silver

The Miser Is Owned by His Wealth

THE MISER DOES not own his wealth; his wealth owns him.

Judah Jeiteles

Learning to Want What We Get

IN OUR PREOCCUPATION with material riches, we are also in danger of growing insensitive to the riches of the spirit. These can be cultivated even in the soil of adversity. The anonymous author of the following piece reminds us that if we do not get what we want perhaps true success means learning to want what we get:

I asked God for strength, that I might achieve: I was made weak, that I might learn humbly to obey. I asked for health, that I might do greater things; I was given infirmity, that I might do better things. I asked for riches, that I might be happy; I was given poverty, that I might be wise. I asked for power, that I might have the praise of men; I was given weakness, that I might feel the need of God, I asked for all things, that I might enjoy life; I was given life, that I might enjoy all things. I got nothing that I asked for—but everything I had hoped for. Almost despite myself, my unspoken prayers were answered. I am among all men, most richly blessed.

Sidney Greenburg

CHAPTER 19

A NOBLE HERITAGE

Democracy's Vast Debt to Ancient Israel

THE DEBT THAT democracy in general, and American democracy in particular, owes ancient Israel is indeed vast. For generations of pious Bible readers, the Scriptures created the moral and spiritual climate, in which a free government could function. The basic content of democracy, if not its forms, existed in ancient Hebrew society, with its insistence upon individual dignity, its hatred of caste, its uncompromising love of liberty. Above all, democracy in action would be inconceivable without the Hebrew Prophets, who proclaimed the truth without fear or favor and established the right to dissent, which is the living breath of democracy.

Robert Gordis

Judaism Embodies Some of Mankind's Most Exalted Ideas

IF ONE WERE to transcribe every phrase in the Hebrew Bible that deals with righteousness, justice, honesty, the need to care for the poor, the orphan, the widow, the needy; if one were to include the important and painstaking investigation of how to adjudicate property in the courts according to the Talmud, one would be faced with hundreds upon hundreds of pages of some of the most exalted ideas and concepts in the history of mankind.

Marshall T. Meyer

Torah Is More Than Law

THE GENERAL NAME in Hebrew for revelation of the Divine will is Torah. "Law" is not an incorrect translation, but it is inadequate. Torah includes law, but its basic meaning is guidance, direction, instruction.

Bernard J. Bamberger

What Is the Sacred?

THE SACRED IS that dimension of being which propels us into the search for love, awe, and reverence . . . . which allows us to create for the morrow a world that is better than yesterday . . . . the power of decision to ensure, as much as we are able, that there will be a morrow.

Marshall T. Meyer

A Continuing Conversation Between the Generations

SOME YEARS AGO, Professor Saul Lieberman, one of the great Talmudic scholars of this century, won some kind of an award. And so the *New York Times* sent a reporter out to visit him. The reporter came into his study and asked him, "What's that book on your desk?" He said, "that's a Humash, the five books of Moses." The reporter asked, "And what's that book next to it?" Dr. Lieberman said, "That's a Mishna." "What's a Mishna?" asked the reporter. "The Mishna is a second-century commentary on the laws in the Humash," answered Professor Lieberman. "What's that stuff below the Mishna?" asked the reporter. Professor Lieberman said, "that's the Gemora." "What's the Gemora?" asked the reporter. "The Gemora is the Aramaic exploration of the meaning of the

Mishna, that was completed in the fifth century." "What's that stuff on the right-hand margin?" asked the reporter "That's the commentary of Rashi," said Dr. Lieberman. "Who's Rashi?" asked the reporter. "Rashi was a French commentator on the Gemora, who lived in the tenth century." "And what's that stuff on the other margin?" asked the reporter "That is the work of the Baaley Tosafot, who lived in Germany two centuries after Rashi." The reporter said, "Oh, I get it. Judaism is a continuing conversation between the generations!"

Dr. Lieberman said afterwards that this reporter was a non-Jew and yet, that was the shortest, simplest definition of Judaism that he had ever heard. "Judaism is a continuing conversation between the generations.

This Shabbat, we have listened in on what seven different generations have had to say. May we listen well to what they have to teach us, and may we, in turn, add our voice and our insights to the continuing conversation, the continuing application and explanation of the words first heard at Sinai, which is the meaning of Jewish life.

Jack Riemer

The Contribution Judaism Can Make in Our Time

JUDAISM CAN, IN our time, make a significant contribution through its unrivaled tradition of the preeminence of Torah, the character-building, soul-cultivating emphasis on learning, calling on man to develop ethical alertness, to master himself rather than to rule over others.

Max Arzt

The Jew Was the Prophet

THE GREEK GRASPED the present moment, and was the artist; the Jew worshipped the timeless spirit, and was the prophet.

Isaac M. Wise

A God-Obsessed Religion

IF THE PROVERBIAL gentile who came to Hillel over two thousand years ago and asked him "Teach me the whole Torah while I am standing on one foot" were to come to me with the same question, I would answer him: "To be aware of God's presence at all times is the essence of Judaism. The rest is commentary. Go and learn it." *Judaism* is a God-obsessed *religion*. The *mitzvot*, the commandments, are designed to make man more sensitive to God's presence, to enable man to be in constant communion with the Divine. From the moment he wakes up in the morning until he goes to sleep at night, the religious Jew is surrounded by behavior patterns (that tell him what to do and what not to do) whose purpose it is to keep man from forgetting his Creator, the source of his being. The observance of *mitzvot* stimulates man's awareness of the transcendent, gets him in touch with the ineffable. Occasionally, it elevates him to such heights that he has the potential to become *shutaf lehaqodosh barukh hu bema-aseh bereishit*, a partner in God's creation.

David Weiss Halivni

CHAPTER 20

WHERE IS HOLINESS?

The Spirit of Holiness

IF THERE BE a spirit of holiness in the synagogue it comes from the spirit of those who enter to pray.

Sidney Brooks

The Higher Forms of Meditation

THE PURPOSE OF the higher forms of meditation is to break through the masks that deceive us, the lies that hinder us, the ephemeral that depresses us. They seek to move us through normal reality (while never leaving it behind) to actually experiencing the Divine. Additionally, it's important to remember that for Jews, interacting with the world is a component of experiencing the Divine.

Avram Davis

Every Man's Privilege

HOLINESS IS EVERY man's privilege. This democracy of holiness is one of the most magnificent creations of the Jewish religious genius.

David De Sola Pool

Where Is Holy Ground?

THE PLACE WHERE men meet to seek the highest is holy ground.

Felix Adler

Our Gift to Mankind

NONE OF THE resplendent names in history—Egypt, Athens, Rome—can compare in eternal grandeur with Jerusalem. For Israel has given to mankind the category of holiness. Israel alone has known the thirst for social justice, and that inner saintliness which is the source of justice.

Charles Wagner

Lead Our Natural Hungers to Holiness

IT HAS BEEN the genius of Judaism to accept the natural hungers of man and, instead of frowning upon them as a source of temptation, to welcome them and direct them into paths that lead to holiness.

Alan S. Green

Who Is a Holy Person?

JUDAISM DOESN'T SEE holiness as a holier-than-thou concept. A holy person is not someone distinguished with a halo and wings, rather merely an average person reaching exceptional heights, dedicating himself to a lifetime of effort and growth.

Eli Glaser

Confronting All That Life Has to Offer

IN SOME RELIGIONS the sphere of the holy is the sanctuary of escape from problems and difficulties. But this has never been the Jewish way. The spiritual strength, the assurance that these days have always brought to us, do not come from a magical resolution of our problems or a flight from them. Rather, it is the result of confronting all that life has to offer, recognizing, amidst the turmoil that every trial comes to God, and that He can be served in truth as one moves forward in obedient acceptance.

David J. Seligson

Our Holy Obligation

I UNDERSTAND THAT both the religious and the nonreligious Jew cannot remain faithful to their historical legacy if they are insensitive to injustice, violence, and terror in our society. Our people have suffered too much historically because of the silence of others. I cannot tolerate a Jew who turns his back to other men, be it Jew or nonJew, in time of need. I should say to the nonaltruist that the Jew cannot survive for long in a society where both the theory and practice of Human Rights do not prevail. For the religious Jew, the holiness of life is the Summum of the Torah. The religious Jew who really knows his tradition knows that the purpose of all Mitzvot is "*letsaref et habriot,*" to unite mankind. The union of mankind doesn't mean that one must convert others or that he must agree with them. Judaism says that the just men of all people deserve divine salvation. It also teaches that man cooperates with God in the continuing work of creation of the world. Judaism considers the sins of omission as much as the sins of commission. For me it is very painful that in the Argentina of today the words "Human Rights" have become ugly and cannot be expressed. It is even more painful for me that many Jews feel this way so few years after Auschwitz.

I, as a Jew, must fight for human rights, decency and human sanctity because God commanded me to do so regardless of whether or not society commands it.

There are too many forces trying to block out the light of hope for a tomorrow of peace and creativity. Everyone has the holy obligation to keep alive at least a small spark of this light.

Marshall T. Meyer

Where Are You?

"AND THE LORD God called to Adam, and said to him, *Ayecha/*Where are you?"

"And he said, I heard your voice in the garden, and I was afraid, because I was naked; and I hid myself."

*Ayecha/*Where are you? Is the first question. It is the eternal question. I believe that it is the role of the Jewish people to ask that question of the world. As we stand on the cusp of a new century, I believe that it is our mission to America as well. The truth is that America is confronting a deep crisis. It is as bad as a financial crisis or as a military crisis. America is facing a crisis in the meaning of holiness. America has lost its sense of the holy. It is our role—we whose job description is to be an *am kadosh*, a holy people.

Jeffrey K. Salkin

Holy Choices

KASHRUT IS A system that our tradition defined in order to accomplish several goals: to make Judaism distinct and to create a discipline in eating and cooking that would remind us that our choices of what we eat are holy choices.

Felicia Sol

Where the Shekhinah Rests

The feeling of the sacred,
The presence of the divine
Is called by the sages: the Shekhinah.
She rests on a person who cheers the sick,
On a havurah that studies Torah
On the warm welcome given to a stranger, or a new Jew.
She rests on a husband because of his wife's love,

On a Jewish parent at a child's Bar or Bat Mitzvah,
On a Jew standing at the Western Wall
    May she rest on us
    In the flames of the Yom Tov candles
    In the blessings spoken by the mothers of Israel
    In all generations past
    For all generations to come.

Allen S. Maller

CHAPTER 21

HOME

Judaism Begins in the Home

JUDAISM BEGINS IN the home. It doesn't begin at a meeting or a conference or at a philanthropic campaign. It begins in homes where Judaism lives in the atmosphere and is integrated in the normal pattern of daily life. It begins in homes where the Jewish words re-echo, where the Jewish book is honored, and the Jewish song is heard. It begins in homes where the child sees and participates in symbols and rites that link him to a people and culture. It begins in homes where the Jewish ceremonial object is visible. It begins in homes where into the deepest layers of a child's developing personality are woven strands of love for and devotion to the life of the Jewish community.

Morris Adler

The Jew's Home—His Sanctuary

THE JEW'S HOME has rarely been his "castle"; throughout the ages it has been something far higher—his sanctuary.

Joseph H. Hertz

The Center of Judaism

THE CENTER OF Judaism is in the home. In contrast to other religions, it is at home where the essential celebrations and acts of observance takes place—rather than in the synagogue or temple. . . . The synagogue is an auxiliary. . . . A Jewish home is where Judaism is at home, where Jewish learning, commitment, sensitivity to values are cultivated and cherished.

Abraham J. Heschel

Let There Be Light . . . In Your Home

LET THERE BE light . . . in your home. Let it be warm, Jewish spiritually significant light . . . the gentle light of the neighborliness, friendship and love . . . the radiant light of knowledge and wisdom . . . the light of justice, truth and peace . . . the light shed by the presence of God in our midst.

Albert S. Goldstein

The Jew's Castle

THROUGHOUT THE AGES the Jew's home has been his castle. Frequently it contained only the poorest furnishings—a few benches, a wooden table and hard beds or straw for the floor. But the home was sacred because it contained a *mezuzah* on the doorpost, religious books on the shelves, a *Tzedakah* box above the oven, candlesticks and a wine-cup ready for the Sabbath and the Festivals. With these ornaments, the home was beautiful. From these homes came Jews with a great love of God and a quiet dignity born out of a pride in their legacy. Our homes have added beautiful furnishings. Their comforts have increased. But will they produce Jews with the same love of their faith? Will they evoke the hidden feelings that kindle Sabbath lights deep in the Jewish soul? To the extent that they do, will they contribute to the enrichment of the lives of their inhabitants and strengthen the faith upon which they must draw for meaningful creative living.

Sidney Greenberg

The Home—Reservoir and Fortress

JUDAISM TEACHES THAT the home is the great reservoir and fortress of our faith. The home is even more important than the synagogue, for Judaism could conceivably survive without the synagogue if the Jewish home was to remain intact. For the most part, whatever is done in the synagogue can be done equally well in the home. The Sabbath is observed in the home. When we pray in the home with a *minyan* and a *Sefer Torah* the home is virtually converted into a synagogue. Judaism instructs that the home is the *Mikdash M'aht*, the Sanctuary-in-miniature. Ideally, the Jewish home is holy and sanctified. There is religion in the home, there is learning in the home, values are taught, character is molded. In the home there is security, protection, beauty, warmth, serenity and inspiration. The home generates a feeling of being wanted, of being needed, of being loved.

Hillel E. Silverman

Jewish Living Begins in the Home

THE SIMPLE TRUTH is that, like charity, Jewish living begins in the home. It is there that the Jewish child makes his first contact with Judaism. Through the home symbols and ceremonies the historical dramas of Judaism are regularly re-enacted. Through the holidays he learns the appealing story of his people and its heroes. The very atmosphere of the Jewish home exercises a profound influence in molding the attitude of the child toward his heritage.

If, therefore, we are genuinely concerned with Jewish survival, we should pay careful attention to the spiritual interior decoration of our homes. A truly Jewish home is not only a place where Jews live but a place where Judaism is lived.

Far too many Jewish parents today feel that their obligation to their child's Jewish education begins and ends when they enroll him in a Hebrew or Sunday school for a few years. How little do they realize the inadequacy of the religious school without the active cooperation of the Jewish home. The child spends a comparatively short period in the school but his home is his constant environment. The school can only teach textbook Judaism that is abstract. It teaches him how Jews should live and yet the Jews he worships most, his parents, do not live in the way he is taught. Can it be that his parents are wrong or is the school wrong? Obviously they cannot both be right. In this way, the school which should inspire and guide the child, finds itself at cross-purposes with the home, and this battle is waged on the battlefield of the child's confused soul. In the end, both the child and Judaism are the losers.

This loss to the child is usually greater than would appear on the surface. Something very vital is missing from his life for he has failed to come to terms with his heritage. In later life, an unkind world may penalize him for his heritage. If that happens, he will be paying a price for something which he hardly understood and rarely enjoyed. He shall be lacking the necessary defense which can only come from a whole-hearted acceptance of his Jewishness based on a knowledge and appreciation of it. No parent would deliberately expose his child to winter's cold without adequate protection. Yet many parents think nothing of exposing their children to the icy winds of intolerance without the necessary inner protection of Jewish values, Jewish learning and Jewish pride.

Sidney Greenberg

CHAPTER 22

HOPE

To Keep Alive That Little Spark

LET US REDISCOVER the place where we can pray together, study together, and work together for the fulfillment of that beautiful dream. Let us try to recapture that sense of *kavanah*, that sense of piety and inner devotion, so that whatever we do will become a sacred act. Let us strive to keep alive that little spark that brings us here each year at this time. May the spark become ignited and may the torch of our faith burn more brightly in the days that lie ahead.

The story is not over. A new chapter will be written this year as we are inscribed, individually and collectively, the Book of Life. With faith in God and confidence in our people, I believe that we shall one day climb the mountain and view, at close range, the cloud of glory.

Norman Kahan

Your Children Shall Return

IN RACHEL'S TOMB in Bethlehem there is a mosaic on one of the walls which consists of the verses from Jeremiah which tell of Rachel's weeping and God's consolation that her children will return to their own border. The mosaic is signed, "This was made by one of her children who returned."

Sidney Greenberg

Our Secret Weapon

WITHOUT THE TORAH the Jew is a body without a soul. It is the reason for his existence. It is his secret weapon. It is his hope in the future.

Albert A. Gordon

Where There Is Hope, There Is Life

LIFE WITHOUT HOPE is hopeless. If we could not hope for a second chance when life inflicts a severe defeat on us, if we could not hope for strength when we have been betrayed, if we could not hope for healing when we have been bruised, if we could not hope for eternity when the winter of our lives drives home the inescapable fact of our mortality—if in all these trials hope did not sustain us, then the burden of life would become insufferable.

"Hope," it has been said, "is the promissory note of life on which the principal never matures but which pays compound interest to those who render their best services each day."

According to an old parable, on one summer night two frogs fell into a bucket of milk. The first frog, realizing the hopelessness of his situation, promptly gave up and drowned. The second frog began thrashing about furiously with all his might. The following morning the farmer was surprised to find his bucket of milk turned to butter and there was a frog sitting on the top of it.

Let us cling stubbornly to our hopes. They keep up alive.

Sidney Greenberg

Hope Has Spanned Jewish History

DURING THE MONTH of Elul, when God and Israel say to each other: "I am my beloved's and my beloved is mine," the concluding prayer of the daily service itself concludes: "I should despair unless I believed to see the goodness of the Lord in the land of the living: wait for the Lord; be strong and let thine heart take courage; yea, wait thou for the Lord."

The rejection of despair leads to hope; hope leads to patient waiting—it is only a matter of time. *Hatikvah,* hope, is the national anthem of Zionism and the State of Israel. Hope has spanned history for the Jew from Abraham to America.

Jacob Chinitz

Hope Is Rooted in Our Faith

HOPE, CENTRAL TO Jewish thought, is rooted in the basic assumptions of our faith. It derives from three fundamental Jewish teachings; the inherent goodness of every man, the power of man to choose good over evil, and man's improvability.

Melvin S. Sands

Hope Is a Duty

THE UPSHOT OF the prophetic message is that hope is a duty.

Lewis E. Bogage

No One Can Live Without Hope

DR. ALFRED ADLER once said while physically it may be true that where there is life there is hope, psychologically the opposite is true: where there is hope there is life. No one can live without hope.

I. Nathan Bamberger

Hope Amidst the Ruins

AN ANCIENT JEWISH teaching consoles us with the startling announcement that on the day the Temple was destroyed the Messiah was born. Amidst the smoking ruins our ancestors felt not the paralyzing chill of death but the invigorating breath of birth. The Messiah was born out of the ashes to lead his people forward with the stubborn faith that the dark night of despair would give way before a bright dawn of hope.

Sidney Greenberg

I See an American Jewry

I SEE AN American Jewry, emancipated along with all other Americans from the restraints of prejudice, secure against violence, free to fulfill itself without hindrance.

An American Jewry alight with a religious faith hallowed by antiquity and responsive to the mystery of all things, yet sanctioned by the best in modern thought and clean with reasonableness.

An American Jewry standing four square by Judaism's great moral ideals, sharpening them into the keenest contemporaneous, applying them boldly, imaginatively—so that the name Jew is a synonym for the practice and advocacy of justice, compassion, freedom and peace.

An American Jewry literature in both its heritages, the American and the Hebraic, creative in both, cross-blending and fertilizing the two until all devotion to one shall connote blessing for the other as well.

An American Jewry whose household is set in order.

An American Jewry which, having labored that Zion be rebuilt, now draws waters in joy from the fountainhead of the Jewish spirit.

I see a Jewry which in its inner life has made of Judaism what it is intended to be, what it is now in some measure, and what it can become in infinitely greater degree—that is to say, a source of blessing.

And I see all this set in a new, brave and free world which Jews, together with all men of goodwill, have helped to set free, laboring as individuals but also as Jews, as members of a fellowship consecrated from the womb to the ideal of a new, brave and free world. . . .

Shall not Jewish dreams and ideals, hands and hearts, blood and anguish have contributed to this end so long desired and prayed for? Will it then be a little thing—will it not rather be accounted a very great thing—to have played a part, not the largest perhaps but not the meanest either, in the building of the Kingdom of God on earth?

Milton Steinberg

What We Hope For

THERE ARE GREAT areas of common interests in which all religions can cooperate in mutual helpfulness and respect, influencing one another and learning from one another.

Judaism, which differed and continues to differ from other religions in significant matters of belief and practice, has sought and seeks opportunities of friendly cooperation with them in all things which may contribute to the building of the good society, firm in its own convictions, reverent of theirs, hoping for the great day of universal reconciliation of all peoples, which "they shall not hurt nor destroy in all My holy mountain, and the earth shall be full of the knowledge of God as the waters cover the sea."

Abba Hillel Silver

The Last Word Is One of Hope

THE HAFTARAH FOR Rosh Hashanah concludes on an optimistic note, reminding us that the last word is one of hope, of confidence in Israel's future, in man's ability to "return." It thereby reinforces the notion that the Days of Awe are not intended to be occasions for melancholy, pensive brooding over past failures, but rather for a joyous, though solemn, reaffirmation of the possibilities inherent in life, in the world which God has created. It strengthens us in the determination to live by the highest as we know it, even as it gives us the courage to face our own weakness and seek to overcome it.

David Lieber

Were You an Optimist?

THE TALMUD ASKS, *Tzipita lishu'a*? "Did you look forward toward redemption?" Were you an optimist? Did you look forward to a brighter future? Do you remember the scene in *City Slickers* where Billy Crystal looks in the mirror and says, "This is the best I am going to look for the rest of my life!" It is all downhill from here. It was a fun movie, but even if Mr. Crystal is Jewish, that is not a Jewish way of looking at the world.

We Jews are the most optimistic of people. Who else but we, after the destructions and massacres and pogroms and Holocaust and evil, could take as our national anthem *Hatikvah*, the Hope. Who else could go to the death camps with Maimonides's words, "I believe in the coming of the Messiah, and even if he tarries, every day I will wait for him to come." We will be asked, were you optimistic?

Michael Gold

Merger—A Vision of the Future

And then all that has divided us will merge
And then compassion will be wedded to power
And then softness will come to a world that is harsh and unkind
And then both men and women will be gentle
And then both women and men will be strong
And then no person will be subject to another's will
And then all will be rich and free and varied
And then the greed of some will give way to the needs of many
And then all will share equally in the earth's abundance
And then all will care for the sick and the weak and the old
And then all will nourish the young

And then all will cherish life's creatures
And then all will live in harmony with each other and the earth
And then everywhere will be called Eden once again.

Judy Chicago

We Have Reason to Be Optimistic

ROSH HASHANAH COMES to remind us that we have reason to be optimistic. Though the liturgy enumerates a host of moral sins and perversions of justice of which we might be guilty—it views all of this as a temporary condition. For the divine instinct within us calls us to *t'shuvah*—to a return to our true self. As long as this divine instinct remains operative within us and informs us to be loving, decent, and just—we shall continue to be optimistic about the human condition and shall view any veering from what we consider to be basic values as a temporary deviation.

Martin S. Rozenberg

The Optimism of Jewish Ethics

JEWISH ETHICS IS inspired with a great optimism. It is not optimism in the sense that it proclaims that everything that is is good; but in the sense that Browning makes Rabbi ben Ezra say: "Grow old along with me, the best is yet to be."

The Jew's vision embraced a glorious future for the whole human race. Jewish ethics is pure idealism, not only in motive, but in hope. That is what is meant by the Jew's Messianic days.

The Jew has never admitted that his ideals have as yet been completely realized by any man or by any society. The refrain of Jewish history and Jewish aspiration is that the Messianic age is still to come.

Revere, as the Jew does, the past, he does not glorify it. He roots in it, but he spreads out, as a good, old, strong, and beautiful tree must do, toward the sky.

He looks to the rising sun of the future and beholds it, with healing on its wings, shining for all humanity.

When man shall have completely learned the law of life, in justice and love, when men and nations shall come to be taught of the Eternal so as to learn of His ways, then will be made manifest the effect of perfect righteousness.

Then will swords be beaten into plough shares and spears into pruning hooks, men will learn war no more, there will be peace.

The culture of humanity will only then be complete and perfect, when the law of righteousness comes to be written in human hearts, when men follow it instinctively, when they carry out in their lives, with joy, what in thought they recognize as law and duty.

Then will God's Kingdom be established. He will be acknowledged as One, with one united humanity worshipping Him and realizing the perfect ethical life, in the name of Him who said, "For I am the Lord, Who exercises mercy, justice and righteousness in the earth, for in these things I delight."

Samuel Schulman

CHAPTER 23

ISRAEL

Israel and Haunted Houses

OF HAUNTED HOUSES it is said that they yield peace of mind only to the descendants of the original owner. Even so the soil of Eretz Yisrael will yield its sustenance and its beauty only to the descendants of those who wrote the *Tehilim* and who bled at Masada.

Solomon Goldman

We Did Not Forget

THE OATH WHICH the first exiles pronounced at the streams of Babylon . . . Jews did not forget! Eras came and went, civilizations grew and decayed, empires rose and fell, historic trends flowed and ebbed, but Jerusalem was yet prized above all joys and remembered in all sorrows. Under the *hupah* (the wedding canopy) when two hearts are beating in unison, when joy reigns supreme, there comes from the depth of the soul the prayer, "May there soon be heard in the cities of Judah and in the streets of Jerusalem the voice of gladness, the voice of the bridegroom and the voice of the bride." And when in the house of mourning, sorrow oppresses the heart and longing tests faith, the lips murmur, "He who fills the world, comfort ye together with all those that mourn for Zion and Jerusalem . . ." And when death claimed the Jew and the cold earth opened its mouth . . . the head (of the Jew) rested on a bag of Palestinian soil.

Solomon Goldman

The Reward of Love

OUR LOVE FOR Zion is one of our proudest titles. For no nation has ever loved its country with such a surpassing love as the people of Israel has loved the land of Israel. Though driven from Palestine nearly two thousand years ago, the Jewish people, which the world, knowing it only on the surface, considers a nation of hard-headed, sober-minded traders, has loved its ancient land with an undying love, with a romantic love, with a love one reads of in books of fiction, a love that expects no reward, a love that is happy in the privilege of loving. And yet, though expecting no reward, Israel receiving the amplest reward for its love. For it is this love which has enabled the Jewish people to survive until this day. The love of Eretz Yisrael was the torch that illumined the thorny path of our people. It was the anchor that kept our ship from drifting out into the boundless ocean. And when the eternal wanderer seemed to sink under the burden of his suffering, he looked up into the sky and saw the light that shone from Zion, and with renewed courage he continued on his journey.

Israel Friedman

A Vital Israel Will Inspire Jews

IT IS NOT speeches and proclamations that will move Diaspora Jews but rather Jewish society which inspires the individual to want to participate in the three-thousand-year-old legacy of the Jewish nation. Aliya must first address Israelis and educate them to appreciate the crucial role they can play in determining the future of Jewish life throughout the world.

Israelis are not only asked to address the persecuted and frightened Jew, but also, and above all, Jews who have lost their sense of memory and history and whose Jewishness has ceased being necessary and self-evident.

Israeli society must convey the excitement and importance of living as modern Jews, who combine a sense of history and tradition with a profound belief in new human possibilities. The final chapter of our people's spiritual drama has not yet been written.

Israel as a vital Jewish society will awaken Jews to become active participants in shaping the future of the Jewish people's moral and spiritual legacy.

David Hartman

The Spiritual Climate of Israel

THERE IS ONE thing that Israel possesses in greater abundance than any other country and that is the freedom to be Jewish. In Israel the environment is your ally. There are no economic considerations to reconcile with observing the Shabbat or the festivals. There is no counter-pull of a dominant and often aggressive Christian civilization. There are no problems arising from the delicate problem of balancing loyalties and contributions to two civilizations. The calendar is Jewish, the radio is Jewish, the language is Jewish, the headlines are Jewish, the names of streets and boulevards are Jewish. The largest crane in Haifa harbor with a lift capacity of one hundred and twenty tons has a Jewish name. It is called "Samson." Israel is a place where you can attend, as I did, a Talmud lesson on Shabbat morning in Jerusalem and share a volume of *Baba Metziah* with the President of the State; a place where you can attend a magnificent all-youth service, replete with choir, cantors and Torah readers in the Bilu Synagogue in Tel Aviv on Shabbat morning and a lecture in the "Ohel Shem" in the afternoon on "Aristotle and Maimonides"; a place where a *Lag B'omer* pilgrimage to Miron can become an unforgettable and thrilling experience; a place where *Bik-kurim* on

Shevuot is not a faded memory but an exciting reality; a place where your radio brings you Bible lessons and Talmud lessons, the music of the synagogue, the classics of our heritage; a place where bank entrances have *Mezuzot* and post-office clerks feel free to wear *Yarmulkes*; a place where the ideals of the Prophets have been translated into political and social realities; a place, in brief, where *Am Yisroel Chai*—the people of Israel lives. When you get caught up in its rhythm and its people insinuate themselves into your heart, you can begin to understand the embarrassing chauvinistic statement of our sages that "he who dwells in Eretz Yisrael is like one who has a God while he who dwells outside of Israel is like one who has no God."

We must have faith in the inherent religious genius of our people, which has already begun to assert itself in a hundred ways and will do so with ever-increasing vigor as Israel strikes firmer roots in the soil in which its spiritual productivity once found its most impressive flowering. The sainted Rabbi Kuk, a passionate believer in the spiritual future of the *Yishuv*, once made the crisp prophecy: "The ancient will be revitalized; the contemporary will be sanctified." That prophecy is already on the road to fulfillment. We can shorten that road.

Sidney Greenberg

CHAPTER 24

JUDAISM AND DEMOCRACY

The Golden Thread of Jewish History

"DEMOCRACY," DECLARED HITLER, "is fundamentally Jewish, not Germanic." The so-called Aryan must trace his political traditions back to the oriental despotisms and ring worship of ancient Persia and to the caste system of India. Even the Greeks had no strong consistent democratic tradition. Thucydides, Plato and Aristotle opposed the democratic form of government. Aristotle actually defended slavery. . . . But the Semite of the desert, from whom Israel is descended, neither knew nor tolerated any despotism. The democratic motif runs like a golden thread through the whole political, social, economic and religious history of Israel from the earliest nomadic period unto the present.

Abba Hillel Silver

Judaism Incompatible with Totalitarianism

JUDAISM IS NATURALLY incompatible with totalitarianism of any kind—not only political totalitarianism, but coerced conformity of any kind. Dictators always found their Jewish citizens indigestible. Fascists and Communists alike have never tolerated the maintenance of the Jewish tradition because it represents a denial of the repression for which they stand.

The Prophet Jeremiah exhorted his followers to seek the welfare of the country in which they live. And Jews have always felt the obligation to participate fully in the life of the community.

The voice of the synagogue will therefore be heard in all issues that would have aroused the ancient Prophets of Israel; integrity in public office; just labor-management relations; civil rights and civil liberties; equality of economic opportunity; decent education, housing and health standards for all citizens; peace among the nations of the world.

One of the rabbis of the Talmud said: "If a man of learning participates in public affairs, he gives stability to the land. But if he sits at home and says to himself: 'What have the affairs of society to do with me? . . . Let my soul dwell in peace,' he brings about the destruction of the world."

Morris N. Kertzer

When Religion Was Greatly Democratized

FOR THE FIRST time in the history of mankind a whole people conceived itself as having been consecrated into an everlasting priesthood and as having been commissioned to perform those functions which among other peoples were relegated to a small official group of priests. Religion was never so democratized.

When our sages speak of Israel as "the chosen of the Lord," "His peculiar inheritance," "His first-born," "the light bringer of the world," "the one indispensable nation"; when Halevi declares that "Israel is the heart of the world, that the gift of prophecy was bestowed upon Israel alone and that all mankind exists for the sake of the prophets"; when Gersonides declares that "this people of Israel must dwell alone in order that it might be separated from all other peoples and be holier than them"; when Bachya declares that "the people of Israel are God's fighting hosts on earth even as the ministering angels are His hosts in heaven";

when Judah Low ben Bezalel declares that "Israel is the essence and goal of all creation," one might take these declarations, and the ten thousand others like them in our literature, to be nothing more than decadent chauvinism, unless one remembers that the people from whose soul these sentiments arose conceived of itself as a covenanted people, as having been summoned by destiny to assume the role of religious leadership, and as having consented to bear the crushing burdens of such a leadership . . .

These sentiments were employed not to impress the Gentile world but to call forth the utmost devotion on the part of the Jew, to remind him of his calling, to challenge him to prove himself worthy of the role assigned to him by God, and to strengthen his morale whenever his ministry made him "despised and forsaken of men."

Abba Hillel Silver

Judaism and Democracy

THE LAW OF acting fairly toward one's neighbor is the starting point for all Jewish teachings. Judaism has no elaborate philosophy of justice. Unlike that of Plato and Aristotle, Jewish teaching made little attempt to develop a systematic democratic philosophy. In point of fact, there is no Hebrew word for democracy, except that which is borrowed from the Greeks. But the social creed by which the Jews have lived for centuries is in democracy's highest traditions.

Basic to Judaism are these fundamental principles which are also basic to democracy: (1) God recognizes no distinction among men on the basis of creed, color or station in life; all men are equal in His sight. (2) Every man is his brother's keeper—we bear responsibility for our neighbor's failings as well as for his needs. (3) All men, being made in God's image, have infinite potential for goodness; therefore the job of society is to evoke the best that is in each man. (4) Freedom is to be prized above all things; the very first words of the Ten Commandments depict God as the Great Liberator.

The theme of freedom and equality runs constantly throughout the three-thousand-year history of the Jewish people. The frequent taste of injustice, as they wandered from country to country, reinforced a tradition already rooted in their faith. Thus, Jews responded readily to the thrilling challenge of the American Declaration of Independence and the Bill of Rights. And the French Revolution also found Jews sympathetic to the cries of Liberty, Fraternity, and Equality. It is no accident that the words, "Proclaim ye liberty throughout the land to all the inhabitants thereof," found on the American Liberty Bell, stem from the Old Testament. For love of liberty is woven into the fabric of Judaism.

Morris N. Kertzer

CHAPTER 25

JUDAISM AND THE JEW

Judaism Is Rooted in the Jewish People

JUDAISM IS ROOTED forever in the soil, blood, life-experience and memory of a particular folk—the Jewish people.

Solomon Goldman

When Is a People Chosen?

A PEOPLE IS chosen not because of any racial superiority; there is no such thing. All men are the children of Adam; all are created in God's image—Jew and Gentile, Hebrew, Ethiopian, Philistine or Aramaean. A people is chosen when it has the will to live in a way which would express God's spirit on earth. A people is chosen when it measures its growth by moral and spiritual and not by material and geographic standards. A people is chosen when it is held together by spirit and not by might. A people is chosen when its highest ideal is not to get as much as possible from the world but to contribute of its best to the world, when it endeavors to live as the "Servant of the Lord—a blessing unto the nations." Israel did not always live up to this position. But it is a historic fact that Israel, of all the peoples, always considered itself a candidate for such a position. When one is a candidate one is often elected; when one is not a candidate, one can hardly be elected.

David Aronson

Judaism Requires Investment of Time

JUDAISM CANNOT HOPE to transform our lives, let alone our world, if we will not invest the time necessary to let it work its wonders in our hearts.

If we don't sanctify the Shabbat day, if we don't regularly attend our synagogue's worship services, if we don't put aside time for Jewish learning on a regular basis, then we can't hope to realize the potential that Judaism offers.

Instead, we find it too simple to fall into the Babylonian fallacy—to regard a willingness to sustain a sacred place as sufficient to safeguard our values and our dreams. While contributing to the upkeep of Jewish institutions is indeed a necessary base, it is but a start.

The task of the Jew, to establish the sovereignty of God in the here-and-now, takes much more than just its proper place. It requires a good deal of heart and soul. And cultivating those precious and evanescent virtues takes time.

Bradley Artson

When Judaism Functions

JUDAISM FUNCTIONS ONLY so long as it is co-extensive with the whole of the Jew's life.

Mordecai M. Kaplan

The Goal of Judaism

INDEED, THE MAJOR thrust of religion as conceived by the Torah and practiced by our people is the achievement of sanctity. "And you shall be unto me a kingdom of priests and a holy nation" precedes the giving of the Ten Commandments. And why are we to strive for holiness? "You shall be holy because I the Lord thy God am holy." The goal of Judaism is thus to bring man as close as possible to the holiness we call God.

Hillel Hyman

Can the Jewish People Survive Without Judaism?

THE JEWISH RELIGION is the crowning achievement of our people and our supreme gift to civilization. It possesses such vast reservoirs of spiritual truth that it has been able to sustain and inspire generations upon generations of our people and to retain their sacrificial loyalty under all circumstances and upon all levels of culture. It thus became the strongest factor in the survival of our people, the *kesher shel kayama*, the enduring tie. It is doubtful whether the Jewish people can long survive in the Diaspora without it. . . . Those religious leaders, therefore, who are today teaching the religion of Israel to their people are not only leading them to fountains of living truth, which can sweeten and refresh their individual lives, but are also conserving the most potent force which, throughout the ages, has preserved the Jewish people.

Abba Hillel Silver

Judaism—The Soul of Jewish Civilization

JEWISH RELIGION IS nothing less than the soul of Judaism, or of Jewish civilization. Through the Jewish conception of God and the various practices connected with it, the contents of Jewish living have always assumed meaning. Through the teaching about God and the observances with which they were associated, the Jews have been able to interpret their experiences, their hopes and their sufferings in a way that enhanced their lives. It was undoubtedly the conviction that those religious teachings constituted religion as its truest and its best that instilled in the Jew the courage to face stoically a hostile world.

Mordecai M. Kaplan

Judaism—The Unique Culture of the Jewish People

THE ONLY NAME which adequately describes the Jewish heritage is civilization or culture. Judaism is, then . . . to be defined as the unique culture of the Jewish people. Like any civilization, it represents an organic complex of a literature, language, religious outlook, folkways, group hopes, aspirations, ethical values and esthetic judgments. In this living whole, religion is at once the driving motif and the most ideal expression, but it is by no means the whole nor the largest part.

Milton Steinberg

What We Want from Judaism

1. We want Judaism to help us to overcome temptation, doubt and discouragement.
2. We want Judaism to imbue us with a sense of responsibility for the righteous use of the blessings wherewith God endows us.
3. We want the Jew so to be trusted that his yea will be taken as yea, and his nay as nay.
4. We want to learn how to utilize our leisure to best advantage physically, intellectually and spiritually.
5. We want the Jewish home to live up to its traditional standards of virtue and piety.
6. We want the Jewish upbringing of our children to further their moral and spiritual growth and to enable them to accept with joy their heritage as Jews.
7. We want the synagogue to enable us to worship God in sincerity and truth.
8. We want our religious traditions to be interpreted in terms of understandable experience and to be made relevant to our present-day needs.

9. We want Judaism to find rich, manifold, and ever new expression in philosophy, in letters, and in the arts.

10. We want all forms of Jewish organization to make for spiritual purpose and ethical endeavor.

11. We want the unity of Israel throughout the world to be fostered through mutual help in time of need, and through cooperation in the furtherance of Judaism at all times.

12. We want Judaism to function as a potent influence for justice, freedom and peace in the lives of men and nations.

Reconstructionist Prayer Book

The Rewards of Jewishness?

WHAT DO I get out of my Jewishness to justify the expenditure of time and energy upon it? How am I the better off for my adherence to it?

From the Jewish heritage, I derive my world outlook, a God-centered interpretation of reality in the light of which man the individual is clothed with dignity, and the career of humanity with cosmic meaning and hope; a humane morality, elevated in its aspirations yet sensibly realistic; a system of rituals that interpenetrates my daily routines and invests them with poetry and intimations of the divine.

Beyond this, my life is enriched by the accumulated treasures of over three millennia of Jewish history—a large literature in which I read extensively, not as an outsider but with a sense of belonging; music for me to sing, art for me to enjoy. I have the privilege of companionship with the great personalities of Jewish history. At my disposal is a second fund of folklore when I spin tales to my children. Mine literally is a double past—the American and the Jewish. My horizons are distant, not in one direction but in two. I am twice anchored in traditions, and hence twice secured against the peril of being rootless and "un-possessed."

And because my Jewishness is something positive, anti-Semitism looms less large in my life than in that of many of my fellows. I am not hagridden by it as they are. To them, it is the whole of what is otherwise a senseless identification; to me it is an unfortunate, a tragic incident in an inherently worthwhile enterprise. Like them, I am prepared to do anything I can to resist it. I, too, man the walls. But I have shrines, libraries and family altars to defend as well as jobs, legal rights and memberships to clubs. And I know that while much will be taken from me in the event of defeat, my Jewish heritage will still remain to sustain and give me direction. The de-Judaized Jews, on the other hand, recognize quite clearly that they will be left with nothing. Little wonder that their preoccupation with anti-Semitism approaches a hysteria.

I am furthermore quite confident that by virtue of my attitudes, I am less susceptible than escapist Jews to infection by self-contempt. I am undeniably exposed to the same psychic influences that play over them. But in my case, as I have already indicated, participation in and appreciation of the Jewish tradition operate as immunizing elements. I am not tempted to flight from myself, nor bitter because I know in advance that it will prove futile. I cannot despise my identity: it is associated with a process I enjoy and respect. Not the least of the significances for me of a meaningful Judaism is its contribution to my mental health.

Milton Steinberg

CHAPTER 26

JUDGING

We Are Too Liable to Misjudge

THOSE WHOM WE misjudge do not usually get the opportunity to defend themselves. Would we therefore not do well to pray in the words of the Sioux Indians: "Great Spirit, help me never to judge another until I have walked two weeks in his moccasins." Ought we not to search diligently for the good in others, humbled by the realization that they may have to search even harder to find the good in us? It is this charitable motivation which prompted our sages to say: "Judge not thy fellowman until thou art in his place." Until we understand his fears and his frustrations, his hopes and his hungers—until we know all that, we ought not to judge for we are too liable to misjudge.

Sidney Greenberg

The Impulse God Loans Us

GOD LOANS US the impulse to judge ourselves and to forgive our own actions. If we use this impulse wisely, then we can create an admirable pattern of life.

Israel Berger

Do Not Judge Until . . .

OUR SAGES CAUTIONED: "Do not judge your fellow human being until you are in his place."

The poet Shelley once said it in another way: "A man, to be greatly good, must imagine intensely and comprehensively; he must put himself in the place of another and of many others; the pains and pleasures of his species must become his own."

There is a desperate shortage in contemporary society of precisely this quality which Judaism prescribes. We all need a more sympathetic imagination to enable us to get under another human being's skin.

There would be more harmony in the home if children would try to understand the fears, the dilemmas, the insecurities of parents; and if parents would try to imagine the anguish and anxiety of growing up.

Sermons would sound less self-righteous if rabbis could imagine themselves into a pew. And congregants would be less critical if they could sympathetically put themselves in the rabbi's place.

Hospital patients would get more thoughtful treatments if their physicians were obliged to spend one week a year in a hospital bed. And perhaps patients would be more understanding of their doctors if they could follow them on their harassing and demanding daily rounds.

More of us would visit parents and grandparents in old-age homes if we could project ourselves into those bleak institutions and try to understand how much a visit can relieve the burden of loneliness and a sense of being unwanted.

"If we could read the secret history of our enemies," wrote Longfellow, "we should find in each man's life sorrow and suffering enough to disarm all hostility."

Sidney Greenberg

The Goal—Be a Mensch

"THAT YE MAY remember and do all my commandments, and be holy unto your God." And that—the goal of all that precedes—is to be a *mensch* [a human being], to treat your fellowman in keeping with those ideals of behavior which the founder of our city emphasized in the names given to its streets. Recall the names of our streets: Peace, Benevolent, Benefit, Hope. Live with your fellowman on a street called peace. Let your attitude toward him be a benevolent one. Be as ready to confer benefits as you are to demand them. And in your dealings with your fellowman always be sure, so to speak and so to act, that the hope within him will stay alive.

William G. Braude

CHAPTER 27

LEARN AND LIVE

Tablets Without Letters

EVERYTHING I AM trying to say about the indispensability of knowledge to the Jewish tradition has been anticipated by the tradition itself. In myriad epigrams and metaphors, the teachers of Israel from Moses on insisted that only as Jewry was informed could it be assured of life. But nowhere has this been stated more colorfully than in a legend spun by ancient rabbis.

When Moses descended from Mount Sinai, they relate, he held in his arms, as Scripture informs us, the tablets of stone engraved by the finger of the Holy One, blessed be He. And such was the virtue of the inscription, that it was not Moses who carried the tablets, but the tablets which carried Moses. So it came to pass that his descent over jagged rocks, on the verge of crags and yawning chasms, was effortless and safe. But when the Prophet neared the mountain's base and caught his first glimpse of the Golden Calf, when God's words and the idol were brought into confrontation with each other, a wonder ensued. The sacred letters detached themselves from the stone in which they had been inscribed and vanished into thin air. Moses was left holding a blank, inert thing, too heavy for him. It is not true, the sages assert, that Moses threw the tablets to the earth, so shattering them. The fact is he had to let them go or be crushed. The lettered stone which had carried Moses was, once letterless, too much for him to bear.

It is not difficult to discern what the ancient rabbis are trying to say in their parable: given knowledge and insight, Judaism sustains the Jew; without them it is a crushing burden, too heavy for even the strongest to withstand.

Milton Steinberg

What Study of Torah Can Do for Us

STUDY OF TORAH was more than a religious duty. The Jew found in study "Life and length of days"—meaningful days, exciting years. And study of Torah can still confer this blessing upon us. I am happy to see so many adults enrolled in our Bible study groups, in the Akiba School, and in the Ulpan classes. I welcome the increasing numbers of mature women who are returning to the University, not only to develop new professional skills, but simply to study, and to learn. For as long as we keep our minds open and alert, as long as we are willing to try a new skill, entertain a new thought, surrender an old prejudice—so long do we remain vital people.

And life would be richer if through the years we invested time in the present, cultivating communal interests and becoming involved in activities that can become full-time at retirement. Our Jewish community, our synagogue, our Talmud Torah need countless volunteers to carry on this work.

Kassel E. Abelson

The Hebrew Language Has Been Set Apart

FLOWING DOWN THE hills of eternity, the Hebrew language has been set apart for truths destined to sway mankind and humanize the world.

Sabato Morais

Judaism Requires Knowledge

DRAWING STRENGTH AND inspiration from the Torah, Israel has weathered all storms. Israel withstood exiles, persecution and misfortune, but will it withstand ignorance?

Bereft of Torah, Israel is bereft of power. Our enemies can burn our books, but only we by our neglect can destroy their spirit.

Samuel S. Cohon

Teaching—A True Act of Giving

IN THIS CLASSIFICATION of those who give, I see at the head of the list the teacher. Not only the teacher in College, or Public School or Hebrew School, but also the Scout and Cub Master, the Youth Leaders, the father who instructs his son in responsibility and the mother who enables her daughter to love in wholesomeness and kindness. Teaching is a true act of giving for it leaves a vestige of oneself in the development of another. If you have ever seen the light of understanding shine in another's eyes where no light shone before, then you have gathered the treasures of teaching. If you have ever guided the unsteady and unpracticed hand and watched it suddenly grown firm and purposeful, then you have had the gain of giving. If you have ever watched a young mind soar to new heights and you have helped to launch a career, then you have felt within you the sense of being a humble instrument in the furtherance of mankind.

Bernard S. Raskas

Hebrew—The Golden Hinge

THE KNOWLEDGE OF Hebrew is the golden hinge upon which our national and religious existence turns. Flowing down from the hills of eternity, the Hebrew language has been set apart by God as the receptacle of truths destined to sway mankind and humanize the world.

Sabato Morais

The Object of Education

THE OBJECT OF education is not merely to enable our children to gain their daily bread and to acquire pleasant means of recreation, but that they should know God and serve Him with earnestness and devotion. Are you thus training your children? Is it your care that they be educated as Jews and Jewesses?

Hermann Adler

Strengthening Resistance

THE ADVANCEMENT OF social and economic progress, the dissemination of the truth regarding Jews and Judaism, the futhering of community movements in which all groups can participate and the utilization of legal means against the embattled forces of prejudice, these constitute the most effective means of fighting anti-Semitism. But their efficacy depends upon utilizing not one or two, but all these means in unison, in a broad, unified attack on the menace.

It must be confessed, however, that even the most effective campaign cannot possibly banish anti-Jewish prejudice within our lifetime, or that of our children. The virulence of the disease may be reduced, but it is too much to hope for its early extirpation.

Under these circumstances, it is obvious that the resistance of the victims must be strengthened, so that they may be better able to endure the ravages of the affliction. Increased Jewish loyalty and courage can come to American Jewish youth and its elders only through a growing understanding and love of the Jewish heritage. In no other way can a harried generation avoid the crumbling of morale. The Jew who is ignorant of his religion, history and culture is an easy prey for the shafts of prejudice. It is not that he remains entirely uniformed on things Jewish. On the contrary, the world about him is only too eager to fill the void with misinformation. From spheres which he has been taught to regard as beyond reproach, the university, the lecture forum, the public press and the printed page, comes propaganda which persuades him that the Jewish heritage is worthless and even dangerous. For this reason, the most cultured and sensitive spirits within the Jewish group, when they lack any Jewish background that would enable them to evaluate their heritage fairly, are often the first victims of self-hate.

Moreover, without meaningful Jewish values in their lives, all Jews are in imminent danger of identifying Jewish life with "anti-anti-Semitism" and Jewish activity with an unending process of fund-raising. That would be a tragedy not only for Judaism, but for the Jew, whose heart would be filled with bitterness and suspicion. On the other hand, in striving to build Jewish loyalty and self-respect, American Jewry is taking the most constructive step toward protecting the psychic health of four and a half million men, women and children. Efforts in this direction still fall woefully short of the necessary maximum in extent and in resourcefulness.

An active program for fighting anti-Semitism and a positive attitude toward Jewish values are the only sure means of preserving the Jewish people in a dark age. But the modern Jew who observes anti-Semitism at large in the world knows that he is fighting for more than his own preservation. Destiny has made him the custodian of those dynamic ideals which alone offer promise of a better world and fate of which quivers on the balance today. Self-defense needs no apology, but the proud consciousness of serving a cause beyond oneself gives this desperate task a touch of glory.

Robert Gordis

The Book and the Jew

JEWS, SURVEYING THEIR own past, often express astonishment at the breadth and depth of the civilization which they have inherited. It seems unreasonable that such exquisite and variegated flowers should have blossomed on a sterile soil and in an uncongenial atmosphere. Amazement disappears when one considers the urgency which impelled Jewish cultural life. For, since the Jew would not die, he had his choice of only two alternatives. He must either cultivate a compensating culture or go stark mad. This accounts for the passionate devotion of the Jew to ideas, for his intense absorption in books, for his reverence for scholarship. With other peoples, culture was an afterthought, a by-product of normal living, an amusement for leisure hours. With this Jew it was a condition for sanity.

Out of rigid necessity, the Jew concerned himself with study and instruction. In no other society was education taken so seriously as in the ghetto. Mothers in their lullabies assured their infants that Torah was the best of all wares. Jewish parents held always before themselves the example of the mother of Rabbi Joshua ben Chananyah who "used to take her child to the door of the academy in his crib so that he might early become accustomed to the sound of learning."

Milton Steinberg

In Judaism Education Is a Lifelong Process

EDUCATION IN JUDAISM is a life-long process. It never stops. In reaching for the highest aim, there is no such thing as completing requirements, passing the tests, and graduating. Requirements are never completed, study is never finished, examinations and tests confront one every day. Where the goal is dedication to God, passing and failing is a lifelong experience, and what our score is should be our lifelong concern.

Hayim Halevy Donin

The True Index of Jewish Vitality

IN THE LONG run the future of American Jewry will be determined not by the level of its material prosperity, not by the size and number of religious edifices which it is able to erect—but by the quality and quantity of *talmiday chachomim* and academies of learning which will thrive in its midst. This is the true index of Jewish vitality.

Joseph M. Baumgarten

What Keeps Us Alive

ISRAEL IS THE tree, we are the leaves. It is clinging to the stem that keeps us alive.

Abraham J. Heschel

What Self-Renewal Requires

TO BE SELF-SUSTAINING, a people has to attend to its economy.
    To be self-renewing, it has to attend to the education of its youth.

Mordecai M. Kaplan

The Best Books

THE BEST BOOKS are those which best teach men how to live.

Israel Abrahams

Torah—Worship of God Through Study

TORAH IS THE worship of God by means of study. It is the prayer of the mind. It is the science which seeks to discover the laws of the moral universe and thus it deals with the realities that lie above and beyond the world of visible nature. It is man's pilgrimage through life in search of himself.

    Torah is the shrine which the Jew builds of thought and feeling and aspiration. It is the tree of life and in its shade alone can the Jew find completeness, peace and serenity.

Morris Adler

What Education Is

EDUCATION IS SOMETHING more than the acquisition of facts. Education is the power and love of thinking.

Bernard Revel

What Jews Discovered About Adult Education

LONG BEFORE THE creation of the modern science of education and the founding of the adult education movement, Jews discovered the basic truths that adults are teachable, that study is enjoyable, and that learning is a life-process.

Robert Gordis

Teaching Torah with Love

THE RIGHT YESHIVA is a place where there is so much love that it's awesome. God gave us Torah with so much love, so if I want to give over the Torah to my children, it has to be done in that same way.

Shlomo Carlebach

What Makes a Man's Face Shine

JUDAH BAR ILAI, a second-century sage, deeply impressed a pagan in the marketplace by his radiant face. "This man," said the pagan, "must either be intoxicated or he has just discovered a hidden treasure."

Rabbi Judah overheard him and said, "Friend, I do not drink except when I must for ritual purposes. Neither have I found any treasure. I am a poor man."

"Then what makes your face shine so?"

"That is quite simple," Rabbi Judah answered: "I study all the time, and the quest for knowledge makes the face of a man to shine."

As long as we keep our minds open and alert, as long as we are willing to try a new skill, entertain a new thought, develop a new friend, surrender an old prejudice—so long do we remain vital people, so long do we gain ground and move forward in the search for more abundant life.

Sidney Greenberg

Paradise Is in the Teachers

SOMETIMES PRAYER IS more than a light before us; it is light before us; it is light within us. Those who have once been resplendent with this light find little meaning in speculations about the efficacy of prayer. A story is told about a Rabbi who once entered heaven in a dream. He was permitted to approach the temple of Paradise where the great sages of the Talmud, the Tannaim, were spending their eternal lives. He saw that they were just sitting around tables studying the Talmud. The disappointed Rabbi wondered, "Is this all there is to Paradise?" But suddenly he heard a voice, "You are mistaken. The Tannaim are not in Paradise. Paradise is in the Tannaim."

Abraham J. Heschel

Unreasonable Jews

JEWS WHO REFUSE to study about Judaism but want to be convinced of its worth and greatness are as reasonable as people who refuse to go into the water before they have learned to swim.

Mordecai M. Kaplan

Our Answer to Anti-Semitism

FOR THE JEWS the moral is to answer anti-Semitism with more Semitism, if by Semitism we mean greater devotion to the great ideals which Judaism proclaimed to the world.

Israel Abrahams

Why We Should Study Our History

WE SHOULD STUDY the history of our people—not for the purpose of learning what to boast of, but for the purpose of knowing what we are.

Mordecai M. Kaplan

CHAPTER 28

WHAT LIFE REQUIRES

The Need for Moral Courage

WITHOUT MORAL COURAGE, all virtue is merely a way of speaking.

Mordecai M. Kaplan

Being Good to Ourselves

MANY PEOPLE GO throughout life committing partial suicide—destroying their talents, energies, creative qualities. Indeed, to learn how to be good to oneself is often more difficult than to learn how to be good to others.

Joshua Loth Liebman

Impossible to Do What We Wish and Get What We Want

MANKIND HAS NOT as yet invented a social order in which it is possible both to do what we wish and get what we want.

Mordecai M. Kaplan

Majoring in the Minors

SO OFTEN THE word "religiously" is used by people who perform a host of secular activities "religiously," while they fulfill their religious obligations spasmodically or not at all.

They are capable of ultimate devotion to marginal concerns but only marginal devotion to ultimate concerns. In the curriculum of their lives, the electives have become required courses. The required courses have become electives.

What one father said of his teenage daughter fits many of us uncomfortably well: "She's a good student," said the father, "but she is constantly majoring in the minors." Majoring in the minors—that's what makes so much of our living trivial and inconsequential."

Sidney Greenberg

We Run Away from Our Duties

OUR LIVES ARE filled with unread books, broken promises, unkept resolutions, unanswered letters, and neglected friendships, all because we have in matters great or small run away from our duties—run away from God. We are all little Jonahs.

Morris Bekritsky

Let Us Live Up to Our Masks

WE COULD ALL grow into finer human beings if we learned to wear the mask of the finest human being we know—not in order to pretend to be what we are not, but rather as a means of aspiring to be what we can become. If we would become kinder and more sympathetic, we would do well to assume the pose and strike the attitude of the kindly and sympathetic person. If we would become more understanding and more merciful, we could profitably don the masks of understanding and mercy. Someone has said with fine insight, "Act human and you will become human." In the very process of playing the role of a better person, we can take an impressive forward stride in actually becoming better. All aspiration is partial realization.

One of the most dramatic illustrations of this truth was provided by the actor Richard Berry Harrison, who played the role of "De Lawd" in the original production of *Green Pastures*. Harrison was chosen for the role because of his powerful build and deep resonant voice, not necessarily for any spiritual qualities. People who watched him perform in the play testified, as did Harrison himself, that after seventeen hundred performances as the Lord, he had become a highly spiritualized individual. As he himself explained it, he strove to become godlike, to be worthy of the role he played. He tried with conspicuous success to live up to his mask. He demonstrated the truth of Professor Hocking's assertion: "There is a deep tendency in human nature to become like that which we imagine ourselves to be."

Let us select our masks carefully, and then let us live up to our masks.

Sidney Greenberg

The Eleventh Test

GOD TESTED ABRAHAM ten times," says the Midrash. The tenth testing: To offer up his beloved Isaac.

But there was an eleventh testing—the greatest and hardest testing of all.

Raise not your hand against the lad. Release him, let him go.

To deny himself the martyrdom which he craved with all his being, which would give him nobility and distinction, to grant Isaac his own God-given individuality, to do with as he wished, to live his life, and in giving to gain release for self—to begin to live his *own* life—hard, hard thing to do. But this is what life demands!

Abraham J. Karp

We Can Do Little Things in a Great Way

IN OUR PERSONAL lives little things play a far greater role than we usually realize. Little things give us pain, and little things give us pleasure. A cruel word can cast a dreary cloud over the brightest of days; a word of appreciation can send our spirits soaring. A small act of kindness can often make a big difference in the delicate machinery of the human spirit.

When the English writer Oscar Wilde was being led handcuffed from prison to the Court of Bankruptcy, a friend waited for him to pass through the dreary, drafty corridor. As the prisoner passed, his friend tipped his hat to him. Of this gesture Wilde wrote later, "The memory of this little, lovely, silent act of love has unsealed for me all the wells of pity."

Few of us are ever asked to do great things, but we are always given the opportunity to do little things in a great way.

Sidney Greenberg

Not Trapped but Tested

ACCORDING TO JEWISH traditional teaching, man is not trapped but tested. His vicissitudes should serve as a challenge to his faith, and patience in the face of the retardation of that blessing which he has a right to expect with the gift of life. To deny the worth of life and to fall into despair because the promise is slow of fulfillment is to fail in the test. This is the main point in the cycle of Abraham stories, which culminates in the account of the test to which God put Abraham when He commanded him to offer up Isaac.

Mordecai M. Kaplan

Great Consequences from Little Things

LITTLE THINGS HAVE not only been responsible for high losses but have triggered great discoveries. A child's soap bubble led Newton to his important optical discoveries. A spider web over a garden path suggested the suspension bridge. A teakettle singing on the stove was the inspiration for the steam engine. A falling apple led to the discovery of the law of gravity. A lantern swinging in a tower was responsible for the pendulum. On both sides of the historical ledger, great consequences have come from little things.

Sidney Greenberg

The Need to Stop Running

LEVI YITZHOK ASKED a man, who seemed to be in a great hurry, why he rushed so. "I am in pursuit of my livelihood," replied the man. "And how do you know," asked the rabbi, "that your livelihood runs ahead of you? May be it is behind you, and what you need is to pause till it overtakes you."

Abraham Kahana

Why Abraham Planted a Tamarisk

A FAMILIAR RABBINIC interpretation of the word *"eshel"* (tamarisk tree) sees in it an acronym for the three Hebrew words *ahilah, shetia, leenah*—food, drink, lodging. This was the rabbinic way of reminding us that Abraham's genuine contribution to the landscape was not simply adding the beauty of a tree, but the nobility of hospitality.

The Vilna Gaon made the brilliant observation that Abraham's purpose in providing these three forms of hospitality was designed to counteract the evils that had been perpetrated in precisely these areas by his predecessors. Adam had sinned through eating, Noah through drinking, and the people of Sodom by denying lodging. In Abraham these transgressions are repaired.

Abraham becomes an inspiration to us to address ourselves to the legacy of evil we have inherited from the past, even as we look to him as an inspiration to perpetuate some of the virtues which are part of our Jewish heritage.

Sidney Greenberg

May We Feel Divine Discontent

MAY WE, LIKE our fathers, still stand out against the multitude, protesting with all our might against its follies and its fears. May a divine discontent give color to our dreams, and a passion for holy heresy set the tone of our thoughts. May the soul of the rebel still throb in us as it throbbed in our forefathers, that today and forever we may still be a light unto those who stumble in darkness.

Lewis Browne

Not by Might

IF THERE IS any holiday on the Jewish calendar which celebrates military might, it is Hanukkah. After all, the rededication of the Temple occurred only because the Maccabees succeeded in vanquishing the Syrians on the field of battle and thereby recapturing the holy Temple that the enemy had defiled. Without military valor there would have been no miracle to celebrate and no Hanukkah.

How profoundly paradoxical then, that on the holiday which owes its very existence to might and power triumphant, we should read the pacifistic put-down by the prophet: "Not by might, nor by power, but by My spirit, says the Lord of Hosts."

Nor is this verse likely to capture any popularity prizes among contemporary world leaders. At a time when billions are being spent on armaments by rich and poor nations alike, when nations buy missiles before they build schools and hospitals—at such time the words of the prophet seem too removed from the world of reality to be taken seriously. The mood of our time was perhaps captured more precisely by Mao Tse-tung when he said: "Every communist must grasp the truth that power grows out of the barrel of a gun."

Because the words of the prophet seem so remote from our way of thinking, they merit special emphasis. Their truth, however, unpopular, is worth considering.

The history of the Jewish people provides a dramatic illustration of Zechariah's teaching. The Jews have outlived great and powerful empires which once strutted noisily and arrogantly across the stage of history. Their conquering armies, their massive might did not rescue them from oblivion. The Jew witnessed their rise and their fall, their coming and their going, while he was armed only with his Torah, his traditions, his faith.

Moreover, the Jew has enriched the larger human family very disproportionately with the gifts of his spirit. David Lloyd George could therefore say with much justification, "God has chosen little nations as the vessels by which he carries his choicest wines to the lips of humanity, to rejoice their hearts, to exalt their vision, to strengthen their faith."

Sidney Greenberg

We Must Live by the Truth

THE DIFFICULTY IS not that men are ignorant of the truth; it is that they have not yet dared to live by it.

Morton J. Cohn

The Necessary Assumption

LIFE IS FULL of coercions. Indeed, life itself is a coercion. As an ancient rabbi long ago told us: "Against your will were you born." And the young never tire of reminding their parents: "I didn't ask to be born." One of Sholom Aleichem's characters makes the wry observation: "The way life is, you're better off not to be born. But who can be so lucky? Maybe one in ten thousand."

The Talmud records a philosophical debate between the schools of Shammai and Hillel on this very question. "Was it better for man to have been created than not to have been created." The discussion continued without resolution for two and a half years. Finally, they put the question to a vote, and it was decided that it were better for man not to have been created. "However," they added, "having been created let him pay heed to his actions."

Life is indeed a matter of coercion, but we must accept it gladly and use it wisely. George Santayana reflected the spirit of our Sages when he wrote: "That life is worth living is the most necessary of assumptions, and were it not assumed, the most impossible of conclusions."

Sidney Greenberg

To Save a Life Haste Is Required

THE PALESTINIAN TALMUD rules [Yoma 8:5] that if one stops to ask a rabbi whether it is permissible to desecrate the Sabbath and Yom Kippur in order to save a life, this delay is a form of murder. While he is busy asking the question, the patient might die. When a life is at stake, haste is required.

Ovadia Yosef

The Art of Discrimination

OUR MINDS CANNOT harbor all thoughts. If we clutter them up with prejudices and hatreds, with pettiness and poisoned memories, we are abusing a delicate and precious instrument. The art of discrimination involves great care in the choice of thoughts to which we grant a seat in the arena of our minds.

Sidney Greenberg

Realizing One's Own Worth

IF ONE DOES not recognize one's own worth, how can one appreciate the worth of another?

Yaakov Yosef of Polnoye

Respect the Old

OUR ANCESTORS PLACED the broken stones in the *aron* and from it we may glean the important lesson this Rosh Hashanah, to remember and honor those who played significant roles in our lives and not permit their abandonment and neglect.

"Dishonor not the old," cautions Rabbi Ben Sira, aware that we teach the young generation how to conduct themselves by our own example, "for," he reminds us, "we shall be numbered among them."

Jay Kaufman

Wanting What We Need

THE THINGS WE want may or may not be necessary to our existence. They may be only superfluities whose possession is really inconsequential for our lives. But they may also be the very opposite of what we need—they may be the means of our injury. The card addict wants to gamble desperately, but he does not need it. What he needs is strength of character to shun it.

The things we really need we often don't want at all. The child needs food, but fights against it. Is there anything we need more than a sense of integrity, than a clear conscience? Yet many people follow the tempting lure of some momentary gain, betraying what they need for the sake of what they want and don't need. Is there anything we need more than the peace of walking humbly with our God? Happy are they who have made this need the object of their wants as well, and who pursue it zealously. There are many who fight against it—like the sick man who fights against the medicine that will heal him.

Many of the things we want so desperately, we could well do without. Some of them, we would indeed be better off without. On the other hand, many of the things we need urgently are readily within our reach—if we would want them. Fortunate are those who really need what they want, and who want what they need.

Ben Zion Bokser

The Purpose of Our Religion

ANYONE WHO HAS read even one page in Jewish history knows that the purpose of our religion isn't to guarantee you protection against tragedy, but to teach you how to live with tragedy, and not lose faith. Those generations of Jews gave the world an example of man's ability to save himself from meanness and pettiness of spirit by not letting persecution and suffering undermine or embitter the grandeur of their faith.

Some people are permanently embittered by tragedy. They never get over it; they never forgive the world for not having treated them better. And there's no way of reasoning with them to change their position. Once they've lost their innocent faith that God will never let anything bad happen to them, they have nothing with which to replace it.

But then, there are people who can turn an ordeal into an occasion for refining and deepening their faith. There are people like Aaron, who was able to return to his duties as High Priest; people like the author of the thirtieth Psalm, who chose to devote the rest of his life to trying to teach people what he had learned from hard experience—that even if sorrow lingers for a night, joy comes in the morning. Our childish faith is then replaced by a more mature and realistic one, by a belief in God that doesn't depend on God's reciprocating and doing us favors. Such as the men who, after reading the thirtieth Psalm, rise to recite the Mourners' Kaddish, to proclaim before the congregation that "despite the fact that something sad has happened to me, I'm still able to come to *shul* and praise the name of God, and affirm the goodness of the world He created."

Harold S. Kushner

The Goal of Life

THE RELIGION OF Judaism can teach us . . . how to understand the goal of life in the presence of mortality. That goal is that we should create a pattern that will be a blessing and inspiration to those who come after us. When we die, those who have been touched and illumined by the flame of our being should rejoice to think of us with joyous reminiscence.

We can face death nobly when we resolve so to live and to work in the years allotted to us that no one shall cry in frustration or anger when we have gone, that no one shall silently curse the day of our birth but rather that they shall recall our day upon the earth in the concert hall of memory and shall laugh, with the over-brimming joy that a dear one walked the earth bravely and lovingly once upon a time.

The thought of death need not fill us with dark and despairing anxiety, but rather with a creative determination to be for the little world of which we are a part the center of the target toward which all the archers shall send the arrows of their aspiration, to be the oak tree, tall and stately, in the shelter of whose branches the young can sit and play and the old can find shade from the heat of the day. Let us live in such a way that our spirit shall be the rain causing the soil of other souls to grow moist and verdant, to be the sunlight making chlorophyll in the filigree leaves of other hearts and other minds, to be the star, the guiding North Star, but which the mariners and the navigators in our family and in our circle of friends can set their compass across the unchartered sea of being. This is the goal of life, so to live that men shall rehearse the story of our being with inspiration and with deep gratitude that we have walked the earth rejoicing to tell of our strong youth, the manliness of our maturity, the wisdom of our old age. Then indeed our memory shall be a blessing.

Joshua Loth Liebman

Laughter Is the Best Medicine

SHOLEM ALEICHEM, THE greatest humorist in Yiddish literature emphasized the importance of laughter, "*Doktoren heisen lachen*—doctors call upon us to laugh."

Surprisingly, there are many who do not know how to laugh properly, a smile, a grain or a chuckle is not to be considered beneficial laughter.

It was Dr. Norman Cousins in his *Anatomy of an Illness* who enumerated the medical benefits of laughter, which he designated as "internal jogging," and that a belly laugh actually massages the internal organs.

Leo Rosten, author of the *Joys of Yiddish*, abhorred those without a sense of humor and warned us to stay away from them.

Laughter is the best medicine and doesn't require a doctor's prescription or a pharmacist to fill it.

The value inherent in laughter can be summarized as: easing pain, reducing stress and tension, fostering recovery from illness and even helping to sleep better.

The Biblical verse, "A merry heart is a good medicine" [Proverbs 17:22], should become our personal motto to further a fresh outlook in confronting our daily problems in a relaxed and optimistic manner.

A noted Chassidic Rebbe would often conclude his discourses with the Yiddish words, "*Lebedig, kinderlach, lebeding*—Lively children, always be lively."

David W. Gordon

God the Endorser

THE BARON DE ROTHSCHILD was once approached by a man who needed a loan of $1000. The baron agreed to grant the loan, if only the client would provide an endorser. The man could think of no one he knew who would accept the responsibility. Finally he told the baron the only one who trusts him is God Almighty. The baron looked puzzled for a moment, but then he replied, "He will be fine. I'll accept Him as an endorser." He asked the man to sign the note and on the back he wrote, "Endorsed by God Almighty."

Six months later the client returned to repay the loan, but the baron refused his payment. The man was astounded and begged for an explanation. With a gentle smile the baron replied, "My dear friend, the Endorser has already repaid the loan."

Rothschild realized that material affluence was a gift of God given in trust, and that the prosperous man is only a steward, charged with the task of administering God's property. God tests us with the blessing of material affluence and then waits to see what we do with it.

Howard B. Greenstein

In Each of Us There Is a Spark

THE STORY IS told of a Hassidic sage who was asked by his followers when he expected the Messiah to arrive. To their amazement he answered that he did not expect a Messiah at all. He went on to explain that in each of us there is a spark of the Messiah. When we put together our individual little sparks, then we create the great light that will illumine the world with Messianic peace and harmony for all mankind.

That is our dream as Jews, to have our spark of the Messiah burn bright, to have it burn brightly on the altars of our homes, in our occupations and in our lives as mature men striving to right the wrongs of our immediate world. We have vowed to do so, we have cause to pray on Yom Kippur for another chance to fulfill the vows. How inspired will we be with our High Holy Day resolutions!

Jay Kaufman

The Search to Which We Are Committed

THE BIBLE NOWHERE calls upon men to go out in search of peace of mind. It does call upon men to go out in search of God and the things of God. It challenges men to hunger and thirst after righteousness, to relieve the oppressed, to proclaim liberty to the captives, and to establish peace in the world. These objectives must be elaborately sought. As often as not, such enterprises are attended by persecution and suffering. Judaism as a prophetic religion could not offer its faithful the compensation of peace of mind, except insofar as the confidence of faith lessens the tensions of doubt and despair; but it did offer them other and more precious compensations—the nearness of God, an uplifting interest in life, a nourishing pride and dignity and, on occasion, the ineffable ecstasy that derives from moments of spiritual daring and adventure. There is a lyrical vibrancy to such moments when man drinks of the wine of life and partakes of the very manna of heaven.

Personal sacrifices are often involved in the pursuit of the good life. Sometimes even martyrdom is called for. The moral commitments of the faithful are never of a limited liability. The Jewish people gave the first religious martyrs known to mankind, and through many dark and weary centuries of exile and persecution, its noblest sons and daughters never denied God the supreme tribute of martyrdom. True love of God is to serve Him "with all your heart, with all your soul and with all your might" [Deuteronomy 6:5]. Akiba defined the term "with all your soul" to mean "even if He takes away your life." He attested it with his own martyrdom.

Abba Hillel Silver

CHAPTER 29

LEARNING TO LISTEN

Listening Is Done with the Heart

WHEN GOD APPEARED to King Solomon in a vision in the night and offered him any gift he wished, the wise monarch asked for neither power nor wealth, nor glory. He asked instead for a "listening heart." It is a gift worth cultivating. For ultimately, true listening is not done with the ears. It is done with the heart.

Sidney Greenberg

God's Faith, Not Mine

HOW SURPRISING THAT when faith is mentioned in our morning liturgy, it is speaking of God's faith, not mine. *Raba Emunatecha!* How great is your faithfulness!

The times when I have risked to speak or cry a prayer into the abyss that stretches out before me, when I have sung out my own essence, when the spark within me has flown out into darkness with the force and heat of my longing, only then have I been met by a Presence, a Mystery.

The universe responds to my turning. Suddenly my eyes are opened to the smallest miracles. Messages are brought to me—the breeze caresses my cheek, blue overflows from the sky into the cup of my heart, my own breath arises out of nowhere as a gift of soul for me to use and transform into giving. Suddenly the world is filled with hidden meaning and this hiddenness beckons me deeper into my own mysteries.

In the silence that follows my song, I listen as God speaks a resounding Amen (which is related to the word *emunah*). It is God's faith in my essence, my uniqueness that allows me to then know my own beauty and purpose. And so I listen intently . . . for I find my faith in the light of this response.

Shefa Gold

We Should Talk Less and Listen More

ANATOMICALLY SPEAKING, WE are so constructed that we should devote more time listening than to speaking. The Divine Architect endowed us with two ears but only one mouth. Yet for most of us the mouth is a sorely overworked organ and the ears are in a state of semi-retirement.

A bartender who was breaking in a young apprentice saw the novice hard at work trying to be witty and humorous with customers. Unhappily, he wasn't making much of an impression. Finally, the veteran called the young man aside and gave him the distilled wisdom of years of experience: "Listen, kid, listen. Don't talk. These guys want to talk. If they wanted to listen, they'd go home."

Sidney Greenberg

We Are Instructed to Listen

SURELY ONE OF the great lessons of Judaism is represented in the opening statement, the opening words of that most important of all affirmations of faith, "Hear, O Israel." We are instructed to listen, not to noises, not to sounds, not to distractions, but to the echo of Sinai, the lesson of our tradition and to the voices of our hearts.

I urge you to treat yourselves to a walk in the park, to be alone, to communicate with nature, to listen to the rustle of the wind in the trees, and to turn away from the constant barrage of noises which deprive us of the chance of hearing our own conscience and finding out what our thoughts are.

Simeon of old was right. There is value in silence, sometimes greater than that which comes in a multitude of sounds and of words.

Manuel Laderman

We Need to Take Time to Listen

OUR TRADITION IS vitally concerned with the proper use of the power of speech. Three times every day we conclude the Amidah with the prayer: "O God keep my tongue from evil and my lips from deceit." But our Sages remind us too that the power to keep silent should also be used frequently and wisely. We often regret having spoken; rarely, having kept silent. In silence there is the opportunity to reflect quietly, to resolve nobly, to probe deeply. In a noisy world, we need to make time to listen to those voices within us and above us which will only be heard when all is hushed around us. Daily the prayer book reminds us too, that we can worship God not only with "the words of my mouth" but also with "the meditations of my heart."

Sidney Greenberg

CHAPTER 30

The Art of Loving

Self-Love

A HASIDIC BOOK states: "All the souls (in their root) are one essence. Even when divided into parts, there exists in each part the whole essence. So a person's love of his neighbor is not love of another, but—love of himself." Hasidim call this exalted level, of loving another in the same way that you love yourself, "essence-love" (*ahavah atzmit*), because you see all souls as part of the same divine essence and as extensions of yourself.

Yitzhak Buxbaum

Love Involves the Confirmation of the Other

THE I-THOU RELATION is most fully realized in love between a man and wife. Here arises what Martin Buber calls the exemplary bond, two people revealing Thou to each other. Love involves the recognition and confirmation of the other in his or her uniqueness, and to this end, marriage affords the greatest length of time and greatest degree of intimacy.

Malcolm L. Diamond

Love is the Job of a Lifetime

FIDELITY IS ROOTED in love. The object of love is not only "union" but unity. It represents a life of truth, such as loving husbands and wives can perceive and share. It is unity in the full sense of the word. To reach that stage of complete oneness calls for unreserved absorption, both physical and spiritual. It is the job of a lifetime.

Morris Mandel

Self-Hate Is Wicked

NOT ONLY IS one who hates another soul called wicked—but someone who hates oneself is also called wicked.

Menachem Mendel of Kotzk

To Turn the Heart to Love

WHENEVER I CAME across anyone whom I had an inclination to dislike, I would utter many blessings for his welfare, so as to turn my heart to love him and to desire his good.

Yoel Frumkin

The Gifts of Love

GIVING AND RECEIVING love clears the nervous system of its muck and mire. You feel strong when you give love and worthy when you receive it. You can't be distressed, confused or unhappy in an atmosphere of love.

David Goodman

Open Love for All People

WHEREAS TRADITIONAL JEWS focus on the love for fellow Jews, sometimes neglecting the universal love for all people, less traditional and more modern Jews sometimes focus on the love for non-Jews, neglecting the special love Jews should have for each other. We must increase our love for Jews *and* for non-Jews. We require a restatement and renewal of a traditional Jewish religious humanism that begins with a special, fervent love for fellow Jews and extends to an open and unabashed love for all people.

Yitzhak Buxbaum

We Will Not Live with Hate

MY FELLOW SURVIVORS, touched by the madness of our nightmare, we have tried to live normal lives. Scarred by the acid of barbarous hatred, we have tried to give love to our children. Forgotten by a silent world, we have tried to avoid cynicism and despair. Despite all we have known, we affirm life—despite the most ferocious of efforts to steal it from us. While we shall never forget, we will not live with hate.

Ernest W. Michel

Causeless Love

THE SECOND TEMPLE was destroyed because of causeless hatred. Perhaps the Third will be rebuilt because of causeless love.

Abraham Isaac Kook

Love Sees More

LOVE IS NOT blind—it sees more, not less. But because it sees more, it is willing to see less.

Julius Gordon

True Love

SUPERFICIAL FEELINGS COME and go; physical attractions are merely temporary; true love is a decision based on judgment.

Sol Landau

A Powerful Love for All

I AM NOT able not to love all people and all nations. I desire from my deepest depths that all be raised to glory, that all be fully brought to perfection. My love for the Jewish people is more fervent and deeper, but the inner desire expands and spreads outward in a powerful love for all.

Abraham Isaac Kook

What We Love in the Neighbor

THE COMMAND TO love one's neighbor is to love the Divinity which is in him.

Mordecai M. Kaplan

Love for Humanity

THE TORAH IS astonishingly bold in using the parable of an idol-maker to portray God's creation of man. And the lesson conveyed through this startling device is profound. The essential teaching is that love and worship of God are best expressed through love of humankind. Moreover, the statement that man is in the "image" of God contains a deep mystic truth: God is not only far away in heaven and separated from us. He appears on earth before our eyes in the form of our fellow human beings. We see from this insight into the Genesis story of man's creation that love for humanity as the essence of Judaism and a belief in the divine dignity of humanity were not invented later by the rabbis. They are found at the beginning of the Torah and at its very heart.

Yitzhak Buxbaum

To Bring the Divorce Rate Down

IF HUSBAND OR wife were less eager to make each other over to please themselves, and more eager to make themselves over to please each other, the divorce rate would come down a good deal.

Mordecai M. Kaplan

We Need Loving Critics

WHAT AMERICA NEEDS, what each of us needs, are neither uncritical lovers nor unloving critics. The uncritical lovers overlook faults. The unloving critics are blind to virtues. Truly needed are loving critics. Because they criticize out of love, they bring growth and blessing. They also prove themselves worthy descendents of the prophets in whose footsteps they follow.

Sidney Greenberg

How to Love Your Neighbor

I UNDERSTAND THE commandment "Love your neighbor" as implicitly obliging us to do what we can to make it possible for our neighbor to act lovingly towards us. This means that we have a responsibility to make it clear to others what it is we need. Our neighbor is not a mind reader. He or she might not even be intuitive, but this does not make the person a bad or unloving neighbor.

So, don't just love your neighbor, make sure you give your neighbor a chance to love you.

Joseph Telushkin

Love Means Giving

LOVE MEANS GIVING not receiving. When you give you feel fully alive. He who has much is not wealthy, but rather he who gives much.

The most valuable possession is not that of material things, but lies in the human realm. When a person gives of himself, he is giving the most precious commodity he has had in his life; his joy, his interest, his understanding, his knowledge, his humor, his sadness—all that is alive in him. By giving of his life, he enriches the other person. He enhances the other's sense of aliveness by enhancing his own sense of aliveness. Love is the power which produces love.

The experience of union with man or God helps us to overcome the sense of separateness.

Israel Gerstein

Let Us Not Hold Back Words of Love

CAN YOU IMAGINE what pain there must be? Can you imagine what shame there must be if you have to stand at a grave and bid farewell and realize then what you didn't say when you could have, when you should have, when there was still time? Can you imagine having to live the rest of your life with the knowledge that you loved someone, and that once you almost told her?

Let none of us ever have to live with that kind of regret in our hearts. Let none of us hold back the words of love, the words that could help and heal. Let none of us keep them choked up and bottled up inside where they can do no good, until it is too late.

Jack Riemer

Unending Love

WE ARE LOVED by an unending love. We are embraced by arms that find us even when we are hidden from ourselves. We are touched by fingers that soothe us. Even when we are too proud for soothing. We are counseled by voices that guide us even when we are too embittered to hear. We are loved by an unending love. We are supported by hands that uplift us even in the midst of a fall. We are urged on by eyes that meet us even when we are too weak for meeting. We are loved by an unending love. Embraced, touched, soothed, and counseled . . . ours are the arms, the fingers, the voices; ours are the hands, the eyes, the smiles; we are loved by an unending love

Rami Shapiro

God Is Not Limited to One Religion

I DON'T BELIEVE in a monopoly. I think God loves all men. He has given many nations. He has given all men an awareness of His greatness and of His love. And God is to be found in many hearts all over the world. Not limited to one nation, to one people or to one religion.

Abraham J. Heschel

God's Love Does Not End at the Grave

EARLY IN THE morning service, we read *"Ahavoh raboh"* (with great love hast Thou loved us). Who at this hour could not sincerely echo that prayer? As we think of our dear parents, the love and inspiration and memories they gave us; of a husband or wife with whom we shared the deepest, the most satisfying and the richest experiences of life; of brothers or sisters who stood loyally by our side through the tribulations of life; of children who blessed us with their sweetness and their joy; of friends and leaders whose name is as precious ointment; as we remember them, shall we too not say "With great love hast Thou loved us."

But is that all we can say? Toward the close of the Yom Kippur service there is a change in one word. No longer "With great love has Thou loved us" but now *Ahavas olom*, with "ever-lasting love has Thou loved us." God would not create such wonderful human beings only to doom them to eternal annihilation. His love does not end at the grave. Our loved ones live on in lives better because of them and in the bonds of eternal life.

The ultimate answer to dying is faith in the living God Whom we all love and move and have in our being. When we walk through the valley of the shadow of death, we will fear no evil for He is with me.

Philip S. Bernstein

CHAPTER 31

LIVING AS A JEW

Our Problem Is How to Make the World Better

AN OPTIMIST IS one who believes that this is the best of all possible worlds, and a pessimist is one who is afraid that the optimist is right. The problem is not whether it is best or worst, but how to go about making it better.

Mordecai M. Kaplan

Why the Jew Must Remain a Jew

TO BE A Jew is the least difficult way of being truly human. It is for this reason that the Jew must remain a Jew.

Bernard Lazare

Where He Is

THERE IS A significant Midrashic comment on the verse: "God heard the voice of the lad where he is." The Midrash imagines the angels protesting: "How can Ishmael be spared in that his descendants will torment Israel?" God replies: "At this moment he is worthy to be saved"; God hears the voice of the lad where he is. Man is a creature of moods and cannot live ever on the heights. The firm resolves he makes on Rosh Hashanah may weaken when the days of self-examination are gone. But at least, the Rabbis might have said, let man's purpose be strong on these days that God might hear his voice where he is.

Louis Jacobs

Torah—A Living Tree

ETIZ HAYYIM HEE, the Torah is a living tree. It is up to each generation to water and fertilize the tree, to prune it and to harvest its fruits. The gardener, not the plant, is the ultimate arbiter of what shape the tree will assume.

Bradley Artson

Being a Jew

BEING A JEW in the broadest definition means first, the accident of birth; secondly, the act of choice, choosing to remain Jewish despite the difficulties; thirdly, the act of cognition, learning to know the history and literature of his people so as to understand its soul and appreciate its place in the world; and finally, the act of transmission, transmitting to the next generation his heritage and the will to carry it on so that the Jewish people may not perish from the earth.

Israel Goldstein

Things That Do Not Change

THE PROPHET ISAIAH said to his people, in the name of God: "For the mountains may depart and the hills be removed: but My kindness shall not depart from you, neither shall My covenant of peace be removed, says the Lord who has compassion on you" [Isaiah 54:10].

To the prophet, the mountains and the hills represented the most enduring of physical things. But more enduring than the physical things, he said, are the spiritual values of life—God's kindness and God's promises. These are the changeless realities in a changing world; these are the things one could cling to in a slippery time, the things that the teeth of time would not chew to pieces.

The redeeming power of compassion, the healing power of forgiveness, the transforming power of love—these things do not change.

The purifying power of repentance, the energizing power of prayer, the sustaining power of faith—these things do not change.

The nourishment that comes from beauty, the strength that comes from adversity, the joy that comes from generosity—these things do not change.

The supreme value of character, the ultimate worth of human life, the permanent perpetuation of personality—these things do not change.

Our capacity to change and improve ourselves, out ability to change the world for the better—these things do not change.

Living at a time of accelerated change, we need desperately the wisdom to cling to the things that do not change.

Sidney Greenberg

We Must Hold On to Our Past History

MAN IS MADE by history. It is history that causes the men of historic nations to be more civilized than the savage. The Jew recognizes that he is made what he is by the history of his fathers, and he feels he is losing his better self so far as he loses his hold on his past history.

Joseph Jacobs

When Not to Do as the Romans Do

THE OLD ADAGE counsels us: "When in Rome, do as the Romans do." The Bible would add—provided that what the Romans are doing ought to be done. Otherwise, "You shall not follow a multitude to do evil."

Sidney Greenberg

Worshipping God and Feasting with the Devil

MAN CANNOT WORSHIP God and feast with the devil.

Isaac Mayer Wise

A Sign of Maturity

WE HAVE SUCCEEDED in teaching large numbers of Jews to carry their communal obligations, in terms of their contribution to Israel, overseas national and local causes, as a normal and constant item in their annual budget. We shall have reached maturity as a Jewish community when equally large numbers of Jews include in their personal budget of time and duty such responsibilities as Jewish study, the Jewish education of their young, Jewish symbols and disciplines in the home and a commitment to the advancement of Jewish learning, art and literature.

Morris Adler

Guilt—Guardian of Our Goodness

CONSCIENCE IS A great servant but a terrible master. It is somewhat like an automobile horn. It is useful for warding off impending danger. But if a horn gets stuck it's a terrible nuisance.

However, because guilt can be neurotic and unearned, it does not mean that all guilt is suspect. Certain acts (including perhaps the attempt to abolish guilt) should indeed produce guilt feelings. Cheating, lying, stealing, breaking promises, malicious gossip, failing to honor commitments, indifference to suffering, insensitivity to others' feelings, failure to expand our horizons and deepen our sympathies—shouldn't these things produce within us at this holy season a profound sense of spiritual discomfort? And if we do not feel guilt for such sins, haven't we already suffered the greatest of all punishments—a coarsening of the fabric of our lives, an abdication of all that makes us human?

Dr. Willard Paylin, a psychiatrist, calls guilt "a guardian of our goodness. . . . It represents the noblest and most painful of all struggles."

Sidney Greenberg

True Jewish Life Is Living Always with God

LIVING THE TRUE Jewish life is living always with God, when we feel adequate as well as when we feel inadequate, when we are secure as well as when we fear. Such a God is never a stranger. Things happen *b'ezras Hashem,* with the help of God; *Boruch Hashem,* thank God; *im yirtzeh Hashem,* if God wills.

The Torah life, the constant dialogue with God, enables the Jew—as it enabled Abraham—to make sacrifices, and it assures him of blessing. Even the greatest tragedy is tempered by the joy of the *mitzvah.* In the midst of desolation, there is the oasis of Torah, or God's word, the faith of a True Friend. There is the confidence that "they who observe His commandments shall return to their strength." There is also God's recognition and appreciation, in Jeremiah's words which we read today: "I remember the tenderness of thy youth, the love of thy betrothal, thy going after me in the desert."

Only Torah life gives man this close identification with God, his constant Guide and Companion. Such life has not faltered in the wanderings of the ages. It is this Godly life that the Jew transmitted to his children—a life of loving faith, practicing beliefs, constant recognition of God—so that man is never helpless, never overwhelmed by mystery, never in fear or despair. God knows Abraham not only for this faith: "Now do I know that you hold awe for God." God also knows Abraham because of this dialogue of action: "I know him that he will command his children and household after him, and they will observe the way of God to do righteousness and justice."

Simon A. Dolgin

Beware of the Half Truth

BEWARE OF THE half truth. You may have gotten hold of the wrong half.

Seymour L. Essrog

"Did You See My Alps?"

SAMSON RAPHAEL HIRSCH surprised his disciples one day when he insisted on traveling to Switzerland. "When I stand shortly before the Almighty," he explained, "I will be held unanswerable to many questions. . . . But what will I say when . . . and I'm sure to be asked, "Shimshon, did you see my Alps?"

Martin Gordon

We Must Teach and Learn from Each Other

JEWISH STUDY IS not a solitary endeavor, carried out by a lonely scholar in his cubicle. Once the Torah was brought down from heaven, the attainment of truth has been the responsibility of human beings, teaching and learning from each other.

Richard N. Levy

Thinking Apart and Acting Together

THE BUSINESS OF the American teacher is to liberate American citizens to think apart and act together.

Stephen S. Wise

When Judaism Becomes a Complex

WHERE JEWISH EDUCATION is neglected, the whole content of Judaism is reduced to merely an awareness of anti-Semitism. Judaism ceases then to be a civilization, and becomes a complex.

Mordecai M. Kaplan

Great Accomplishments in Secret

IN THE JEWISH world, the greatest accomplishments of life are most often done in private, in the home where no one sees, in the privacy of one's own heart and mind, where moral strength and determination, coupled with an ability to turn one's back on the ever-present temptation of sin and passion, are private battles to be waged and won. The ability to say "no" to sin, passion and temptation is an achievement performed in secret.

Pinchas Stolper

Don't Scorn the Little

WHO SCORNS THE little was not born for the great.

Isaac Friedmann

What Happens on the Third Day?

A NUMBER OF commentators, including the Kotzker Rebbe, point out the significance of the fact that Abraham does not actually reach the mountain on which the Akedah is performed until a lapse of three days. His willingness to honor his commitment after an interval of several days is especially worthy of note and emulation.

All too familiar is the initial burst of enthusiasm in response to a profound emotional appeal or stimulus. We witness it on the High Holy Days when all kinds of lofty resolves well up within us. But what happens on the third day? What happens when the spell is broken and the memory of the synagogue recedes into the background? Are we still as determined to honor our commitments and redeem our promises to ourselves and to God? A true test of our zeal is not the immediate response—"And Abraham rose up early in the morning." The true measure of his spiritual stamina was revealed on the third day.

The Midrash in commenting on this verse quotes Hosea 6:2. "He will revive us for two days and on the third day He will establish us and we shall live before Him."

Sidney Greenberg

A Link Between Two Eternities

UNLESS IT IS a present which forms a link between two eternities, representing an answer of Amen to the past and an Opening Prayer to the future, it will be a very petty present indeed.

Solomon Schechter

Vulgarity

BY VULGARITY I mean that bite of civilization which makes man ashamed of himself and his next of kin, and pretend to be somebody else.

Solomon Schechter

We Talk One Way and Live Another

THERE ARE MASSIVE contradictions and hypocrisies which stain our lives. Who can estimate how much they contribute to our emotional ailments? We are split spiritual personalities.

We swear allegiance to one set of principles and live by another.

We extol self-control and practice self-indulgence.

We proclaim brotherhood and harbor prejudice.

We laud character but strive to climb to the top at any cost.

We erect houses of worship but our shrines are our places of business and recreation.

We are "proud" to be Jews but make too little effort to live out our Jewishness.

We talk one way and live another.

We embrace lofty ideals and then demean them by shabby acts.

We are suffering from a distressing cleavage between the truths we affirm and the values we try to live by. Our souls are the battlegrounds for civil wars while we try to live serene lives in houses divided against themselves.

The integrity which is so indispensable to vital and creative living is thus denied us. We are fragmented and fractured when we yearn to be intact and whole.

It was Harold Laski who warned that "the surest way to bring about the destruction of a civilization is to allow the abyss to widen between the values men praise and the values they permit to operate." We overlook this warning at our own peril.

Sidney Greenberg

As We Think

If you think you are beaten, you are;
If you think you dare not, you don't.
If you'd like to win, but think you can't,
It's almost a cinch you won't.
. . . Life's battles don't always go
To the stronger or faster man;
But soon or late, the man who wins
Is the one who thinks he can."

Author Unknown

Duty to Be Oneself

THE RIGHT TO be different is only the obverse of the duty to be oneself.

Mordecai M. Kaplan

Cleaning the Soul

EACH MORNING, WHEN you arise, say the words of the *Elohai N'shamah*. Sit in a quiet place for a few moments, and focus on the *hametz* you are discarding and what needs to be done for this to happen. See yourself making it happen. Then, in the fourteen days from *Rosh Hodesh* to *Pesah*, cleanse your soul with intention, effort and hard work. This will not be easy, just as cleaning your entire house is not easy. However, when the first bit of *matzoh* is in your mouth at the first *sedar,* your soul will be just as ready for freedom as your house is. And this is the deeper meaning of the Exodus.

This *Pesah,* help your soul to be pure, your heart to be joyous—this will make your house even cleaner.

Joshua Levine Grater

The Need for Sentiment

THE JEWISH RELIGION has always been sensitive to the need of sentiment in our lives and to its role as a most enriching source of inspiration. Expressions of tenderness, Judaism has taught us, add poetry to our lives . . . they drive out dullness and monotony, and introduce color and meaning. Life without sentiment is like a world without flowers and without music.

Baruch Silverstein

Ideals Will Not Let Go

IDEALS ARE CONVICTIONS with sharp teeth that bite into the mind and heart and will not let go.

Alexander Alan Steinbach

The Delicate Mitzvah

RABBI PINCHAS OF Koretz has taught that "a man may often live out the entire span of his life for the purpose of performing a single *mitzvah* or gaining a single chosen end." If that be the case, I would devote my rabbinic career to an emphasis on the *mitzvah* of *bikkur cholim* which has been termed the 'delicate *mitzvah.*' I welcome the day when every Jewish community will contain a *bikkur cholim* society as an integral part of the synagogue structure. I hope for the time when all Jews, professionals and laypeople alike, will make visitation of the sick and the aged a high priority in their weekly activities. I believe that we are witnessing the day when hospital and institutional chaplaincy is rapidly becoming more widely regarded as a full-time and professional option within the rabbinate, no less important to our continued spiritual health than leadership on the pulpit and in the classroom. Let us always remember the Psalmist's plea to God that we recite throughout the High Holy Day season:

"Do not cast us off in old age; when our strength fails, do not forsake us!" Let us re-establish our faith in the dignity of our fellow human beings who cry out to us. Let us choose life by loving the Lord our God and heeding Adonai's commandments of working with and involving the elderly in the affairs of our community and visiting the sick and giving them strength in their hour of need.

Stephen Shulman

Jews at Heart

HAVING A JEWISH heart is great. But merely being a Jew at heart is placing an overwhelming burden upon a single organ of the body. The privilege and responsibility of being a Jew is so great that entrusting it only unto the heart results in a cardiac Jew. Furthermore, as stated by learned doctors, overburdening the heart can lead to heart failure. Perhaps this is why so many contemporary American Jews are ill with afflictions of the heart.

The Psalmist said: "All my bones shall praise you."

We ought not overburden the heart. Rather all the organs, limbs, and bones of the body should help in being a Jew. The head should be directed toward the study of the Torah. The eyes must seek truth and justice while the hands kindle the candles, don the *tefillin* and give to the poor. And the feet should hurry us to do the bidding of God while the lips move in prayer.

Herbert M. Blalik

Money—Servant or Master

MONEY IS A liberal's faithful servant and a miser's hard master.

Israel Friedman

Who Is Said to Have Lived?

ONLY HE WHO has been a force for human goodness, and abides in hearts and souls made better by his presence during his pilgrimage on earth can be said to have lived.

Joseph H. Hertz

Where the Essence of Judaism Lies

THE ESSENCE OF Judaism does not lie merely in entertaining a concept of God, but in the ability to articulate the moments of illumination by His presence. Our whole program of Jewish living is to help us to become articulate and express our wonder as we stand in awe before God.

Abraham E. Halpern

Demonstrate Our Loyalty by Our Lives

THIS IS THE message that we should hear as the *Shofar* is sounded three times this day. As the Shofar proclaims the *Malkhuyot*, "the sovereignty of God," we need to recapture a vivid sense of the presence of our Father, our King, who has made us, His children, the instruments for the fulfillment of His will. When we rise to proclaim the sovereignty of God, let us resolve that during this year, if the good Lord spares us, we will demonstrate our love and loyalty to Him by our lives and actions, but raising the level of our Jewish practice at home and in the street, in the Temple and the school, on the Sabbath and on the Festivals.

Robert Gordis

How to Live

DRAW FROM THE past, live in the present, work for the future.

Abraham Geiger

Tradition Asks "Use Me"

JUDAISM EMPHASIZES REASON, not blind faith. It stresses understanding, not intellectual surrender; knowledge and inquiry, and not helpless submission. No, for Judaism, at least, tradition is not a voice from the dead which commands, "Obey me!" It is rather the thrilling call of living experience which says, "Use me!"

Joseph Lookstein

Enjoy This World

OTHER RELIGIOUS TRADITIONS speak of asceticism as the path to holiness, living in a monastery, taking vows of abstinence, celibacy, poverty. That has never been the Jewish way to God.

Judaism says, Enjoy life. The book of Ecclesiasties reads, "Go thy way, eat thy bread with joy and drink thy wine with merry heart . . . let thy garments be always white and let thy head lack no oil. Enjoy life with the wife whom thou lovest . . ." [Ecclesiastes 9:7–9]. Other traditions may speak of the pleasures of the next world; Judaism asks, Did you really enjoy this world?

Michael Gold

Hebrew Necessary for Our Survival

THE JEWS OF America cannot live without English but will not survive without Hebrew.

Solomon Schechter

Basic Qualifications for Being a Jew

THE BASIC QUALIFICATIONS for being a Jew are (1) the identification of oneself as a Jew, i.e., the acceptance of the Jewish People with its past, its present and its future as one's own People; (2) belief in the spiritual values of the Jewish tradition, i.e., the conviction that the Jewish spiritual heritage affords inspiration for living, and constitutes a worthy contribution to the totality of man's spiritual wisdom; and (3) participation in Jewish life, i.e., sharing in those activities which help to insure the perpetuation of the Jewish People and the advancement of its civilization.

These qualifications, and not Jewish parentage, have been stressed in the bulk of our tradition. Jews were enjoined to qualify themselves for the story of Torah (i.e., Judaism) "because it is not subject to inheritance." Converts, on the other hand, were told to address God in worship, in the same terms as born Jews, as "our God and God of our fathers, God of Abraham, God of Isaac, and God of Jacob," because converts are regarded as authentic Jews *(na-asu ikkar k'yisrael)*.

Mordecai M. Kaplan

Judaism—A Way of Life

JUDAISM IS A way of life which endeavors to transform virtually every human action into a means of communion with God. Through this communion with God, the Jew is enabled to make his contribution to the establishment of the Kingdom of God and the brotherhood of men on earth. So far as its adherents are concerned, Judaism seeks to extend the concept of right and wrong to every aspect of their behavior. Jewish rules of conduct apply not merely to worship, ceremonial, and justice between man and man, but also to such matters as philanthropy, personal friendships and kindnesses, intellectual pursuits, artistic creation, courtesy, the preservation of health, and the care of diet.

So rigorous is the discipline, as ideally conceived in Jewish writings, that it may be compared to those specified for members of religious orders in other faiths. A casual conversation or a thoughtless remark may, for instance, be considered a violation of Jewish Law. It is forbidden, not merely as a matter of good form, but of religious law, to use obscene language, to rouse a person to anger, or to display unusual ability in the presence of the handicapped. The ceremonial observances are equally detailed.

Louis Finkelstein

Why I Go to Synagogue

I COME TO the Synagogue to probe my weakness and my strength, and to fill the gap between my profession and my practice. I come to lift myself by my bootstraps. I come to quiet the turbulence of my heart, restrain its mad impulsiveness and check the itching eagerness of my every muscle to outsmart and outdistance my neighbor. I come for self-renewal and regeneration. I come into the sadness and compassion permeating the Synagogue to contemplate and be instructed by the heaving panorama of Jewish martyrdom and human misery. I come to be strengthened in my determination to be free, never to compromise with idolatry or bow to dictatorship, cringe before autocracy or succumb to force. I come to orient myself to the whole of Reality, to the thrusts of power beyond the comprehension of my compounded dust. I come to behold the beauty of the Lord, to find Him who put an upward reach in the heart of man.

Solomon Goldman

Life Is Good

LIFE IS GOOD and a gracious gift of God. To love God one need not hate the world. Life should not be feared or renounced, but sanctified and enjoyed through wholesome living in which the whole of man—body, mind and soul—is fulfilled.

Abba Hillel Silver

Our Quarrel Is with Indifferent Jews

OUR QUARREL IS not with Jews who are different but with Jews who are indifferent.

Stephen S. Wise

Bind the Injured Relations

RECOVERY IS A return. Go home to your families and love them. Go home to your houses with your Sabbath lights and wine and white Challah and make peace. Go home to your families and bind the injured relations. Cast aside invective and sharpness of tongue and irony and sarcasm and judgment and blame. Go home to your family and learn to listen and enjoy and share legend and story and laugh together, sing together and study together and come to Shul together. And go home to your friends. Do not let small things, jealousies, demeaning envies destroy the health in your life.

Harold M. Schulweis

Room for Different Versions of Judaism

BY REASON OF the prevailing diversity in world outlook, there has to be room in Jewish religion for different versions of it.

Mordecai M. Kaplan

Tradition Oils the Wheels of Progress

TRADITION IS NOT the grit and the rust in the wheels of progress. Not infrequently it is the oil that lubricates those wheels.

Joseph Lookstein

The Idea of Eternal Life

THE MAN OF Halakhah is not a secular, cognitive type, whose mind is not directed at all toward the transcendental, but is limited to the temporal. Torah has planted in the consciousness of the man of Halakhah the idea of eternal life and the yearning toward immortality . . . he is the man of religion in all his elevation and beauty, whose soul thirsts for the living God, and rivers of nostalgia sweep him into transcendental seas, to the hidden God . . . the man of Halakhah begins with refinement and ends up in this world.

J. B. Soloveitchik

Enjoying the Richness of Jewish Living

THE RICHNESS OF Jewish living is apparent only when you are living it. In this respect, it is no different than most experiences. You can read all you want about parenting, for example, but any parent will tell you that the experience of holding your baby for the first time is something you can't fathom in advance.

The philosopher Franz Rosenzweig described the challenge of conveying Judaism to assimilated Jews as the process of moving from the Jewish periphery to its center. He suggested that people who stand on the outside watching other Jews practice are like deaf people who watch people dance without being able to hear the music to which they are dancing.

A description of the meaning of Yom Kippur, no matter how well it is written, cannot convey the transforming power of the experience.

The challenge of outreach, then, is to get those on the outside to read, or even to watch others practice. The challenge is rather to get them involved so that they can hear the music and experience the warmth and the richness, to move them to a place where they can feel that their heritage is their own.

Jacob J. Staub

He Goes and Shouts

IN CAESARIA AND again in Beth Shean, I saw the ruins of Roman amphitheaters, imposing structures. In these arenas, gladiators once fought for the entertainment of spectators. To the ancient Rabbis who taught that man was fashioned by the Creator in His own image, that saving or destroying a single life is tantamount to saving or destroying the entire world, these arenas were the embodiment of evil. It was unthinkable that a Jew should ever be seen in an amphitheater. But the Talmud records that Rabbi Nathan disagreed.

Said Rabbi Nathan: "He goes and shouts!"

By shouting "Thumbs up" it was possible to save the life of a gladiator. A Jew was obliged to descend to the amphitheater if there was a chance of saving a life. God's voice was in the anguished cry of a defeated gladiator. Man must hear, and respond; go and shout, to save a life.

Abraham J. Karp

Taking Along One's Youth

ABRAHAM TOOK ALONG to the Akedah "two of his servants." The Hebrew words are *Shnay na'arav*. These words, a Hasidic interpretation points out, can also be translated, "The years of his youth." It is worth noting in this regard that according to tradition, Abraham was 137 years old at this time. He could have pleaded infirmity and the disabilities of age as an excuse for not fulfilling the onerous Divine command. But the Bible makes a point of letting us know that despite the anguish and the indescribable heartbreak involved in fulfilling the Divine command, Abraham gathered up his youthful energy and determination in order to fulfill God's word. His zeal not only commands our admiration but also calls for emulation.

Sidney Greenberg

To Live as a Jew

TO LIVE AS a Jew! Is there a better phrase in which to sum up in a few words the whole burden of our prayers on this day, what we ask of God, and what in return God asks of us, than the phrase to live as a Jew? For what is it that we ask of God? Like the clang of a hammer on a plate of brass, the reverberating of *"Zochrenu l'Chaim"* ("Remember us, O Lord, for life") resounds throughout our whole prayers. Inscribe us for a good life; take us not hence in the midst of our days. Grant that we may enjoy life, for "the dead shall not praise God." And what is it that God demands from us in return for that boon of life? That we live as Jews, proud and conscious of our responsibilities to Him and to ourselves.

Louis Rabinowitz

The Rabbi Who Worried About the Maidservant

THE WIFE OF Rabbi Wolf of Zbaraz accused her maidservant of having stolen a costly vessel. The girl denied the deed. The woman, being wroth, prepared herself to go out and appeal to the rabbinical court. Rabbi Wolf, seeing her preparations, put on his Sabbath garment also. His wife said that it was not fitting for him to go, too, and she knew well enough how to bear herself in the court's presence.

"Truly," replies the Zaddick, "you do. But the poor orphan, your maid, as whose counsel I am going does not. And who but I will see that justice is done to her?"

Louis I. Newman

An Ideal Is a Port

AN IDEAL IS a port toward which we resolve to steer.

Felix Adler

No Sacrifice Is Ever Wasted

IN PIRKE R. ELIEZER, 31 we are told that no particle of the ram which was ultimately used by Abraham went to waste. The ashes were later used to form the foundation of the altar on which atonement was made for Israel. The sinews were used for strings for David's harp. The skin was converted by Elijah into his girdle. One of its horns became the shofar which was sounded at Mount Sinai when the Torah was given and the other horn will be sounded at the end of days.

This picturesque midrash hammers home to us the reassuring conviction that no sacrifice, indeed no portion of a sacrifice is ever wasted.

If we achieve without sacrifice in any area it is because of the sacrifice of those who have gone before us. If we sacrifice and see no immediate results we can rest confident in the faith that others will reap the fruits of our exertions. There is a staying power to goodness. The good that men do lives after them. In God's economy nothing good is ever lost. Nothing noble is ever wasted.

Sidney Greenberg

Drawing the Line

TO LEARN TO have respect for the lines, that is the point of the book of Vayikra, and that is why they started children with this book in ancient times, and that is why we need to take it seriously in our own time. That is why it is a book that our children need to study, and that is why it is a book that we need to take to heart. For without lines, there is no human life, without Havadalah there is no Shabbat and no work week. Without Havdalah, there is no sea and no dry land, only swampland. Without Havdalah, there is no day and there is no night, only murky, muddy gray. Without Havdalah, there is no right and there is no wrong, only a gray zone in between where you can do whatever makes you happy until you come to understand that living that way makes you miserable.

Let us learn the lesson of the book of Vayikra, let us learn how to draw the line.

Arnold Turetsky

Avram Ha-Ivri

IN ITS DESCRIPTION of this ancient battle, the Torah introduces a new appellation for Avram: "Avram the Hebrew (*ha-ivri*)" 14:13. The exact origin and meaning of the label is not known. Midrash Bereisheet Rabbah 42:13 offers the possibility that it derives from the word, side; i.e. "all the world was on one side *'eiver'* and he on the other side." In other words, Avram was on one side of a moral and spiritual divide and the rest of the world was on the other. To be a true descendant is to live out Avram's nonconformism and to feel that Judaism has something to say that is different from what secular society glorifies and rewards.

Lee Buckman

Avoid Dishonesty at Work

BEFORE YOU GO to work, have a time of preparation to make yourself ready to be careful about all forbidden things and ready to fulfill God's warning, and not transgress, God forbid, such things as theft and robbery, fraud, lying, cheating, false weights and measures.

After eating your midday meal, and before you go back to work, prepare yourself again as you did in the morning, going over in your mind the various things to avoid. And happy are you if you fulfill all this.

Hayim Yosef David Azulai

Stay Away from Stealing Even One Cent

LET YOUR "YES" be true and let your "no" be true, and let all your business dealings be honest. Stay far away from theft and robbery, even from stealing one cent from a non-Jew.

David ha-Levi of Steppin

Give Charity Before Lighting Shabbat Candles

IT IS CUSTOMARY to give some *tzedaka* right before lighting the *shabbat* candles.

A. Y. Eisenbach

The Chain of Jewish Tradition

OUR CONTRIBUTION TO the world will be positive and constructive to the extent that it follows in the chain of Jewish tradition.

Uri Miller

CHAPTER 32

LIVING WITH OTHERS

Why We Can Love God

MAN CAN LOVE God with an all-consuming love not only because he needs Him, but also because He needs him.

Jack J. Cohen

Take Others Along

ON THE WAY to the highest goal I must take my fellow-beings with me.

Felix Adler

As We Give We Receive

THE ACT OF giving is simultaneously an act of receiving. The benefactor is also the beneficiary. To give is to become enriched.

As we feed, we are fed. As we give, we receive. As we lift, we are raised. As we go out of ourselves into something bigger than ourselves, we become bigger in the process and we provide the most nourishing sustenance our craving hearts demand.

"Help your brother's boat across the river and lo, your own has reached the shore."

Sidney Greenberg

Sharing

THE STORY OF the binding of Isaac is the story of a family undermined by an inability to share. They did not talk to one another and they did not listen. The story helps us to understand how imperative it is that we share our failures, our pain and our sorrow as well as our longings and our triumphs. It insists that we be honest with ourselves and seek what we need. And further, the story of the binding of Isaac underscores how essential it is that we listen for others' pain and that we do so with a caring ear and a kindred heart.

Aaron Benjamin Bisno

The Immortal Part of Us

WHAT WE HAVE done for ourselves alone dies with us. What we have done for others and the world remains and is immortal.

Albert Pine

No Throwing Stones

BECAUSE WE LIVE within a stone's throw of each other is no reason we should throw stones at each other.

Stephen S. Wise

Ways of Robbing Others

ROBBING DOES NOT always involve taking from another what already belongs to that person; sometimes we rob by failing to give that person what he needs. We impoverish others by the gifts we withhold from them, by the support we fail to extend. We can rob without taking. We can rob by not giving.

This kind of robbery never shows up in the crime statistics and is punishable by no court of justice. But upon reflection we realize that it is far more prevalent than we suspect. And not only where material things are concerned.

Consider, for example, how often we withhold a word of appreciation and encouragement to those who desperately need to be praised and given a lift. How quick we are to criticize, but slow to compliment. One little boy on his first day in nursery school was asked by the teacher what his name was. He replied: "Billy don't."

Thomas Carlyle's wife was a higly gifted person, one of the most clever women in England in her time. She loved her husband dearly, and to the extent that he was capable of loving any woman other than his mother, he loved her too. After her death, he read this entry in her diary: "Carlyle never praises me. If he says nothing, I have to be content that things are all right."

He had been living for decades with a woman whose heart hungered and ached for a word of appreciation—a word which this prolific writer of words had never been kind enough to utter. Did he not rob her by failing to give her what she so much needed to have?

Sidney Greenberg

The Religion for All

THE RELIGION OF the Prophets by its very nature seeks to be the religion for all; it imposes upon everybody the same demand; it offers to everybody the same promise. The religious personality which it seeks to inform is to be the personality of every man.

Leo Baeck

Kindness—The Universal Language

KINDNESS IS A universal language which even an animal can understand and even the mute can speak. The person who has not learned kindness remains uneducated no matter how many diplomas adorn his office walls or the number of degrees that follow his signature. The person who has learned to be kind has mastered the most vital subject of life's curriculum. His formal schooling may be meager, his familiarity with books not very intimate. If he has learned how to bring a ray of light where there is darkness, a touch of softness where life has been hard, a word of cheer to lift drooping spirits—that person is best equipped to live life as it should be lived.

Sidney Greenberg

A Vegetarian for Health Reasons

WHEN ASKED IF he was a vegetarian for health reasons, Isaac Bashevis Singer answered: "Yes, for the chicken's health."

Ephraim Bennett

No Backward People

THERE ARE NO backward people. There are people who are held backward.

Louis L. Mann

What the Rabbi Worried About

WHEN RABBI ISRAEL Salanter became ill one *Erev Pesah*, he was unable to supervise the baking of the Matzot, and someone was therefore appointed to take his place. His replacement came to Rabbi Salanter to ask if he had any special instructions for him. "Yes," said the Rabbi, "there is one very important precaution I want to impress upon you. The woman who bakes the Matzot is a widow. Be especially careful how you talk to her."

Sidney Greenberg

What Pluralism Is

PLURALISM IS MORE than tolerance. Without saying that anything goes or that all are the same, without yielding its own standards, the pluralist group affirms that the others, despite their limits and even misdeeds, make a contribution to Clal Yisrael, which God wants and which the group alone cannot make.

Irving Greenberg

The Evil of Indifference

THERE IS AN evil which most of us condone and are even guilty of: indifference to evil. We remain neutral, impartial, and not easily moved by the wrongs done unto other people. Indifference to evil is more insidious than evil itself; it is more universal, more contagious, more dangerous.

Abraham J. Heschel

How to Control an Argument

IF SOMEONE YOU are with is provoking you to anger, be silent; if you have to speak to him, make it a point to speak in a low and gentle voice, as this will keep anger from overcoming you. This is a good device to see that an argument that starts does not continue and get bigger.

Hayim Yosef David Azulai

As We Lift We Are Raised

GOD SO FASHIONED us that we are not satisfied merely to be satisfied. We have a deep-rooted craving to give satisfaction.

Erich Fromm, the noted psychologist, has underlined this truth: "Not he who has much is rich, but he who gives much. The hoarder, who is anxiously worried about losing something is, psychologically speaking, the poor impoverished man, regardless of how much he has. Whoever is capable of giving of himself is rich."

As we feed, we are fed. As we give, we receive. As we lift, we are raised. As we go out of ourselves into something bigger than ourselves, we become bigger in the process and we provide the most nourishing sustenance our craving hearts demand.

"Help your brother's boat across, and lo, your own has reached the shore."

Sidney Greenberg

A Sign of Maturity

ONE SIGN OF maturity is the ability to be comfortable with people who are not like us.

Virgil A. Kraft

We Hold Each Other Up

NONE OF US has solid ground under his feet; each of us is only held up by the neighborly hands grasping him by the scruff, with the result that we are each held up by the next man, and often, indeed most of the time, hold each other up mutually.

Franz Rosenzweig

Treat Every Person with Gentleness

YOU SHOULD RECEIVE every person with warmth, and bear his yoke, and treat him with gentleness, as if he were your king. It is part of human kindness to listen to him talk, even if he overdoes it; but at the very same time you should not forget the Creator, blessed be He, at all.

Yaakov Yitzhak

Never Express Anger When Upset

THE RABBI OF Gastinin, of blessed memory, made it a practice never to express anger on the same day when he was upset or annoyed with someone. Only on the following day would he tell him, "Yesterday I was annoyed at you."

Siah Sarfei Kodesh

Anger Brings Regret

ANGER BEGINS WITH madness, and ends with regret.

Abraham Hasdai

Love Is Always a Refuge

THERE IS ONE fundamental difference between love and hate. Love is always a refuge. Hate is never a refuge. Only a mentally sick person can find refuge in his hates. But love is the enduring sanctuary of life. Life may rob you of things. It often does. But it can never bereave us of love itself.

Abba Hillel Silver

Charity and Loving-Kindness—The Differences

THE RABBIS POINTED out the distinction between giving charity and performing an act of loving-kindness. Charity involves financial help, while an act of loving-kindness can be performed with money or with one's person. Charity is given only to the poor, but an act of loving-kindness can be shown to the rich as well as to the poor. Charity is extended only to the living, while an act of loving-kindness can be conferred even upon the dead.

An act of loving-kindness is a humane response to human need. It is your pain in my heart.

Sidney Greenberg

Nobody Is a Stranger

WHEN WE LET God into ourselves we open our hearts to a world where we see others made like us in the common image of Divinity. The ancient Jews were told by their lawgiver Moses to remember the stranger; this was a challenge to them to build a future world where nobody would be a stranger.

Charles E. Shulman

Cultivate Difference Creatively

WHAT IS WRONG with difference is not difference, but man's reluctance to allow and encourage it, and to cultivate it creatively.

Milton Steinberg

Faithful Love Rejoices for Others

EVERY BELOVED KNOWS himself to be chosen. Nor does his awareness of election require that no other should be elected. Faithful love rejoices that others are also beloved.

Dudley Weinberg

The Highest Service—To Evoke Love

WOULD YOU NOT agree with me were I to say that the baby does for the mother more than the mother does for the baby? The mother tends the baby unselfishly, but the baby does more; the baby evokes the mother's love. And no higher service can one human being render another.

Abraham Cronbach

We Have What We Give Away

Love that is hoarded moulds at last
Until we know some day
The only thing we ever have
Is what we gave away.

Louis Ginsberg

What Is Tolerance?

TOLERANCE IS THE positive and cordial effort to understand another's beliefs, practices and habits, without necessarily sharing or accepting them.

Joshua Loth Liebman

The Illusion

THE CHIEF VALUE of history, if it is critically studied, is to break down the illusion that people are very different.

Leo Stein

What Our Aim Should Be

OUR AIM SHOULD be, not one civilization, supreme at the cost of others, but as many types flourishing on this earth as possible.

Felix Adler

Life's Most Sacred Function

THE ANCIENT ROMANS regarded bridge-building as a sacred pursuit.

That is evident from the name they gave to the priest, whom they called "pontifex," which means bridge-builder.

A bridge unites those whom nature divides.

Can there be a more sacred function in life?

Mordecai M. Kaplan

The Whole Torah

A FAMOUS STORY about Hillel, the greatest rabbi of ancient times, tells that a gentile once came to him and said, "Rabbi, I would like to convert to Judaism, but only if you can teach me the whole Torah while I am standing on one leg." Hillel taught him the Golden Rule, saying, "The essence of the Torah is: Do not do to others what you would not like done to you. The rest is commentary; but go home and study it."

The ancient rabbis considered the Golden Rule as the "rule of thumb" to fulfill the Torah's commandment to love your neighbor *as yourself*. How do you know how to love your neighbor? By realizing that your neighbor is *as yourself*, by reflecting on how you would want to be treated if you were in her place. The negative Golden Rule—not doing to others what you would not want done to you, not to hate or to harm—is the beginner's lesson; the positive Golden Rule—treating others as you would want them to treat you, to love and to help—is the advanced lesson.

This Hillel story is so familiar to Jews that they may neglect to see how radical it is. What happened to love of God? How can love of neighbor be "the whole Torah"? The answer is that Hillel so closely associated love of God with love of people—that a person should love God *by* loving people—that the former did not even have to be explicitly mentioned. Hillel's approach was thoroughly humanistic.

Yitzhak Buxbaum

The Darkness in the Heart

A TEN-YEAR-OLD *yeshivah* student studied for the first time about the plagues that were visited upon the ancient Egyptians.

The ninth plague, he learned, was darkness, a darkness so "thick" that "they saw not one another" [Exodus 10:33].

He asked the rebbe: "What kind of plague was that? After all, they could have lit their lamps and been able to see despite the darkness. Isn't that what they did every night when it got dark?"

The rebbe's smile indicated that he was not displeased by the question. Patting the boy on his head, he said: "The darkness from which the Egyptians suffered was a special kind of darkness that affected the eyes; it was a darkness that affected the heart. Physically, they were able to see, but they didn't feel for each other; they didn't care for one another. This is what the Torah means when it says, 'They saw not one another.' They were blind to each other's needs. Each person saw only himself. And that is a terrible plague."

Perhaps the rebbe's answer cannot be harmonized with the literal meaning of the Torah text. But this much is certain, he taught the boy a lesson that goes to the very essence of Judaism.

Much as Judaism is concerned with the relationship between human being and God, "*beyn adam la-makom*," it is no less concerned with the relationship between one human being and another, "*beyn adam la-haveyro*."

Judaism expects of us that we shall "see" each person as a human being who has needs, feelings, fears, hungers, hopes just as we do; who is a child of God just as we are; who is fully entitled to be treated with the dignity, justice, and compassion we claim for ourselves.

Sidney Greenberg

Why Prejudice Is Held Against People

PREJUDICE IS NOT held against people because they have evil qualities. Evil qualities are imputed to people because prejudices are held against them.

Marshall Wingfield

We Are Tied to the Community

TRUE RELIGION AFFIRMS two great principles, neither of which is complete without the other. One is man's faith in God; the other, God's faith in man. It is the faith of our Divine Father in us that ultimately spurs us and enables us to overcome frailty and rise to a higher fulfillment of the potentialities He has implanted within us. We should go forward from worship purified in purpose, fortified in resolve and elevated in vision.

This confrontation of self by the individual does not take place in solitude and withdrawal. It occurs in the midst of the Congregation and in the company of one's fellow-worshippers. The spiritual enhancement of an individual's life is bound up with the community of which he is part. The community must resolve to raise its corporate life to a higher point of spiritual awareness and content if its constituent individuals are to attain greater cultural and spiritual heights.

Morris Adler

Meeting in the Middle

TWENTY CENTURIES AGO, Hillel spoke words that have puzzled Jews for two millennia: "If I am not for myself, who will be for me? But if I am only for myself, what am I?" Hillel recognized the tension between self-interest and self-sacrifice, between being selfish and unselfish, obsequious and supercilious, humble and haughty. It is a delicate balance that serves as a challenge to Jews everywhere. Its foundation stone is centered on *efshar*, on the possibility of meeting in the middle, on genuine dialogue, on boundaries with fringes. Its keystone is the little known blessing once regularly utilized by sages upon addressing a Jewish audience: "Blessed is He who discerns secrets, for the mind of each is different from the other, as the face of each is different from the other" [Berachot 58a]. May this blessing serve as our compass when we dig tunnels toward one another, so that we may meet in the middle!

Steven S. Pearce

The Promise of Our Religious Genius

THE THREE RELIGIOUS parties, Orthodox, Conservative, and Reform, constitute what has been felicitously called catholic Judaism. Wide as are some of their differences in belief and practice they are not separatist sects but differing members of one religion. They are united not only by kinship and history and the bonds of a common destiny but also by a deep abiding faith in religious principles, which they hold to be immortal and which they cherish for the happiness of humanity.

Common to them all is the belief that Israel has a divine and prophetic role to play in the concert of nations and in the progress of united humanity toward an era of universal justice and peace. The millennial vision abides eternally in the Torah and illumes the hope of all its children. The creative religious genius, which has produced the world's greatest Prophets and has given the greater part of mankind its religion and ethics, still holds great promise for endless generations to come who will build the foundations of "a new heaven and a new earth." Whatever interpretations a religious party or individual may give to this Jewish Messianic faith, its essence is spiritually alive with optimistic faith in God and the future of mankind. Therein lies the strength and the unity of Judaism.

Abraham A. Neuman

The Evil Tongue

LOOK HOW MANY sins in our prayer book refer to sins of the mouth. For the sin we have committed against you by gossip, and by tale-bearing, and by mocking and scoffing, and by falsehood, and by needlessly judging other people. In Hebrew, the sin of gossip is called *lashon hara*, the evil tongue. It is the subject of centuries of moral advice. Our sages, of blessed memory, wrote entire volumes about it. Entire *yeshivot* in Vilna and Slobodka existed where the curriculum was nothing but the laws of *lashon hara*—where the students became as expert in the laws of speaking as some were in the laws of slaughtering. *Lashon hara* means saying anything bad about anyone, even and especially if it's true. *Lason hara* means insult, ridicule, and jest. *Lashon hara* means denigrating someone's possessions (never laugh at someone's car) or work or merchandise. It means commenting on someone's body or commenting on someone's mind and someone's money or someone's medical history. It means saying anything that might cause another person harm, embarrassment, or displeasure.

Jeffrey K. Salkin

We Are All a Single Family

WE CANNOT LIVE alone, nor can we live frightened, nor can we live in desperation. We live today at the best that we are today. We do today what is given into our hand today: the kindly word, the visit, the compassionate deed. We let our spirits touch the lives about us, husbands, wives, children, friends, strangers. We see today as an opportunity. We see tomorrow as a bright and shining possibility. We see life as a continuous dynamism, as an endless stream. We are part of that stream. We enrich it with our years.

Humankind is a single family and who serves one of its members serves them all. The truth is that the view from my hospital window was the world; and I, obscure, unimportant and of not much value, was the beneficiary of all that the world had learned, so that I might be kept alive.

Should I not be grateful? Should I not be bound to take the roses of the spirit outside and help transform mankind's winter world into a shining and everlasting loveliness?

Jacob Philip Rudin

The Ultimate Goal of Religion

THIS IS THE ultimate goal of religious affirmation: a life free from oppression, from wrong action, as from wrong thought. It endorses both, love, the honest acquisition of property as the enjoyment of anything acquired in integrity. It established the line between right and wrong. Enjoy what is rightly yours, but do not cast envious or predatory eyes on what belongs to others. Religion has never been defined more adequately than by the fact that the Ten Commandments commence with, "I shall be the Lord thy God" and end with "all that belongs to your neighbor."

Leo Jung

In Hebrew Life Is a Plural Noun

IN ALL LANGUAGES of the world, the word "life" is a singular noun. In all languages except Hebrew. In the sacred tongue of our Bible and prophets, life is *chai-im*. It is a plural form and there is no singular for it in the holy tongue. Why? Because a good life cannot possibly be lived in the singular. It must be in the plural.

Joseph Lookstein

We Claim No Monopoly on Truth

JEWS REGARD JUDAISM as the only religion for Jews. But we neither judge nor condemn the honest, devout worshiper of any faith. The Talmud tells us: "the righteous of all nations are worthy of immortality."

We believe in certain basic ethical concepts: decency, kindliness, justice and integrity. These we regard as eternal verities. But we claim no monopoly on these verities, for we recognize that every great religious faith has discovered them. That is what Rabbi Meier meant some eighteen centuries ago, when he said that a Gentile who follows the Torah is as good as our High Priest.

There are many mountaintops and all of them reach for the stars.

Morris N. Kertzer

Clapping Hands

THE BAAL SHEM teaches that when people are happy they clap their hands. This is because joy is spreading throughout the entire body. But do you know what it is that I'm really doing when I'm clapping? A person is bringing the left and right to love each other. Let me explain. The right usually tells the left: Listen, you know you're a leftist. I don't want to have anything to do with you. And the left (hand) says to the right: Who needs you? You're so boring; you're always doing something good. Who needs you and your *mitzvot*. I have no strength for you. So the right doesn't speak to the left and the left doesn't speak to the right. But when clapping hands, the left comes close to the right and says, "Hey, you're precious after all." And the right says to the left: "I love you." So let's sing and pray that the Holy One stirs the eyes of our people so that we recognize that we are only one, a holy and sanctified nation.

Shlomo Carlebach

The Gifts of Sharing

SO MANY OF us know Abraham's pain. Who here has not been certain of the path we walk along? Who among us has not struggled alone with a difficult choice? Is there one here who has not suffered in silence?

But when we share the gift of our thoughts and our feelings with another, when we allow ourselves to cry on a friend's shoulder, when we express our innermost feelings with those we love, we forbid loneliness from bruising our soul. And we open ourselves to life's feeling.

And reciprocally, when we offer these gifts to another—a willingness to listen, a shoulder to cry on, a safe place in which one can unburden oneself, we perform an act of loving-kindness for which our tradition holds out the highest of praise. We have been taught that our world is sustained by such actions.

Aaron Benjamin Bisno

The Greater Crime

WHY WAS NOAH'S generation destroyed and not the generation of Babel even though the latter also rebelled against God? According to Rashi, a crime against a fellow human being (e.g., such as one committed in Noah's generation) is more contemptible than a crime against God (such as that which the generation of Babel committed). For this reason, humanity was destroyed only in Noah's generation and not in Babel's where there was unity among the people.

Lee Buckman

Honor a Person's Feelings and Dignity

ON THE SURFACE, the laws of the sacrificial system may seem irrelevant and lacking in inspiration. Yet, in almost every verse, our tradition has uncovered important lessons for living. The very first verse of the Parasha, for example, has given rise to an insightful piece of advice. The verse states: "He called to Moses "*vayikra el moshe*." God spoke to him from the Tent of Meeting, saying . . ." [Leviticus 1:1].

Commentators ask why the verse mentions that God called to Moses before beginning to speak to him. Why doesn't God just begin speaking? The Talmud [Yoma 4B] answers by saying, "the Torah teaches us good manners: a man should not address his neighbor without having first greeted him. This supports the view of Rabbi Chanina, for Rabbi Chanina said: No man shall speak to his neighbor unless he calls him first to speak to him."

Similarly, one should not give instructions to a "subordinate" until he/she has called that person by name, for this is what God did in this verse. God is the Master of the universe and yet, when God speaks to Moses, God first calls him by name in order to set an example for the way we are to treat others with less power, namely, with sensitivity to their feelings and dignity.

Lee Buckman

Breaking through the Prison of Prejudice

ONE OF THE tragedies of our times is that prejudice has enslaved the minds of millions and erected walls that isolate man from man. Prejudice locks us into our own backyard and closes the door on many worlds of friendship, of spiritual and cultural enrichment. It pits brother against brother. It holds up to man the false mirror of a society in which one group can raise itself only by trampling upon the dignity and self-respect of another group. You can say what you will about prejudice: it is costly, it is irrational, it is criminal; it is all of that, but above all else prejudice is a prison that confines the human mind and spirit, and robs man of the opportunity to broaden his understanding and enrich his life through a close and free relationship with his fellowman.

We know that Joseph broke through the self-imprisonment of his prejudices when he made himself known to his brothers with the following words: "Come near to me, I pray you . . . I am Joseph, your brother." When we draw near to our fellowman and call him brother, when we learn to know him and become sensitive to his needs and problems, when we realize that we can grow together with him and share with him common hopes and tasks, common privileges and responsibilities, only then can we claim to have broken through the prison of prejudice.

Israel Mowshowitz

Are We Fit to Celebrate Passover?

WHENEVER AND WHEREVER there is oppression of the weak by the strong, of the poor by the rich, or of one race by another, they who are knit together by the common celebration of the Passover ought to feel righteous indignation, and do all which lies in their power to remedy the wrong. The Jews should ever be foremost in the cause of freedom, or justice, and of charity. Otherwise they are false to the very foundation of their history and creed. Each coming Passover should remind us to ask ourselves, have I done my best to help those whom I can help? Have I cared my best for those for whom I ought to care? Have I been gentle and considerate and kind to those who serve me in my home and who work for me and for my household, whether within doors or without? Have I remembered the poor and sought to help them wisely, if such help be within my power, through my gift, my time, and my thought? Have I made any sacrifice for their sakes? If we cannot say something of a "yes" to questions such as these, are we fit to rejoice at and take our part in this celebration of Passover?

C. G. Montefiore

How Abraham Found God

IN ONE OF the classics of modern Hebrew literature, a story is told which would explain the source of his wise-heartedness. The house of Abraham, according to tradition, was situated on top of a hill. There were doors in all directions, so that the weary traveler, seeking its famed hospitality, might find his way up without undue delay. One morning he saw an old man struggling painfully up the hill. In accordance with his way, Father Abraham rushed out of the house to meet the stranger. He helped him reach the top. He bathed his feet, he offered him food and drink. The old man was profoundly grateful and when he was sufficiently relaxed, Abraham said to him, "And now that you are happy, let us say grace to God." The stranger looked at him without comprehension and said, "What is God? Who is God?" "Well," said Abraham, "He is the creator of the world. He is the father of human beings. He is the provider of everything we enjoy." Said the old man, "I don't know anything about that God. I worship the fire." Abraham lost his patience and he said, "You wicked man! I can't have in my house someone who doesn't acknowledge God. You had better leave." The old man went out, unconvinced, unhappy, more lonely than ever.

That night, God appeared to Abraham in a dream, and He said, "I have suffered the foolish old man for seventy years, Abraham. Couldn't you have been patient with him for one night?"

That dream changed the course of Abraham's life. Through that dream, he found God truly, he came closer to Him. That dream has been the promise and the challenge and the whole purpose of Jewish history. That dream is of profound significance for every one of us, today and tomorrow.

Leo Jung

Pray with People in Pain

WHY DON'T WE pray with people in pain? You don't have to know the "right" words. Just close your eyes and ask them what they want to ask for. If someone you care about is depressed or anxious or hurting, either physically or emotionally, they need not only rational explanations but they also crave spiritual direction. And, most importantly, they don't require a rabbi or a professional to "give" it to them; they need someone they trust to share it with them. How unfortunate that we leave the "religious" aspects of *bikur cholim*, of visiting the sick, to the clergy, to chaplains that have no relationship with the ill person outside of the hospital. We ask rabbis to "pray for" the people we love, but we feel awkward praying for them ourselves.

Spontaneous prayer comes hard to most Jews, yet the desire to say something remains. I'm sure you've all heard about the fact that prayer actually helps. Recently a test group of three hundred patients in San Francisco were divided into two groups: those prayed for—even by strangers—and those not. The prayed-for group had lower statistical instances of the needed antibiotics or second surgeries. I don't believe that saying a *misheberach* will cure a person of disease, but it often cures people of depression. And we get so mad at God when we've prayed for Grandma not to die but she does anyway. Prayer isn't magic. It doesn't take away death, but it often takes away despair. It's a hammock we weave for people to lie on and look heavenward. I never regret the times I prayed with Shelly, even when it seemed hokey. I only regret the times I didn't.

Elyse Goldstein

CHAPTER 33

PARENTING

Teachers of a Lifetime

PARENTS ARE OF course expected to be warm and sympathetic toward their children, and there are times when they should relax and be informal with their sons and daughters. But children should never come to look upon their parents as they would their school chums; they should always look to their parents with respect and reverence. Parents are in many ways like teachers, perhaps even more so, for they are the teachers of a lifetime.

Simon Glustrom

How to Help a Child Become a Person

WHEN WE REASON with a child, we not only treat him as a person but we also help him to become one.

Mordecai M. Kaplan

Our Human Limitations

WHEN WE ACKNOWLEDGE the built-in limitations of the human condition, we avoid the destructive tendency to blame ourselves when children do not turn out exactly as we had hoped. Deluded by a sense of omnipotence, we succumb to the illusion that when kids go wrong it is all our fault. We have done it to them. We forget the many other forces that go into the making and the shaping of a child—the genes of generations past, the environment, the TV, the friends on the street, the teachers in the classroom, the characters the child encounters in books. These are only some of the multitude of forces at work, and while no parent has the right to abdicate responsibility, neither has the parent the right to arrogate unto himself the feeling of invincibility.

Emerson said there is a crack in everything that God has made. Perfection is beyond human reach. Jacob captured this truth in his question, "Am I in the place of God?"

In a letter to William James, Justice Holmes wrote, "The great act of faith is when a man decides he is not God." When we realize that we are not God, we have a better chance of becoming human.

Sidney Greenberg

What Children Need from Parents

IN JUDAISM THE parent-child relationship is a very clear and important one. The parents' responsibility is to teach, to educate. The Hebrew word for parents is *horim*, and it comes from the same root as *moreh*, teacher. The parent is, and remains, the first and most important teacher that the child will ever have.

Being a pal is good and has an important role in a parent-child relationship. But the parent must ever be aware that it is his responsibility to teach, to lead, to set an example.

But unlike classroom teaching, when the aim is primarily conveying facts, the parent is charged with setting standards, transmitting ideals and giving the child a sense of values which will guide him when he is confronted with a moral problem. This type of teaching is done when we "are sitting in our house, when we are walking on the road, when we lie down and when we rise up."

Kassel Abelson

What Parents Owe Their Childen

THE FACT THAT we cannot exercise total control does not justify abdication of all parental responsibility. Our tradition which asks children to honor their parents also demands of parents that they keep themselves honorable. And, above all, that they be parents, not pals to their children. Pals they'll find in the playground. What they look for in parents is something quite different. If we want our child to grow up to be a certain kind of person we have the obligation to be the kind of person we would like the child to become. If we want our child to lead a life of loyalty and commitment to our people's past and future we have to be the child's model in the present.

In raising children, as in so many other crucial areas of life, there are no sure bets. But one thing we owe them is the example of parental behavior worth emulating. Then we must take them, as we take ourselves "frail and full of faults, but moved now and then by a dream so big there are no words for it."

Sidney Greenberg

Our Responsibility as Parents

ROSH HASHANAH PUTS on us the responsibility of determining whether we are the sort of people we want our children to become!

Kassel Abelson

How to Teach Your Son

THERE IS A tale of a man who brought his son to a rabbi to teach him Torah. The rabbi asked, "Why do you want him to learn Torah?" "So that when he grows up, he will bring his son to learn Torah, and so on." The rabbi answered, "Better you should come and study Torah, so that when your son sees you, he will want to."

Michael Gold

Visiting the Mourner

SOMETIMES WE'LL HAVE to visit the mourner. We Jews have lost the art—and I mean art—of *shiva*. You don't have to say anything clever, or spiritual, or religious. You don't have to answer the question "why?" and you don't have to ask it, either. You don't have to defend God or explain God. You just have to be quiet and helpful and confirm that they are still alive although their loved one is not. You just have to bring the coffee or run the errands or pick up the kids from school or make the *minyan* or sit for a while in sad silence and every now and then, offer a supportive sigh. Come during the day, when it's really lonely. If you're invited to stay for a meal, don't decline—they mean it when they say they want your company. The Talmud relates the custom that when someone died, the whole town would stop working when the funeral cortege passed by. Even today, I am deeply touched when I am in a funeral processional and I see gentile workers on the street stand at attention, and take off their hats in respect to the passing cars. When it's us in the big black family car in the front—oh how we long for the world to stop and notice. Take your kids on *shiva* calls. It's not too sad for them. How will they ever learn by experience what it means to be a Jew who comforts the mourners? Even if time slips by and you didn't visit right away, don't worry. People mourn for a long time, not just for the first seven days. The card and the phone call both help the slow, aching, healing process. I never regret the times I paid a *shiva* call, only the times I didn't; even when it's tense or unbearably sad or even unbearably shallow.

Elyse Goldstein

CHAPTER 34

THE BLESSING OF PEACE

A Thirteen-Year-Old's Poem for Peace

IN OUR MORE vigorous pursuit of peace, perhaps we might find some inspiration in a poem written by thirteen-year-old Tali Sorek from Beersheba, Israel:

> I had a box of color—
> Shining, bright and bold.
> I had a box of colors,
> Some warm, some very cold.
>
> I had no red for the blood of wounds.
> I had no black for the orphans' grief.
> I had no white for dead faces and hands.
> I had no yellow for burning sands.
>
> But I had orange for the joy of life,
> And I had green for buds and nests.
> I had blue for bright, clear skies.
> I had pink for dreams and rest.
>
> I sat down and painted Peace.

Sidney Greenberg

We Must Rise to Spiritual Heights

WHEN EACH OF US, as individuals, and collectively as a nation, rises to spiritual heights of the new attitude of self-correction, of fashioning order and contentment in our own little world, can we hope to see a happy mankind walking the road of peace, hand in hand, with the light of God's law as their guide. On this Rosh Hashanah we pray for such divine guidance.

Bernard Mandelbaum

A Song to Peace

LET THE SUN rise and give the morning light, the purest prayer will not bring us back. He whose candle was snuffed out and was buried in the dust, a bitter cry won't wake him, won't bring him back. Nobody will return us from the dead dark pit. Here, neither the joy of victory nor songs of praise will help. So sing only for peace, don't whisper a prayer, it's better to sing a song for peace with a big shout! Let the sun penetrate through the flowers, don't look backward, leave those who have departed. Lift your eyes with hope not through the rifle sights, sing a song for love and not for wars. Don't pray the day will come, bring the day, because it is not a dream. And within all the city's squares, cheer for peace.

Yaakov Rotblit

Be Quick to Reestablish Peace

YOU SHOULD BE careful on the holy Sabbath to cleave to your fellowman in love and brotherhood, peace and friendship—even more is this true between husband and wife. . . . So if two people had some dispute, they should each one approach the other with words of reconciliation and love before the entrance of Shabbat.

Alexander Susskind

When Shalom Is Present

When the blessing of SHALOM is lacking
However much we have of other blessings—
Wealth or power,
Fame or family,

Even health—
These all appear
As nothing.

But when SHALOM is present,
However little else we have
Somehow seems sufficient.

Hershel Matt

The Mezuzah in Space

IN JUDAISM, WE seek to achieve the spiritual goals of *shalom bayit*, peaceful relations in the home, and *darchei shalom*, peaceful relations in our daily lives in the world. Perhaps no ritual object and its traditions teach more about this quest than the *mezuzah* that adorns the doorposts and gates of our homes. Proof of this comes not only from tradition but also from the front page of a recent newspaper. What did Jewish astronaut David Wolf bring with him when he landed on the Mir space station? A *mezuzah*. Why? "The *Sh'ma* represents the oneness of God and all humanity," said the astronaut. It was the most important symbol he could think of for world peace.

Richard M. Litvak

Where Peace Begins

GOD DOES NOT grant peace; He places peace within the reach of man. This is an invaluable lesson. Peace is not to be found in international conferences. These are beyond the reach of the common man who most thirsts after this elusive goal. Peace must begin with man himself, and from within reach out to the family unit. And from there to the community. Inner harmony, the result of obeisance to the will of God, is the only certain road to outer peace.

Henry Hoschander

What We Must Preach Now

IT HAS ALWAYS been the mission of Israel to preach the oneness of God. We have done so for thirty-five hundred years. But now, when a new consciousness of oneness is imperative for our age which is so unlike any that has passed before, Judaism must preach that message—embodied in the *Shema*—again, and say what it means in the language of our day. What does the oneness of God mean? The oneness of God means the oneness of the world and the oneness of all humanity. The oneness of God means the brotherhood of man. It can never mean less than that. For us to preach the oneness of God, and yet to accept the hatred of man is to live a lie. You cannot have the oneness of God unless you have the oneness of man, and you cannot have the oneness of man unless you have peace. For peace is the affirmation that men are brothers and that God is one. Peace is the affirmation; war is its denial.

Mervin B. Tomsky

CHAPTER 35

PRAYER: THE BRIDGE BETWEEN GOD
AND MAN

God Works through Us

PRAYER DOES NOT involve a change in the will of God, but rather a change in the will of man to fulfill the will of God. God is no servant, He is a helper. He works not for us, but with us, within us and through us.

Herman Kieval

When Man Recognizes That He Stands in the Presence of God

WHATEVER ELSE PRAYER may be, it is minimally *what a man does when he recognizes that he stands in the presence of God.* This is the basic truth about prayer. I am not referring now to study groups in which we speculate and philosophize about God; nor do I have in mind the conversations with our children in which we struggle to demonstrate God's existence to them. I mean the immediately experienced reality of our own position in the presence of God. Either we know this reality or we do not. And what I am saying is that prayer is what a man does when he knows it.

Dudley Weinberg

The Power to Transform Life

THE REAL VALUE of prayer lies in its power to transform a man's life. When sincerely and regularly practiced—whether spoken or unspoken—it has the effect of lifting one out of the slough of despair and the mire of fear. It can perform a veritable miracle in our lives by bringing us nearer to God.

Julius Mark

The Power of a Carlebach Tune

IT COULD BE argued that a tune of Rav Shlomo Carlebach or Rebbe Nachman of Bratslav is more convincing than any academic discourse.

Reuven Ben Dov

A New World Every Day

THE REGULAR WORSHIPER enters a new world every day, a world which did not exist yesterday, a bright new world wherein the miraculous and the divine are within his grasp.

Reuben M. Katz

We Can Pray in Silence

THE TZARTKOVER REBBE failed to preach for a long time. He was asked why, and he replied: "There are seventy ways of reciting the Torah. One of them is through silence."

Perhaps the Rebbe was trying to convey the thought that we teach best not by our exhortations but by our examples, not by our lessons but by our lives.

If we can teach silently we can also pray silently. The Psalmist tells us: "To You, silence is praise."

We can praise in silence; we can petition in silence; we can pray in silence.

Sidney Greenberg

What Prayer Can and Cannot Do

PRAYER CANNOT MEND a broken bridge, rebuild a ruined city, or bring water to parched fields.

Prayer can mend a broken heart, lift up a discouraged soul, and strengthen a weakened will.

Ferdinand M. Isserman

At the Door Whisper a Prayer

A HASIDIC RABBI compared the entrance to a synagogue to a border between two countries, where you must have your luggage checked and any contraband must be thrown away before crossing. As you enter the synagogue or briefly pause at the doorway, whisper or pray mentally a short prayer, such as: "God, let me feel awe and love for You within the synagogue. Let me pray earnestly once inside and feel Your presence." Explicitly expressing your intention at the outset helps you to fulfill it.

Yitzhak Buxbaum

Prayer Produces Practical Moral Results

DOES PRAYER PRODUCE any practical moral results? I believe that it does. It is one of the consequences of our involvement with God in prayer that we come to hunger and thirst after righteousness. How else can we return the love with which we are loved? How else can we understand the meaning of the divine concern that makes us human, except by joyously translating our responding love not into merely sentimental declarations, but into specific acts of justice, decency and kindness? How else can we deal with the whole truth about ourselves, including the nasty part, except by struggling to overcome everything in ourselves and in our environment that attacks our precious God-given humanity?

In prayer, if nowhere else; we express our loyalty to the Utmost and thus achieve a clearer knowledge of our duty. When God's love becomes God's commandment, moral consequences *do* follow—not easily, not without struggle and not without the constant need for revision and re-thinking, *but they follow*. And they follow not merely as *knowledge*, as the technical ability to make ethical judgments about theoretical situations and to say what is right and wrong. They follow as the courage to *be* and to *do* what our human nature with its divine dimension requires. The creative effort of prayer moves us from the *knowledge* of the good to the *deed*, which is good.

Dudley Weinberg

Imagine Yourself Face to Face with God

HOW DO YOU meditate to prepare for prayer? Such a meditation can have a number of elements, but the primary one is to simply focus on God. With eyes closed (or open, if you prefer), direct your attention to God. You can imagine the room as full of God's light, the aura of His glorious presence, which totally surrounds you—above, below, left, right, in front and back. You can also imagine God as before you and that you are looking at Him and He at you, face to face.

Yitzhak Buxbaum

The Prayer That Ascends on High

PRAYER, IF OFFERED from the heart and for the sake of heaven, even though the worshiper does not know its meaning, ascends on high and pierces the firmament.

The Baal Shem Tov

Ideal Prayer Reaches God's Responsive Heart

PRAYER IS THAT dimension of language which begins in the human heart and carries that voice through the imagination to God. Ideal prayer returns to the human heart from the responsive heart of God.

Ira Stone

Our Liturgy Is a Higher Form of Silence

IN A SENSE, our liturgy is a higher form of silence. It is pervaded by an awed sense of the grandeur of God which resists description and surpasses all expression. The individual is silent. He does not bring forth his own words. His saying the consecrated words is in essence an act of listening to what they convey. The spirit of Israel speaks, the self is silent.

Abraham J. Heschel

When Our Prayers Are Answered

PRAYER TAKES US beyond the self. Joining our little self to the selfhood of humanity, it gives our wishes the freedom to grow large and broad and inclusive. Our prayers are answered not when we are given what we ask, but when we are challenged to be what we can be.

Morris Adler

We Need to Pray for Our Own Sakes

PRAYER INFLUENCES NOT God, but ourselves. He does not need our worship. Our wants, our yearnings, our lightest thoughts are known to Him as soon as they are known to us. It is for our own sakes that we need to pray. It is a need far greater than the trivial wants that form the burden of many of our petitions. We too often pray for little, even for worthless things, for favors that are more than doubtful. But what we most need, though we do not always see it, is the help that comes from prayer itself—help to bear our load more bravely, to face temptation more resolutely. We need to get the very mood of surrender, to realize that we are but as little children in the hands of a loving, yet infinitely wise Parent, humble servants of an august Master. And, therefore, even when our prayers seem to fail, they succeed; for they effect that spiritual uplifting which is far more worth having than the things we pray for.

Morris Joesph

To Live Out the Dreams of Prayer

PRAYER TAKES US from the noise of the world into the stillness of the soul, not so that we may escape from the world into some mountain retreat or island monastery, but to return us into the world there to perform our task. Before he could know how to lead his people out of Egypt, Moses had to experience the shepherd's solitude in the land of Midian where God found him at the burning bush. The Baal Shem spent the early years of his life in a mountain retreat and far from society. There he strengthened the bonds which joined him to the divine, until he was prepared to disclose his identity and engage in his holy work of redemption. So it is with all of us. Prayer removes us from the marketplace and the counting-chamber to heal us, to wash us clean, to purify us, to strengthen us, to remind us of what we have forgotten, to let our souls touch the Source of all souls, and then to send us back to the crossroads of life so that we may live out the dreams of prayer.

Samuel H. Dresner

The Language of Meditation

MUCH HAVE I seen with the seeing of my eyes and much have I heard with the hearing of my ears. But frequently I must close my eyes to behold revelations that are focused only through the telescope of the spirit. And often I hearken to truths spoken in the hushed corridors of solitude. How much there is to hear from choirs of silence! We track the Unseen and the Unseeable to its hiding place when we learn to speak and understand the language of meditation.

Alexander Alan Steinbach

An Act of Devotion

APPRECIATING BEAUTY IS an act of devotion.

David J. Wolpe

Plead That You Be Worthy

THE MAIN THING is prayer. Accustom yourself to beg and plead before God. Speak to Him in any language and you understand—this is especially important. Beg Him to open your eyes. Ask Him to help you along the path of devotion. Plead that you be worthy of drawing close to Him.

Natan of Nemirov

The Need for Daily Worship

THE INSIGHTS OF wonder must be constantly kept alive. Since there is a need for daily wonder, there is a need for daily worship. The sense of the "miracles which are daily with us," the sense of the "continual marvels," is the source of prayer. There is no worship, no music, no love, if we take for granted the blessings or defeats of living. . . . The profound and perpetual awareness of the wonder of being has become a part of the religious consciousness of the Jew.

Abraham J. Heschel

A Relationship of Father and Child

THE PRAYERS SHOULD raise man in the purest perfection to be as a child toward his Father in heaven, perceiving the Father everywhere, allowing everything to be permeated by the thought of the Father, resolving the whole world, and the whole of life, in a single relationship of Father and child.

Samson Rafael Hirsch

We Need Prayer

GOD SURELY KNOWS our thoughts and desires. What need is there therefore to give expression to them? This is quite true; and still the human soul yearns to give articulate expression to what is uppermost in its consciousness at any one time. Prayer does not affect God, but ourselves. In prayer, the divine within us asserts itself, seeks its union with the divine in the universe and through that becomes ennobled and glorified. God needs none of our praises and supplications, but we feel impelled to pour out our hearts to Him and by doing this we come to be in greater harmony with our spiritual selves, and with God, the spiritual element in the universe.

Julius H. Greenstone

Prayer Taps Sources of Courage and Faith

PEOPLE WHO PRAY for miracles usually don't get miracles. . . . But people who pray for courage, for strength to bear the unbearable, for the grace to remember what they have left instead of what they have lost, very often find their prayers answered. . . . Their prayers helped them tap hidden reserves of faith and courage which were not available to them before.

Harold Kushner

Set Your Heart on Fire for God

A LENS CAN focus the sun's rays to start a fire. Use the lens of your meditation and concentration on the davening to set your heart on fire for God

Yitzhak Buxbaum

Add Short Personal Prayers

IT IS VERY helpful to intersperse short personal prayers during your davening, particularly when there is some short break in the service. For example, say: "God, please draw me close to You!" Or: "God, let me do *tshuvah* (repent)!" Or: "Let me love my fellow humans. Let me treat everyone with respect, never saying a hurtful word." Although you may occasionally miss saying an ordained prayer because of this, this practice falls under the category of it being better to say little with *kavvanah* than much without, for uttering these short prayers inspires *kavvanah*.

Yitzhak Buxbaum

When We Pray, We Join All Souls of All Ages

WE NEVER PRAY as individuals, set apart from the rest of the world. The liturgy is an order which we can enter only as part of the Community of Israel. Every act of worship is an act of participating in an eternal service, in the service of all souls of all ages.

Abraham J. Heschel

Silence—The Language of Prayer

THE LANGUAGE OF prayer should help us to an experience, not get in the way. Perhaps the most powerful language for Jews today is silence: we need more *shohin*—more emptying—in our prayer experience.

Rodger Kemenetz

Many Pray for the Wrong Reasons

HOW MANY OF us pray for the wrong reasons! We have a "slot machine" approach to prayer. All we have to do is insert a prayer and out will come instant fulfillment, immediate gratification, regardless of whether what we are asking for is moral, ethical, or possible; regardless of whether or not it clashes with the needs and hopes of others.

When what we ask for is denied us, we often abandon prayer as an exercise in futility. We forget that prayer at its highest involves praise and thanksgiving and that its primary concern is not getting but becoming. Our prayers are answered when they enable us to grow toward the person we are capable of being, and live as God would have us live.

Sidney Greenberg

The Power of Prayer

BY THE POWER of my Prayer, I can transform this wooden table into gold. But I would be embarrassed to pray to the Holy One for such a trivial thing.

The Baal Shem Tov

A God Whose Ways Are Comprehensible

I WOULD NEVER want to worship a God whose ways are comprehensible to every simple mortal.

Menachem Mendel of Kotzk

The Purpose of Prayer

THE PURPOSE OF prayer is to leave us alone with God.

Leo Baeck

How to Meet God in Prayer

ANY KIND OF injustice, corruption, cruelty, etc., desecrates the very essence of the prayer adventure, since it encases man in an ugly little world into which God is unwilling to enter. If man craves to meet God in prayer, then he must purge himself of all that separates him from God.

J. B. Soloveitchik

A Sermon to Ourselves

TRUE WORSHIP IS not a petition to God; it is a sermon to ourselves.

Emil G. Hirsch

Through Prayer Man Lifts Up All Creation

EVERY PLANT AND bush, every grain of sand and clod of earth, everything in which life is revealed or hidden, the smallest and the biggest in creation—all longs and yearns and reaches out toward its celestial source. And at every moment, all these cravings are gathered up and absorbed by man, who is himself lifted up by the longing for holiness within him. It is during prayer that all these pent-up desires and yearnings are released. Through his prayer, man unites in himself all being, and lifts all creation up to the fountainhead of blessing and life.

Abraham Isaac Kook

The Spirit Within Reaching Out

WE ARE FORMED by the same forces—chemical, physical, and spiritual which hold the stars in their orbit, thrust up the mountains, scoop out the seas, bring the rose to bloom, teach the hawk to fly, the horse to neigh. "If I climb up unto the heavens, behold Thou art there, and, if I go to the ends of the earth, behold Thou art there" [Psalm 139:8].

Prayer is not the lonely cry of a "tailless monkey playing ape to his dreams," nor a shout into an empty void answered only by its own echo. Prayer is the spirit within us reaching out to the Spirit of the universe, and prayer is that Spirit responding to us.

Robert I. Kahn

I Pray That I May Give Myself to God

I PRAY NOT that I may have, but that I may be. I pray not that God may give me, but that I may give myself to God. Nor shall I cease to pray when God withholds from me, for from men God may not withhold the infinite and eternal of themselves. Prayer is the joy, high and unutterable, of the soul's outreaching to Him who is the Soul of souls.

Stephen S. Wise

Moments Auspicious for Prayer

WHENEVER THERE RISES in man's heart a joyous thought, a feeling of happiness, a sense of love for His law, that moment is auspicious for prayer.

Zevi Hirsch Kaidanover

Prayer Is the Soul of Man

PRAYER IS THE soul of man holding converse with the soul of the universe.

Israel Bettan

No Sadness—Only Longing and Yearning

IN MEDITATION A man may discuss his tribulations with God: he may excuse himself for his misdeeds and implore the Lord to grant him his desire to approach nearer to God. A man's offenses separate him from his Maker.

It is impossible to be a good Jew without devoting each day a portion of the time to commune with the Lord in solitude, and to have a conversation from the heart with Him.

Even though a man may feel he cannot concentrate adequately upon the theme of his meditation, he should nevertheless continue to express his thoughts in words. Words are like water which falls continually upon a rock until it breaks it through. In similar fashion they will break through a man's flinty heart.

In true meditation a man cries to the Lord like a child to his father who is about to go on a journey. There is no sadness in this weeping—only longing and yearning.

Nachman of Bratzlav

The Difference

TO PRAY IS not the same as to pray for.

Claude G. Montefiore

Dance Is Prayer

A DANCE BEFORE the Blessed Holy One is prayer.

The Baal Shem Tov

Let No Day Pass Without Prayer

IT MAY BE that we seldom say a word of prayer. We have lost the habit, or perhaps were never taught it. We are like a home with a beautiful piano in the parlor, which is never played. We who do not pray are like that piano. We do not give forth the fine, clear notes of the spirit that lies mute and dormant in our souls.

The Reverend Doctor H. Pereira Mendes had this to say on prayer:

> God gives us much.
> Should we not give Him some time?
> Let no day pass without one prayer.
> Better one prayer than no prayer at all.
> Prayer should be the key to the morning and the bolt at night.
>
> *Herbert S. Goldstein*

To Petition Him Means to Pledge Ourselves

WITHOUT US THE most important tasks in the world will remain undone. That is why our requests of God imply commitment of ourselves. To petition Him means to pledge ourselves. Our prayers become meaningful when we do everything we can to make them come true. "Prayer," wrote Santayana, "is not a substitute for work; it is a desperate effort to work further and to be efficient beyond the range of one's powers." Our prayers are answered when they enable us to act as God desires.

Sidney Greenberg

God Hears Every Word

YOU MAY PRAY in the merest whisper, yet God hears every word. God, who hears the footfall of an ant, certainly listens to your words.

Yitzhak Buxbaum

Do a Good Deed Before Praying

BY BENEVOLENCE MAN rises to a height where he meets God. Therefore do a good deed before you begin your prayers.

Ahai Gaon

If We Understood What It Means to Pray

IF WE UNDERSTOOD what it means to pray, if we understood why prayer has been an indispensable part of Jewish life for thousands of years, what would we gain? From public prayer we would gain the experience of overcoming our loneliness and becoming part of a congregation. From the concept of the *minyan*, we would learn that we are changed by being in the company of others. You are a different person in a group than you are when you are alone, and you are a different person in one group than you are in another. Alone, you may find it difficult to pray. In a room full of praying Jews, you too become a praying Jew (and amazingly, you have the power to help other people become praying Jews as well).

Harold S. Kushner

Prayer—A Source of Serenity and Peace

TO PRAY IS to experience the reality of God, to feel the purity and exaltation that comes from being near Him, and to give to our souls that serenity and peace which neither worldly success nor worldly failure, which neither the love of life, nor the fear of death, can disturb.

Simon Greenberg

Prayer—A Home for the Soul

PRAYER IS NOT a stratagem for occasional use, a refuge to resort to now and then. It is rather like an established residence for the innermost self. All things have a home, the bird has a nest, the fox has a hole, the bee has a hive. A soul without prayer is a soul without a home. Weary, sobbing, the soul, after running through a world festered with aimlessness, falsehoods, and absurdities, seeks a moment in which to gather up its scattered life, in which to divest itself of enforced pretensions and camouflage, in which to simplify complexities, in which to call for help without being a coward. Such a home is prayer.

Abraham J. Heschel

The Bridge of Prayer

PRAYER IS THE bridge between man and God.

With the intellect one figures out what God *is* and also something of what He must be.

In intuition one experiences Him.

In revelation one receives testimony concerning Him, more or less definitive according to the credence given it.

In the good life one charts a course by His light.

In ritual one celebrates Him.

But only in prayer does one establish a soul to soul interchange with Him.

Prayer then consists in two elements: that a soul shall be oriented toward God; and that, whether with words or not, it shall address Him.

Milton Steinberg

The Search for God

TRUE PRAYER IS a search for God, the answer is finding Him.

Israel I. Mattuck

Signposts

PRAYERS ARE SIGNPOSTS along the way, visible even in the fog, pointing in the right direction and reminding us what to remember.

Samuel H. Dresner

Homesick for Our Universal Parents

MORE THAN EVER then do we become homesick; homesick, not for our houses or for our countries, but homesick for the universal Parent of all of us, for that deep affection which is the heart of the universe itself, for the mercy of God; yet a wall of iron has been placed between us and Him, and we cannot find Him. What greater good can a man achieve, either for himself or for the world, than to contribute his effort to piercing this wall, and bring the Father and the children once more into loving communion with one another!

Louis Finkelstein

Prayer Pushes Out the Walls of Normal Existence

PRAYER IS NOT an easy way of getting God to do what He ought to do, and neither is it a way of getting Him to do what we ought to do. There is no escape from the duty that lies upon us. Prayer will not offer us a refuge from the problems that trouble us. Prayer does, however, offer us the opportunity to raise ourselves and our lives to a higher peak. Prayer, if performed in that spirit, will put us in a better position, far better equipped to deal with the harassments and the dilemmas of our lives.

Prayers takes us into a large universe. It pushes out the walls of normal existence.

Morris Adler

The First Step to Prayer

FOR PRAYER TO have real significance, man when praying must disengage himself from mundane, everyday affairs, and must detach himself from the shallow and humdrum materialism which engulfs him when he is engaged in his ordinary daily activities. By doing so, he will reach that vital degree of awareness of the divine side of his existence which is the turning point in his innermost being. That turning point marks the striving of the suppliant, for it lies in the very depths of his heart. When man attains that degree of awareness and is capable of withdrawing from his habitual pedestrianism, he has taken the first step to prayer.

Abraham Kon

Three Fitting Things

THE CHASIDIC RABBI, Menachem Mendel of Premislan, once declared: "Three things are fitting for us: upright kneeling, motionless dancing, and silent screaming."

Kneeling is not only a matter of physical posture: it can also be a spiritual attitude. Thus we can kneel even when we are upright. A man can stand erect and feel humility and reverence in his heart.

Dancing is not only a matter of outward movement; it can also be an inner mood. We can dance motionless.

Prayer is not always articulate; often it is the unspoken yearning alone. We can cry out silently.

Sidney Greenberg

I Pray That I May Give Myself to God

WHO WILL PRESUME to speak of futility in the role of spirit, who will say that aspiration is unavailing because it seems to be what the world calls futile? How can prayer be futile, for through prayer one reaches out—as is possible in no other way—into the life of another, one reaches out into the life of all. Prayer might almost be defined as the mingling of the stream of life of the individual with the seas of infinite life; the stream of the soul is not lost or spent, but regained and enriched through commingling with the tides of life, infinite and eternal. . . .

I pray not that I may have, but that I may be. I pray not that God may give me, but that I may give myself to God. Nor shall I cease to pray when God withholds from me, for from men God may not withhold the infinite and eternal of themselves. Prayer is the joy, high and unutterable, of the soul's outreaching to Him who is the Soul of souls.

Stephen S. Wise

Praise in All Jewish Prayer

"Praised be Thou, O God . . ." is the basic prayer in Judaism: There is no prayer in which, implicitly or explicitly, praise is not an essential element. A Jew recites a *berachah* over bread, wine, other kinds of food; on first seeing a tree or animal of a species previously unknown to him; on seeing the ocean and a rainbow. He recites one *berachah* when he sees a great Jewish sage, and another when he sees a great Gentile one; one on hearing good news and another on hearing bad news. And a series of early morning *berachot* ends with one that discloses the root of praise and hence of prayer itself. "Praised be Thou, Lord our God, King of the world, who removest sleep from my eyes and slumber from my eyelids." A Jew awakens and is astonished and grateful: He is both because sleep has not been death. The Creation is renewed, every day.

Praise is implicit or explicit in all Jewish prayer.

Emil L. Fackenheim

The Difference Between Prayer and Worship

I am a firm believer in public worship.

I want to hold and read the liturgy of my people.

The worship that I love is something finer and wiser than prayer.

Prayer begins in need.

Worship begins in reverence.

Prayer is a measure of man's anxiety. Worship is the measure of man's commitment.

Prayer begins in the overheated heart. Worship begins in the reflective Soul.

Prayer is half-formed—a thing of the moment. Worship is sculptured— a thing of beauty.

Prayer is an urgency. Worship is a discipline.

We pray when life is too much for us. We worship. The better to live.

Daniel Jeremy Silver

Hidden Yearnings

PRAYER IS AT the heart not only of great religion but of significant living.

Without prayer we cannot scale the heights of compassion or attain the peaks of love of our fellowman of which we are capable.

Prayer has been an enduring and universal phenomenon of human life, not because a priesthood ordained it, nor because tradition hallowed it, but because man is ever seeking to probe into his own depths and bring to light his hidden yearnings.

Morris Adler

The Most Authentic Testimony of Prayer

HOW CAN I pray with another human being if I do not know the *needs* of that other? What does it mean to pray together if I do not have the *consent* of the others with whom I pray? But the others may say to me in the course of this process, "Care about me first as a person! Cease oppressing me or merely 'using' me as a member of your religious community. Help me be free enough to join in this search in *my own* way." When we realize that ultimately, we are necessarily joined in a prayer community to all of humanity, since the light of each and every soul is needed for the ultimate *tikkun ha-shekhinah*, the restoration of the One great light, there is no escaping the real life demands that being a person of prayer makes upon us. Here prayer and action are completely united with one another, and for many, action itself will speak as the loudest and most authentic testimony of prayer.

Arthur Green

What Is Special About Jewish Prayer

JEWISH PRAYER IS prayer that uses the idiom of the Hebrew Bible and reflects the Jewish soul. It is prayer that expresses the basic values of the Jewish people and affirms the central articles of Jewish faith. It is prayer that reflects our historical experience and gives expression to our future aspirations. When the prayer of a Jewish person does not reflect one of these components, he may be praying, but it cannot be said that he is praying as a Jew.

A Jew may choose his own words when praying to God; but when he uses the words of the siddur, he becomes part of a people. He identifies with Jews everywhere who use the same words and express the same thoughts. He affirms the principle of mutual responsibility and concern. He takes his place at the dawn of history as he binds himself to Abraham, Isaac, and Jacob. He asserts his rights to a Jewish future in this world and to personal redemption in the World-to-Come.

Hayim Halevi Donin

Second Only to the Bible

MOST REWARDING IS the glimpse into the soul of the Jewish people that one gains through an acquaintance with the siddur. In the prayers one can sense the pulse of the Jewish heart, the innermost feelings of the Jewish people in their moments of exaltation and dejection. One can also discern the Jewish people's aspirations and disillusionments, its ideals, and its profoundest beliefs. As a devotional compendium the siddur is characterized by its numerous supplications and beseechments directed to the God of Abraham, Isaac, and Jacob, its many utterances of gratitude to the Almighty for His blessings and His love, its repeated outpourings of grief over sins committed, and its unending expressions of confidence that the Father in heaven will in His compassion forgive Israel's transgressions and will restore His people to its former glory. Through the siddur one can also fathom the essence of Judaism and grasp "its strong doctrines of duty and righteousness, its moral earnestness, its cheery confidence in the world's possibilities of a sufficing and ennobling happiness, its faith in the purity and perfectibility of human nature, in brief, its ethical optimism." It is a treasure-house of prayers, hymns, psalms, affirmations of faith, and eternal hope. These vital characteristics have raised the siddur from the status of a useful handbook of worship to one of the most sacred books of Judaism, second only to the Bible.

Abraham Millgram

The Prayer Book—The Property of Every Jew

THE PRAYER BOOK was the property of every Jew. Before printing, people repeated prayers by rote, or at least listened to their recital daily. Wealthy patrons hired scribes to write personal copies of the siddur. And after the sixteenth century, the prayer book was the one volume which made a crystallization of the Jewish legacy readily available. True, the literal meaning of the Hebrew words was often beyond the linguistic competence of Jews, whose education was not what they might have wished, but the "message" inherent in the prayer book is transmitted by factors that go beyond comprehension of the prayers. That the prayer book owed its popularity to its unique capacity to carry such a vital message is beyond doubt.

Lawrence A. Hoffman

A Liturgy in Words and Deeds

THE SYSTEM OF sacred duties which makes of Judaism a "portable religion" is buttressed and sustained by certain convictions which transform the Halakhah into a sacred access to God. These convictions are embedded and expressed in our liturgy. In this special sense, Judaism can be said to be a "liturgical religion," for its fundamental beliefs are most clearly reflected in its liturgy. In his prayers, the Jew gave voice to his yearning for God, to his deep sense of moral accountability, to his ecstatic love for the Torah, and to his invincible faith in his people's rehabilitation in a peaceful world. It was the liturgy in word (prayer) and in act (*mitzvah*) which gave our forebears high hope in the face of despair, and perseverance in the midst of persecution.

Max Arzt

The Power of That Ancient Text

IN THE LIFE of prayer we seek to create a constant awareness of the Divinity that surrounds us at all times. We live in the Divine presence as did our ancestors and as will our descendents. Prayer offers to the individual and the community something of an echo of eternity, and that single echo is borne by the multiple echoes of history and antiquity. It is for this reason that I believe the Hebrew language will remain a vital vehicle in the prayer life of the Jewish community. No translation bears for the Jewish soul even a faint reverberation of the tremendous power contained in the Hebrew liturgical text. We may not allow the power contained in that ancient text to be lost.

Arthur Green

The Prayer Book Is Spiritual Training

GREAT RELIGIOUS AND ethical influences were exercised by Judaism over the world through the Bible. But through the prayer book, also, it exercised an influence perhaps equally important. Whereas, through the Bible Judaism taught the world an ideal of religion nobler than any known before, through the prayer book and the Synagogue, it taught the world a mode of communion with God which made this noble religion liveable, intimate, and effective in daily life. The Bible is the meaning of Judaism; the prayer book, its method. The Bible is doctrine. The prayer book is spiritual training.

Solomon B. Freehof

Spiritual Discipline and Spiritual Growth

THE SIDDUR IS a primary path to reliving the formative myths of the Jewish people, reviewing our key memories, reasserting our theology, reconnecting to community, and renewing our commitment to social justice. The siddur, however, is even more than that. It is an introduction to spiritual discipline and spiritual growth. The rhythms of ritual provide a powerful sense of the holy dimension in each day, week, month and year. The words of the siddur and the actions that accompany them create a ritual structure that enables us to sense the dimension of the holy. That ability becomes ours when we take on the aspirations, make commitments of time and energy, and discipline ourselves for the task.

David A. Teutsch

We Are Part of the Fellowship of Israel

PUBLIC WORSHIP GENERALLY is an occasion when we proclaim that we are part of the fellowship of Israel in covenant with God. The prayer book is liturgical agada. Its words are designed to evoke, express, confirm that we individuals—with all the personal agendas and histories which distinguish us from each other—share a common story that is the key to our life's transcendent meaning. The peak moments of authentic worship are moments when we feel that the words of Moses to the children of Israel, or of Jacob to his sons, are words addressed to us. Liturgical agada is the language through which the children of Israel in each generation reaffirm the covenant of their fathers.

Samuel E. Karff

The Values of Regular Public Worship

THE INDIVIDUAL, WHEN he is his own standard, will pray when he feels he needs to. Prayer then, finds its occasion and its value in response to his private moods and feelings. What happens under those circumstances to regular prayer with respect to frequency, intensity, and unselfish content is commonplace of modern versions of religiosity. The man who objects that he cannot pray on schedule often does not pray at all. And when, in this hectic world, he finally allows a conscious desire to pray to take priority over all the important things he should be doing now, he finds he does not have the knack. Obviously prayer in response to the inspiration of a moment has a unique significance, one well worthy of cherishing. But it is a supplement to, not a substitute for, regular public worship—and the acquired habit of turning to God in prayer is readily transferred from the congregational to the private situation.

Eugene B. Borowitz

Praying to God as Process

I KNOW THAT it is very hard for people who have been in the habit of thinking of God as a person to understand how one can address God if one regards God as a cosmic process. I don't think that it is so difficult if you understand that as being really is—I am talking to you, are you just static entities? Isn't every one of you a life, and isn't life a process? Are you to whom I am talking the same being that you were on the day you were born? Are you not constantly becoming something different? You are a process and I am talking to you. I can talk in the same way and with the same freedom with that cosmic process which I regard as the very source and fountain of my own being.

Eugene Kohn

The Bridge

PRAYER IS THE bridge that carries man to God.

Louis I. Newman

A Source of Strength and Comfort

IF THERE WERE not something in the universe that draws us, as the moon draws the sea, man's high aspirations would have no meaning. Tides prove the moon is there, even though clouds may cover it. . . . Aspiration is an expression of something deeper than intellect; a profound certainty that beyond man's body and beyond his mind there is a spiritual content in the universe with which his own spirit can from time to time communicate and from which he can draw strength and comfort . . . this sense of Presence, this central, orienting core of things, is what we mean by God.

Edmond Sinnot

Why the Jew Prays in Hebrew

THE JEW PRAYS in Hebrew, not because God understands no other language, but because it is his language, and therefore is both the form and the content of his thought. His holiest sentiments must be expressed in the tongue that links him with his ancestors and his brothers everywhere. As Schechter said of Bible translations prepared by Gentiles, "We cannot afford to have our love letters written for us by others."

Robert Gordis

Prayer—A Complete Turning of the Heart to God

THE FOCUS OF prayer is not the self. A man may spend hours meditating about himself, or be stirred by the deepest sympathy for his fellow man, and no prayer will come to pass. Prayer comes to pass in a complete turning of the heart toward God, toward His goodness and power. It is the momentary disregard of our personal concerns, the absence of self-centered thoughts, which constitute the art of prayer. Feeling becomes prayer in the moment in which we forget ourselves and become aware of God. When we analyze the consciousness of a supplicant, we discover that it is not concentrated upon his own interests, but on something beyond the self. The thought of personal need is absent, and the thought of divine grace alone is present in his mind. Thus, in beseeching Him for bread, there is *one* instant, at least, in which our mind is directed neither to our hunger nor to food, but to His mercy. This instant is prayer.

Abraham J. Heschel

Speaking and Listening to God

WHEN I PRAY, I speak to God. When I study, God speaks to me.

Louis Finkelstein

A Prayer Before Praying

BEFORE PRAYER IS a good time to join yourself with all of Israel, as is often suggested, and to say: "I join myself and my prayer, in love, with all the congregations of Your people Israel throughout the world."

Arye Levin

Prayer—The Encounter Between the I and the Great Thou

WE MAY NOT be able to meet God in prayer. But prayer makes it possible for us to reach the meeting point between God and man, the moment— that point in time—when the I encounters the great Thou. We cannot reach more, but this point we can reach. And in the rare moments in which we are able to reach this meeting point, we reach beyond ourselves.

Ernst Simon

Prayer—An Invitation to God

PRAYER TAKES THE mind out of the narrowness of self-interest, and enables us to see the world in the mirror of the holy.

The focus of prayer is not the self. Prayer comes to pass in a complete turning of the heart toward God, toward His goodness and power. It is the momentary disregard of our personal concerns, the absence of self-centered thoughts, which constitute the art of prayer. Feeling becomes prayer in the moment in which we forget ourselves and become aware of God. . . .

Prayer is an invitation to God to intervene in our lives, to let His will prevail in our affairs; it is the opening of a window to Him in our will, and effort to make Him the Lord of our soul. . . .

In crisis, in moments of despair, a word of prayer is like a strap we take hold of when tottering in a rushing street car which seems to be turning over.

Abraham J. Heschel

There Is a Special Quality to Group Prayer

OUR SAGES TAUGHT that when one witnesses lightning, comets, thunder, hurricanes, or the like, he should pray, "Blessed is He whose almighty power fills the world." The same men who found the evidence of God everywhere taught the value of the formal prayer. A man can pray well and deeply when he finds God for himself through nature or through spiritual reflection, but there is another profound meaning of prayer when it is performed in association with other human beings who have come together with the avowed intention of searching as a group for the deeper meaning of life. Clinical psychological tests clearly show that a decision reached by a group can be more binding on each of the participants than a decision reached by an individual acting alone. There are decisions to be made when one is alone, and there are decisions which are best made by the group. Anyone who has felt the warmth and good-fellowship present at a congregational service, anyone who has witnessed the sharing of sorrow at a funeral, or the sharing of joy at a wedding, knows that there are things best accomplished in a group situation. The man who feels that he cannot reach God when he is alone is lacking in probing powers which must be trained and sharpened, but the person who feels that he does not need to share the aspirations and moods of the group is deceiving himself. Rabbi Mikhal prayed, "I join myself to all of Israel, to those who are more than I, that through these my thought may rise, and to those who are less than I, so that they may rise through my thought." There is a special quality to group prayer from which all men can benefit.

Our sages taught that God proclaimed, "He who prays with a congregation is credited with redeeming Me and My children." This teaching reflects the strong Jewish conviction against the fragmentation of the community by those who flee from community responsibility and insist that they can gain nothing from the group. He who wishes to serve God cannot do so merely by staying out of trouble. He can "redeem" God only by working and praying with the community.

Our sages also taught that certain prayers such as the "*K'dushah* Sanctification" should not be recited by the individual alone. They were properly recited only in a group. Why did they come to this conclusion? Scripture teaches, "I will be hallowed among the children of Israel," (i.e., not by one child, not by an individual alone, but by the group acting in concert).

In this day, when there are strong pressures upon men to "go it" alone, we need the Synagogue more than ever. Our fathers were wise enough to know that when men pray together, they are less apt to engage in flights of fancy; they are less apt to pray selfishly; and they are the more easily reminded of their covenantal task. When men pray only when they are alone, they are not able to recite meaningfully the prayer which comes as the climax of our religious service, "Fervently we pray that day may come when all men . . . created in Thine image, shall recognize that they are brethren . . ." [*Union Prayerbook*, p. 71]. The ultimate goal of prayer is to unite the hearts of men. Indeed our prayer book reads, "Unite our hearts, that we may serve thee *in truth*."

Herbert A. Baumgard

To Petition Him Means to Pledge Ourselves

"TRUE WORSHIP," WROTE Emil Hirsch, "is not a petition to God. It is a sermon to ourselves." And that is why, for example, the Shema is followed immediately by a host of orders addressed to us. "Thou shalt love the Lord thy God. Thou shalt teach these words diligently to thy children. Thou shalt speak of them. Thou shalt bind them. Thou shalt write them." This prayer is concerned with our behavior most explicitly.

But even when the prayer is not directly addressed to us, even when the prayer is addressed to God, there is implied in it the understanding that we and God work together for the realization and the fulfillment of those prayers. In the Jewish view of things you and I are engaged in a great partnership, in a partnership with God. And we are expected to be active partners. We are expected to work for those things in which we believe and which we would like to see come to pass.

I hope this won't sound blasphemous or irreverent but I think that a mature understanding of God must include an awareness of God's helplessness. As children, we are taught to believe that God is omnipotent. He can do everything. Well, He can't, as a matter of fact.

There is not a single affliction from which we suffer—war, poverty, pollution, injustice, racial strife—that God can remove without our cooperation. There is not a single blessing we crave—world peace, food and shelter for all, clean air, a just society, domestic tranquility—that God can bring without our cooperation. A mature understanding of God looks upon Him neither as a miracle worker, nor a magician, nor as a Messiah who provides instant cure for all the world's ills. God is the power who works in us and through us to enable us to achieve those things that our faith in Him assures us are capable of coming into being.

Without us the most important tasks in the world will remain undone. That is why our requests of God imply commitment of ourselves. To petition Him means to pledge ourselves. Our prayers become meaningful when we do everything we can to make them come true. "Prayer," wrote Santayana, "is not a substitute for work; it is a desperate effort to work further and to be efficient beyond the range of one's powers." Our prayers are answered when they enable us to act as God desires.

Sidney Greenberg

Prayer—Grateful Communion with the Infinite

THE FACT THAT even the petitions are also praises of God and, therefore, not exclusively or even predominantly petitional in mood, clearly reveals a significant attitude toward prayer itself as a spiritual exercise. This attitude has been specifically stated in the following rabbinic statement: "A man should always utter the praises of God before he offers his petitions" [Berachot 32a]. Judging by this mood in the *T'filo*, prayer is primarily the achievement of an affirmative relationship to God, a sense of gratitude and appreciation for the blessings we have received. If our faith can succeed in curing us of the mood of constant discontent and can teach us to find joyous gratitude in whatever happiness we already have, however small it may be, then it will engender a healthy-mindedness within us that makes for a happy life, itself the answer to most of our prayers. This habit of praising God rather than begging from Him has become, through centuries of this type of prayer, a prevalent state of mind which enabled our fathers to find joy even in minor blessings and thus played its part in preserving Israel through the vicissitudes of history. A poverty-stricken, forlorn, exiled Jew, raising his last crust of bread to his mouth, might perhaps be justified in cursing his lot and denouncing God, but instead it would not enter his mind to partake of this bit of bread without first saying, "Praised be Thou O Lord Who bringest forth food from the earth." The rabbis speak even of a higher state of heroism, a more triumphant conquest of bitterness when they say, "A man should praise God even for misfortunes as much as he praised Him for happiness" [Yerushalmi, Berachot 9:5]. Whether this lofty courage is attainable by the average Jew or not, he learns to feel and to express, or perhaps to express and thus to feel, a constant sense of gratitude to the Master of the Universe. Prayer in Israel teaches man to overcome bitterness and self-pity; to think not of what the world owes *him*, but what he owes the world and God. It is not primarily piteous pleading but is essentially grateful communion with the Infinite.

Solomon B. Freehof

The Liberating Power of Public Worship

PUBLIC WORSHIP AIDS us by liberating our personality from the confining walls of the individual ego. Imprisoned in self, we easily fall a prey to morbid brooding. Interference with our career, personal disappointments and disillusionments, hurts to our vanity, the fear of death—all these tend so to dominate our attention that our minds move in a fixed and narrow system of ideas, which we detest but from which we see no escape. With a whole wide world of boundless opportunities about us, we permit our minds, as it were, to pace up and down within the narrow cell of their ego-prison. But participation in public worship breaks through the prison of the ego and lets in the light and air of the world. Instead of living but one small and petty life, we now share the multitudinous life of our people. Against the wider horizons that now open to our ken, our personal cares do not loom so large. Life becomes infinitely more meaningful and worthwhile when we become aware, through our participation in public worship, of sharing in a common life that transcends that of our personal organism.

A sense of common consecration to ideals inherited from a distant past and projected into a remote future means that we have in a sense made ourselves immortal. For death cannot rob our life of significance and value to us so long as we are interested in passing on to our posterity a heritage of culture and ideals. The past before we were born and the future after our death are a part of us, and every moment is eternal that embraces them. Through our worship as part of a religious community that outlives all its members, this sense of our life's triumph over death and all manner of frustration is brought home to us. We thus experience an expansion of our personality, an enlargement of the scope of its interests and its capacities. It is as though by surrendering our souls to God, we admit God into our souls and partake of His infinity and eternity.

Mordecai M. Kaplan

CHAPTER 36

RELIGION

Where Religion Begins

A STRANGER SHALT thou not wrong [Exodus 22]. The Rabbis explain this term to mean that nothing must be done to injure or annoy him, or even by word to wound his feelings. The fact that a man is a stranger should in no way justify treatment other than that enjoyed by brethren in race. "This law of shielding the alien from all wrong is of vital significance in the history of religion. With it, alone, true Religion begins. The alien was to be protected, not because he was a member of one's family, clan, religious community, or people; but because he was a human being. In the alien, therefore, man discovered the idea of humanity" [Herman Cohen].

Joseph H. Hertz

Judaism Is Not a Lullaby—It Is an Alarm Clock

RELIGION SHOULD NOT only comfort us when we are disturbed; it should also disturb us when we are comfortable.

The prophets who could soothe with motherly compassion when their people were heartsick, could also scold with bitter condemnation when their people appeared heartless. Isaiah who called out: "Comfort my people, comfort them," was the same prophet who cried out: "Woe unto the rebellious children."

Of course, it makes better advertising copy to promote Judaism as a comforter rather than as a disturber. Heaven knows that in these difficult days, the need for comfort and solace runs deep. And there are enough things in our personal lives to disturb us without turning to our religion for additional irritants.

And yet we cannot escape the truth that when Judaism offers only serenity and contentment, when it focuses all of our attention upon our personal needs and turns it back on the rest of the world, at that point Judaism betrays its own character.

"The enemy," wrote Norman Cousins, "is any man in the pulpit . . . who is a dispenser of balm rather than an awakener of conscience. He is preoccupied with the need to provide personal peace of mind rather than to create a blazing sense of restlessness to set things right."

It is worth noting that when Jews gather in our synagogues on the holy day of Rosh Hashanah, the central ritual is the sounding of the Shofar. The Shofar, as Maimonides explained it, cries out to us: "Awake from your sleep, shake off your lethargy." The Shofar is not a lullaby but an alarm clock. It does not encourage complacency; it shatters it.

These are surely days when religion should be a disturber of the peace, a goad to conscience and "a blazing sense of restlessness" to address the world's wrongs.

Sidney Greenberg

The Essence of Religion

WE NEED THE ability to thank God for the blessings of each day, for each sunset, for each sunrise, for each new month, for each new year, for each new joy. And this, after all, is the essence of religion to which all else is tributary and commentary.

Stanley Rabinowitz

Religion—A Gamble

I WOULD THINK of my religion as a gamble rather than think of it as an insurance premium.

Stephen S. Wise

We Have to Live Religion Religiously

WE MIGHT FIND it instructive to pause to take inventory among our own priorities and values.

Which activities do we consider a "must?" Do they include spending time with our mates and children, building a Jewish home, visiting parents, attending services, reading a Jewish book, participating in a program of Jewish study, rendering service to the community, performing acts of loving-kindness, giving *tzedakah*? Or are those the things we will do "when I have time," "when I am not so tired," "after the children grow up," "after I retire"?

We have come a long way since the days of Moses. En route we have accumulated a host of scientific discoveries, technological advances, modern gadgets. A thousand servants do our bidding at the press of a button. But with all our progress we have found little happiness, and true contentment too frequently eludes us.

We have many anxieties but few anchors, much outward security but little inward serenity, enlarged means but shrunken purposes, stronger houses but weaker homes. We travel faster but too often without a sense of direction. As someone complained: "We travel at twice the speed of sound but at half the speed of sense."

Perhaps the time has come for us to reexamine our priorities. Perhaps the time has come to live our religion—religiously!

Sidney Greenberg

The Purposes of Religion

RELIGION SUBSERVES MANY purposes. It is a principle of explanation of the universe, in the light of which the individual can find meaning for his own career and that of mankind. It is a sanction for morality. It is an aesthetic, and much else beside. But not the least of its utilities is this: by positing God, it inhibits man from laying claim to being God. It prevents his becoming less than man through the arrogance of claiming to be more. In brief, it helps to keep man human.

Milton Steinberg

The Historic Challenge of Religion

NOT MORE THINGS but higher values—this has been the historic challenge of religion.

Joseph L. Baron

When Civilizations Wane

ARNOLD TOYNBEE IS responsible for the suggestion that every civilization which has perished has died a suicide. When men refuse to give the central position in their thinking and living to moral and spiritual values, their civilizations wane.

Perry E. Nussbaum

Disorganized Religion

WHEN A MAN told the clergyman he disapproved of organized religion, the latter assured him that his was the most disorganized one available.

Victor Solomon

The Fences on Life's Steep Cliffs

THE ROLE OF religion is not so much to pick us up after we have fallen as it is to keep us from falling in the first place. To be sure, it is important to know that no moral defeat need be final: but together with the power to repent after wrongdoing, religion offers us the strength to prevent wrongdoing in the first place.

Religion helps us to develop a rich reservoir of spiritual resources, a firm commitment to a life disciplined by the commandments, and an awareness of what God expects of us. These are the fences on life's steep cliffs.

It has been said that the difference between a clever man and a wise man is that the clever man knows how to get out of a predicament the wise man would never have gotten into in the first place.

The Bible puts it simply: "When you build a new house, erect a fence around your roof" [Deuteronomy 22:8].

Sidney Greenberg

The Everlasting Dialogue Between Humanity and God

RELIGION IS THE everlasting dialogue between humanity and God.

Franz Werfel

Needed—More Religion

THE OLD CONCEPTIONS of religion can be overcome only through more religion, not by irreligion.

Ludwig Geiger

Religion Is a Momentous Possibility

RELIGION IS A momentous possibility, the possibility namely that what is highest in spirit is also deepest in nature—that there is something at the heart of nature, something akin to us, a conserver and increaser of values . . . that the things that matter most are not at the mercy of the things that matter least.

Henry Slominsky

This Is Religion

LONGING AFTER THE highest and noblest attachment to the whole, soaring up to the Infinite, despite our finiteness and limitedness—this is religion.

Abraham Geiger

The All-Encompassing Intelligence

RELIGION, WHILE ASSUMING an endless variety of forms, is at bottom of man's consciousness of the sacred or his response to the Divine as apprehended in the external world and within his own mind, heart and conscience. Religion, in its truest and most vital sense, begins when the human spirit turns toward the mysterious source of its being and seeks to commune with it as with an all-encompassing Presence and all-comprehending Intelligence. It reaches its noblest forms in man's self-consecration to the Holy One and His purposes and in his dedication of heart, mind and will to His service and to the service of his fellowmen. In Judaism, the consciousness of the sacred crystallized itself into the doctrine of Ethical Monotheism, the noblest conception of God known to humanity.

Samuel S. Cohon

The Majestic Meaning of Religion

THE FINAL PRINCIPLE is that one should recite the prayers "in a serious and not in a flippant manner." Our age places a premium on light-heartedness. The greatest compliment we can pay a person is to say that he has a sense of humor, that he is a lot of fun and good company. It is only natural that we look for the light moments in our life; but at the same time, we must remember that life is not merely a comedy, that living is not a joke but entails solemnity and serious considerations. There are responsibilities to fulfill, duties to discharge, and assignments to perform. If we are content to be merry and gay when drinking from the cup of life and consider the bubbles as the genuine wine, then the cup will never become a cup of blessing.

Many find religion wanting because they feel it is too serious and somber. Others have tried to bring religion down from its lofty pedestal by sugar-coating it to make it more appetizing and palatable. Our age, which has seen so much vulgarization in Jewish life, is in danger of having religion debased to the level of entertainment. We come to the synagogue to be entertained; we send our children to religious school to enjoy themselves; we send our youth to synagogue clubs to have a good time. Please do not misunderstand me. Happiness and pleasure are welcome by-products of religion, but they are not ends in themselves. The sweeping majestic meaning of religion must be spelled out in terms of our highest selves; it must never terminate in a joke or a laugh or mere amusement.

Joseph I. Singer

Index